FALL FROM GRACE

FALL FROM GRACE

THE TRUTH AND TRAGEDY OF "SHOELESS JOE" JACKSON

TIM HORNBAKER

First paperback edition 2018

Sports Publishing books may be purchased in bulk at special discounts for sales promotion, corporate gifts, fund-raising, or educational purposes. Special editions can also be created to specifications. For details, contact the Special Sales Department, Sports Publishing, 307 West 36th Street, 11th Floor, New York, NY 10018 or sportspubbooks@skyhorsepublishing.com.

Sports Publishing® is a registered trademark of Skyhorse Publishing, Inc.®, a Delaware corporation.

Visit our website at www.sportspubbooks.com.

10 9 8 7 6 5 4

Library of Congress Cataloging-in-Publication Data is available on file.

Cover design by Tom Lau
Front cover photo courtesy of the Library of Congress
All photographs and documents, unless otherwise noted, are courtesy of The Shoeless Joe Jackson Virtual Hall of Fame website (blackbetsy.com)

Paperback ISBN: 978-1-68358-201-4
Ebook ISBN: 978-1-61321-914-0

Printed in the United States of America

This book is dedicated to three important people who've influenced me during my lifetime:

Neil Jenkins
DS Lee
Jim Cypher

CONTENTS

INTRODUCTION

A single moment can make a hero.

Throughout the history of sports, legends have been born as a result of extraordinary performances by remarkable athletes. In more than a century of Major League Baseball, there are an untold number of time honored moments; occasions in which records were set, championships were won, and heroic feats were performed by individual players, forever establishing their immortality. These defining moments are rare, making them even more special, and the unexpected triumph of a player and team were cherished by fans for their exclusivity. For those at Comiskey Park on the South Side of Chicago on July 4, 1916, such a moment arose in the ninth inning of an emotional game against the St. Louis Browns.

Independence Day was always a big drawing event, and families from throughout the city traveled to the stadium to enjoy the national pastime. This year was no different. An estimated 25,000 people jammed the park, and the local crowd wanted to see the White Sox win the second game of a doubleheader after losing the morning affair, 2–1. Headed into the contest, no one could've predicted how remarkable this event was going to be. In fact, the game was going to be so overwhelmingly special that a superstar was about to become a legend right before their eyes.

Things were going well for the home team until the top of the ninth, when the Browns produced two runs, leaving the Sox in a hole headed into the bottom of the inning. Eddie Collins, the faithful second baseman, started a last ditch rally by singling his way on base. He was succeeded in the lineup by slugger Joe Jackson of South Carolina, then in his sixth full big-league season. Acknowledged for having one of the most distinctive nicknames of the Deadball Era—or any era for that matter—"Shoeless Joe" was an enigma in many respects. Naturally gifted, he didn't play the game with science but rather with an innate flair that differed from his contemporaries. He was known for denting outfield walls with his powerful drives, and extra base hits were commonplace for Jackson. Joe was popular in Chicago, but since joining the Sox in August 1915, had yet to live up to the hype in the minds of some critics.

At bat against the Browns in the ninth, Joe readied himself in the batter's box and waited patiently. His opponent on the mound, Bob Groom, was a tall and imposing right-hander, but to Jackson every pitcher looked the same. He didn't care who was out there, nor did he anticipate any specific pitch.

Groom's offering looked right, and Joe gave the fans what they were hoping for: a tremendous blast to deep right-center. The ball landed safely and Jackson rounded the bases with all of his immense might. He had one thought in mind: scoring. That meant he was going to ignore the halt sign given by manager "Pants" Rowland at third base. But Rowland could see what Jackson couldn't, and knew the ball was already back in the infield. He knew a play at the plate was going to be too close to let him go. Jackson didn't seem to care one way or another.

The Browns' catcher, Hank Severeid, was an experienced man and could certainly hold his own. He eyed the throw and planted himself for a collision while at the same time preparing to make the tag. Jackson was blinded by his determination. The fact that a 6-foot, 175-pound backstop was standing in front of the plate did not deter him for a second. Moments later the inevitable occurred, and Jackson made impact. Home plate umpire Billy Evans saw the ball beat the runner and called Joe out, but reversed his decision after seeing the ball fall free from Severeid's control. The latter had dropped it, and Jackson was safe. Since Collins had scored as well, the game was now tied and the holiday crowd erupted into an immense roar.

Notably, Jackson was unaware of his safe status when Evans made his call. The reason was because he smashed the back of his head on the ground during the forceful slide, and nearly knocked himself unconscious. Within seconds of realizing what was transpiring before them, spectators collectively hushed, acknowledging what apparently was a serious injury to Jackson. A handful of minutes passed—which probably seemed like an eternity—before he was helped to his feet. Again, the crowd responded audibly, grateful that Joe wasn't badly hurt. His teammates tried to allow him to walk on his own, but Jackson fell to the ground en route to the dugout and was quickly carried off the field. He received immediate treatment, including icepacks, and recovered enough to return to the outfield the next inning. It was an amazing display of courage which wasn't lost on the humongous throng of fans.

The Sox would go on to win the game, 7–6, in 13 innings. Sportswriters covering the action were all too ready to lionize Jackson, and relayed vivid accounts to readers the following day. "If it had been a hero play staged for the movies, it couldn't have been arranged better," declared James Crusinberry in the *Chicago Daily Tribune.* He added: "Never before [was there] a greater hero at Comiskey Park."[1] Irving Vaughan explained in the *Chicago Examiner* that the luminary, who spearheaded a Sox victory, received "the greatest applause ever given a player on the South Side lot." Vaughan was sure the player's clutch hit would be "a long time remembered."[2] However, nearly 100 years later, the significance of the game has been lost in the annals of baseball history. But for the man known as "Shoeless Joe" Jackson, it was a defining moment in a turbulent career.

Headed into the 1916 season, sportswriters and fans alike were concerned about Jackson's ability to meet expectations. His career statistics were in decline, and his days of challenging for the league batting championship were a thing of the past. To make matters worse, Joe failed to provide the spark needed for the Sox to win the 1915 pennant, and rumors circulated about a possible trade after the season. The questions about his ability, health, and overall attitude were discouraging to Jackson, but he knew deep down the need to come into his own while wearing a Chicago uniform. He had to demonstrate that he was all-in, and deeply committed to the franchise. Independence Day 1916 allowed him to do just that, and the fans decided that he was one of them. He was a big-hearted warrior on the diamond and his actions earned him a mountain of respect from an eternally loyal group of enthusiasts. And, in effect, his legend in Chicago was born.

Over the years Joe Jackson took on a mythical nature, and a number of mainstream factors played a role. Some of it was indeed legitimate, while other aspects were moderately fabricated to create a sellable product, whether it was a book or film. But Jackson didn't need any additional color to be an interesting story. His rise from a small mill community to the pinnacle of baseball was fascinating, and his accomplishments spoke for themselves. His .408 batting average as a rookie in 1911 is a record that remains to this day. Everything from his personal quirks to his sense of humor and the way he interacted with spectators made him a one-of-a-kind ballplayer. His popularity was genuine because of his natural charisma and the image he portrayed to the public. And for that reason, nothing needs to be manufactured to produce a true representation of Joe Jackson. He lived an incredible life.

F. C. Lane of *Baseball Magazine* described Jackson as having a "clean cut face and dark, curly hair," in a 1916 article, and mentioned that he was "a striking figure in any company."[3] In many ways, he was a typical American ballplayer, possessing the physical characteristics of a professional athlete. He was better than his size, with proportioned muscles and extraordinary strength. Gifted with long arms, which accentuated his abilities at the plate, Joe was able to make contact with pitches far outside the box. And if the ball looked good to him, he'd often reach out and give it a wallop. There was no specific discipline behind his efforts, just a natural gift. His piercing dark eyes saw the ball in all its clarity, and with tremendous hand-eye coordination he rarely had trouble meeting a pitch with perfect timing, speed, and strength. As a result, he exemplified the prototype of a baseball slugger.

Limited by personal weaknesses—particularly a lack of formal education—Jackson was strong-willed, but easily susceptible to the smooth talking of others. Throughout his life he was ensnared by crafty manipulators, and usually his wife Katie was the voice of reason. But there were times when Katie was not around, or when Jackson's own eccentricities took over. In the case of the 1919 World Series scandal, Joe found himself embroiled in a situation way over his head. Although he had options, he made the best decisions he could and, in the end, paid the price for what transpired. The entire story remains haunting to a certain degree, and the truth behind Jackson's exact involvement is shrouded by an overwhelming number of contradictory versions. These inconsistencies hurt Jackson in his attempts to clear his name during his lifetime and impeded advocates in much the same way since his death in 1951.

Of course, the situation damaged the reputation of Jackson and cast him from the good graces of baseball, but "Shoeless Joe" still remains a clear-cut enigma of the game from any history perspective. The absence of his name on a plaque on the walls of Cooperstown at the National Baseball Hall of Fame is evidence of Jackson's cataclysmic fall from the plateaus of the national pastime. Regardless of what happened at the 1919 Series and in its aftermath, Joe was the true embodiment of a baseball idol prior to that horrendous episode. The vivid memories of his powerful drives, his never-ending chase of Ty Cobb and the batting championship, and the way he naturally smiled during the course of a ballgame made him an inspiration to the young and old. These facts made his eventual banishment hurt all the more. There are many layers to Jackson's story, including insight into his perspective and motivations, and it is only when these aspects are digested that the real "Shoeless Joe" is revealed. And the real story is better than fiction.

"SHOELESS JOE"

Toward the end of the nineteenth century, the rapid rise of textile mills in Upstate South Carolina was a blessing to an untold number of impoverished families. The flourishing market opened the door to scores of localized facilities, offering full-time work to people in need of stable incomes. These venues not only provided housing in communities built for its employees, but offered educational opportunities, churches, and organized sports. To a degree, life in these areas revolved around the mill and the people were connected by a palpable sense of kinship. For newcomers to these budding districts, there was high optimism; and for the parents of small children, it was understood that once their kids progressed to a certain age, they too would be welcome to a job. The additional income derived by children was necessary for numerous struggling households.

George D. Elmore Jackson was a product of South Carolina, a first generation American born in 1856, and a man who was ever hopeful about the benefits of life in the thriving textile industry. He was one of fourteen children reared by James Samuel and Jane Littlefield Jackson, and spent his earliest years in Union County, just east of Greenville and Spartanburg, the two largest cities in the region. With the Civil War on the horizon, the Jackson family was fortunately outside the maximum and minimum age limits for conscription in the Confederate Army. James, who was also foreign born (originally from Liverpool, Lancashire, England), was over fifty years old when the conflict broke out.[1] His oldest son, William, was but sixteen in 1861, and it is not known if the latter entered the army once he met the age requirement. Nevertheless, the Jacksons were undoubtedly affected by the war in more ways than one and, as prideful members of the state, helped in the rebuilding.

During the 1880s, George met Martha Ann Jenkinson of Gantt, South Carolina, which was just outside Greenville, and the two were later married.[2] The couple settled in the small town of Easley—an unincorporated part of nearby Pickens County—with less than 500 residents.[3] On July 16, 1887, Martha gave birth to their first child, Joseph Jefferson Wofford Jackson. A unique fact about the future "Shoeless Joe" is that researchers have struggled with his year of birth throughout history, insisting it was either 1887 or 1888. The normal answer to such a question would rest in the reliability of a birth certificate, but since those weren't required in South Carolina until 1915, it is ruled out. However, the usually dependable World War I Draft Registration documents on file with the National Archives and Records Administration indicate that he was born in 1887. Conversely, several books and articles claim it was the year following. But, oddly, his South Carolina Certificate of Death goes one better, and states that Joe was born in 1889.[4]

There is endless exceptionality to the story of Joe Jackson, and with that in mind it is not surprising that his year of birth *and* his legal name are both subjects of dispute. Again, without a birth certificate to put an exclamation point on the matter, historians have had to rely on all available documentation. Per those sources, his middle names of "Jefferson Wofford" are generally acknowledged as fact. This would be completely satisfactory if it wasn't complicated by Joe himself in a 1912 interview with J. A. Fitzgerald. The reporter asked him what his full name was, and Jackson replied: "Joseph Walker Jackson, but don't print the Walker part, will you? Say, I've got nothing against Walker, but I like plain 'Joe' better. Joseph Walker Jackson has a kind of one legged sound."[5] Was it a miscommunication or misinterpretation of his Southern style of speech? It might have been, but four months before his conversation with Fitzgerald, Joe was asked the same question by a different journalist. His answer was again, "Joseph Walker Jackson."[6]

Historian Joe Thompson revealed in his book *Growing Up with "Shoeless Joe"* that "Jefferson Walker" was a nickname Joe had received in his youth.[7] It is altogether likely Jackson was just recalling the moniker given to him by his brother Dave when talking to reporters in 1912, but it confuses the situation nonetheless.

Unsurprisingly, that is not all. In his conversation with Fitzgerald, Joe was asked how many people were in his immediate family. The reporter claimed Jackson used his fingers to count, and came up with eleven: seven boys, two girls, and his parents.[8] In 1924, during a legal proceeding, Joe's lawyer Raymond J. Cannon spent a little time discussing Jackson's history before a jury, and ran through important points of note. During the statement, Cannon claimed Joe was "one of fifteen children," according to the *Milwaukee Evening Sentinel*—*six* more than the Jacksons really had.[9] This was an obvious mistake, but served to distort Jackson's biography for anyone who was paying attention.

As Jackson noted, his parents George and Martha gave birth to nine children. Joe was followed by Lula, Dave, Lee Earl, Ernest, Jerry, Luther, and Gertrude (one brother's name not confirmed).[10] The family relocated from Easely to Pelzer by the mid-1890s, and his father got work at a local mill. News of a promising opportunity on the Western border of Greenville in 1901 caused the Jacksons to move once again, this time settling outside the Brandon Mills textile complex.[11] Their home, on Furman Street, was actually part of the newly developing Brandon Village, an area primed for expansion. Several hundred employees were hired, and Joe Jackson, then fourteen years old, was one of them. Joe was no stranger to the mill culture, as he had toiled at the Pelzer facility since before he was a teenager.[12] Even at that age, he was called upon by his parents to help generate an income, and things weren't any different at Brandon Mills. In fact, for many families, it was the children's duty to step up and contribute financially.

Schooling was simply not a priority. As a result, Joe neglected learning the basic fundamentals of life: reading and writing. Since he was the oldest boy of the family, he assumed much of the workload and did so without complaint. And like his father, who was also illiterate, he would rely on his physical attributes to a greater extent than his mind.[13] Although Joe would miss taking advantage of pivotal lessons during his formative years, the younger Jackson siblings enrolled in the two-story Brandon Mills School and obtained a proper education. Rather than being caught up in scholarly affairs, Joe was putting in 12-hour days at the plant and earning upwards of $1.25 per shift.[14] With the mill swelling from 10,000 cotton spindles to over 40,000 in only a few years, there was plenty of labor to go around, and Joe was a diligent employee in an often hazardous environment. The Brandon facility would be his workplace for six years.

The Jacksons were a determined and close-knit family. Martha referred to her eldest as "Her Joe," and each of the siblings were firmly dedicated to the chores of their homestead. George was known for being obstinate at times, and after a difference in opinion with management walked away from the mill to do a little farming, in addition to work as a butcher during the 1900s.[15] Joe was a dutiful son and just as supportive in his father's butcher shop as he was in the mill as a youngster. He chopped meat, drove the wagon, and did whatever was asked of him. Again, these efforts were at the expense of any education. But Joe plugged along and, as he got older, the expectations for him to take on a heavier responsibility for the family's financial intake grew. It was his birthright to meet the obligation as his father aged.

Around 1902, when Jackson was fifteen, he became preoccupied by baseball—not only as an amusement, but as a way to supplement his income.[16] His initial foray into the sport was as a member of the Brandon Mills squad, and the competition among the textile firms in the region was robust. Saturday afternoons were prime time for the contests, and Joe was thrust into the spotlight for the first time in his life. He began his semi-pro career as a catcher, but quickly found he wasn't right for the position. Martha later explained: "Joe has a scar on his forehead that he got in those early days. He was catching behind the plate and a great burly mill hand was pitching to him. He threw one so swift and strong that Joe didn't have strength enough to stop it. So it forced his hands back, drove into his mask, and dented the mask into his forehead, leaving a deep cut. That was how he got that scar."[17]

The outfield was a more suitable location, and Jackson's speed and throwing power was a great asset to any team. At the plate, hitting came naturally, and he attributed a lot of it to his excellent eyesight.[18] His instincts kicked in on the field, over and above any pregame coaching, and it wasn't long before he was the standout figure, even against older opponents. Of course, his mother and siblings were enthusiastic, and his brothers were itching to follow his footsteps onto the diamond. But his father wasn't pleased. He disliked the idea of playing ball for money, but Joe wasn't going to be swayed.[19] He enjoyed the sport and really liked making the extra cash. He might not have been able to see baseball as a pathway to future endeavors at the time, but that possibility was quickly coming into focus.

By eighteen years of age Joe was starting to see the bigger picture and decided he'd had enough of the mill life. He quit his job and joined the Greenville Grangers, a local semipro ballclub. With the addition of Jackson, the Grangers started to build up quite the reputation. In one season, they reportedly won 30-straight contests, an astounding feat.[20]

Jackson was making great progress as an athlete but, like his father, he was a little mulish and occasionally things got rowdy, even violent. According to a story told in the *Pittsburgh Daily Post*, Joe was spiked by an opposing collegian during one game of note and took great offense to the player's actions. Jackson allegedly removed his spiked shoe and, in revenge, hit the man with it, stunning onlookers. The report claimed the latter "bore some resemblance to a hamburger steak" afterwards.[21] As could be expected, the competitiveness was heated on the baseball circuit, but Joe obviously had a lot of growing up to do.

In terms of his playing abilities, Jackson was much more confident in himself. He soon left Greenville to do a little touring away from home with an independent squad, but often returned to assist his parents. The venture was a big source of discovery for Jackson, and in his travels to various cities met different types of people while gaining a slew of new experiences. At Mobile, Alabama, his teammates decided to purchase him his first pair of trousers—deciding he'd outgrown the knickers he'd been wearing with regularity—and Joe later recalled, "I sure thought I was some man that night."[22] Jackson was also attached to a Greenville-area team known as the "Near Leaguers," managed by twenty-five-year-old Laurens "Lolly" Gray, a well-known local player. But Gray had to promise Joe's father 75 cents for each day the younger Jackson was away playing ball to secure his services. It was worth it to Gray. "We needed him for his hitting," he explained. "And there was always a place to use a man who could hit as Joe did."[23]

The "Near-Leaguers" were a talented bunch, supported by the able pitching of Logan Ferguson. Ferguson grew up about a mile east of Brandon Mills, and was from a large family. Several of his brothers were involved in the woodworking industry.[24] His eldest sibling, Charles Cline Ferguson, as a favor to young Jackson, carved out a sizable 36-inch, 48-ounce bat reportedly dyed black with tobacco juice. Jackson prized the bat, naming it "Black Betsy," and it became the predominant weapon in his baseball arsenal. Years later, Jackson recalled that Captain Wesley Fletcher Martin of the Greenville Street Car system had actually delivered the bat to him, perhaps en route to a local game.[25] Joe long remembered the combination of Ferguson's handiwork and Martin's kindly act, and from there the legend of "Black Betsy" was born.[26]

In 1907, Jackson was hired by the Victor Mills textile firm in Greer, South Carolina, and was making several dollars per game.[27] It was during this time frame that Joe received his first big break. "I found Joe Jackson in the fall of 1907," explained Tommy Stouch, who is credited with "discovering" the slugger for Organized Baseball. "After our season in the South Carolina league was over, I organized a team and played five games against the Greer team. I had heard of Jackson's wonderful hitting so I engaged Billy Laval, a good left-handed pitcher, to pitch in an effort to check this terrific swatting. It did not." In fact, Joe managed to hit every trick pitch Laval threw. Impressed to say the least, Stouch didn't hesitate and asked Jackson to join his Class D Carolina Association franchise, a professional club known as the Greenville Spinners. Joe was receptive, and asked for $60 a month in salary. Stouch did him one better, offering $75, and Jackson replied: "I'll play my head off for that."[28]

In Stouch and Laval, Jackson gained two pivotal mentors. Both men were college coaches at various times and had extensive experience working with young ballplayers. They were able to impart precious information to Joe; concentrating on his weaknesses in running the bases, judging fly-balls, and approaching the plate with a more scientific mind-set. The lessons began as soon as Joe reported to the Spinners in mid-April 1908, and of the many athletes in contention for outfield spots, Jackson's spot was pretty secure. Stouch liked Jackson immediately, seeing his raw potential. But, interestingly, the Greenville press didn't know much about the young player, and, in one report, stated he was from Greer instead of Brandon Mills.[29] That caused one irritated enthusiast from the latter village to write the *Greenville Daily News* and set him straight. A few days later, the sports editor apologized and said it was "pure ignorance" on their part.[30]

But it didn't take long for local reporters to learn about Jackson, and soon they were liberally complimenting his play. Ultimately, they'd broaden the assertion that he was from suburban Brandon Mills, and deem him Greenville's hometown idol, essentially adopting Joe as their own. During a preseason exhibition against Wake Forest College on April 25, 1908, Stouch ushered Joe into the pitcher's box. Jackson displayed a good fastball and control in a 4–0 victory, striking out eight on only four hits.[31] It wouldn't be the last time Stouch went to Joe to pitch, but when the season commenced on April 30, Joe was starting in center field and batting third in the lineup. Producing two doubles and a triple in five at-bats, Jackson performed remarkably in his Organized Baseball debut. A journalist covering the game also asserted that Joe snared a difficult catch "that made the fans want to stand on their heads."[32]

Within the first few weeks of the season, Jackson's notoriety with the public had grown to the point that he was already one of the most popular players on the team. He was consistent at the plate, often achieved more than one hit a game, and was a prime reason Greenville jumped into first place. The season wasn't even a month old when it was revealed that two American League scouts were already observing his work, considering his big-league potential.[33] Joe's play warranted it, and out-of-town newspapers were picking up stories about his remarkable abilities. Amidst the colorful anecdotes about Jackson were tales of his supposed shoeless ball-playing and, of course, sportswriters loved the yarn. They encouraged and nurtured the nickname "Shoeless" until it was a natural part of the baseball lexicon. According to lore, it was first affixed to Jackson by Carter "Scoop" Latimer, a Greenville reporter, but since the latter was a young teenager in 1908, it is rather implausible. Nevertheless, through the years, Latimer and his journalistic brethren took the name and ran with it, creating a plethora of origin stories in the process.

The tales were creative and amusing, and differed ever so slightly depending on the author. But overall the theme was similar, claiming that he either hated shoes or couldn't afford them because of his impoverished status. Neither, in fact, was true. Jackson himself explained what happened:

> I was playing in Anderson, South Carolina, one day and it happened that I played the day before in a new pair of baseball shoes. You know how ill-fitting shoes will act at times. Well, this pair simply raised the biggest blister you can imagine on each heel. So when I put on the shoes for the Anderson game I found I could hardly walk with them on, much less play ball. So the only thing for me to do was to take 'em off or die standing up—so I just naturally took 'em off and played ball in my stocking feet. Some fan in the bleachers with a megaphone voice spied my twinkling toes and shouted with all his might: "Oh, you shoeless wonder!" I guess every baseball fan in the country heard him, for I have been called that ever since.[34]

During a lopsided game against Anderson on June 4, 1908, Stouch again called Joe to the mound to silence the active bats of their opponents. Jackson was successful, but Greenville couldn't overcome the deficit and lost 15–4. At one point, however, an errant pitch by Jackson broke the arm of Anderson's third baseman Lee Meyers, and eventually prompted him to give up his pitching aspirations. The *Greenville Daily News* commented that "No one [regretted the accident] more than Joe Jackson."[35] Despite their talent, the Spinners began giving up ground in the pennant fight near the end of June, and Spartanburg started to close in. Jackson went through several brief slumps and early in July broke his favorite bat, leaving him in search of a replacement.[36] When he did have a first-class piece of timber at the plate, there was no telling how far one of his blasts could go. And for each home run he hit, team president Albert James gave him a $5 bonus. Joe collected a good sum of money by season's end.

While his personal life remained out of the press, it is evident that the twenty-one-year-old Jackson was developing a serious relationship with Katherine "Katie" Wynn, the fifteen-year-old daughter of Charles and Alice Phillips Wynn in 1908. The Wynns were a working-class family from the resort community of Chick Springs, northeast of downtown Greenville. Joe and Katie were lost in love, and although the details of their courtship have been lost to history, they didn't wait long to wed. At 4:30 on the afternoon of July 19, 1908, they were married before Reverend Wesley B. Justus.[37] Jackson was back in uniform the next day, going 2-for-3 in a victory over Winston-Salem. All things considered, this was a tremendously exciting time in his life. Between his marriage, baseball success, and the rumors circulating about possible big paydays in the major leagues, Joe was riding an immense high.

Minor league clubs in Atlanta and Memphis both had an opportunity to purchase Jackson, and Hugh Jennings of the Detroit Tigers was also interested.[38] Connie Mack, manager of the Philadelphia Athletics, had received input about the youngster from at least four sources and was prepared to make a move to obtain him. "Socks" Seybold, Ossee Schrecongost, Sam Kennedy, and Al Maul had each done scouting work for Mack in the South that summer, and watched Joe perform for Greenville.[39] Their recommendations, plus the need for Mack to fill an outfield spot, compelled the latter to invest $900 in Jackson and another $600 for Scotty Barr.[40] The purchase was elevating Joe to the big leagues, and there was a certain amount of elation—though some apprehension as well. He'd never been to the big cities of the North and didn't know anyone up there. He was newly married and the thought of leaving his bride behind to pursue a career in baseball wasn't something he'd come to grips with.

Jackson was to finish out the season with Greenville, then report to Connie Mack. In the meantime, he needed to resolve any internal questions about his baseball future and decide if relocating to Philadelphia was something he cared to do. Ironically, the battle for first place in the league was boiling down to the final games, and a close play at the plate involving Jackson against Greensboro initiated a protest, which held up naming a pennant winner.[41] The season closed in a cloud of confusion, and the time was quickly arriving for Joe to make a decision. Still hesitant, he agreed to venture northward as long as manager Tommy Stouch went with him as a guide. They boarded a train for Philadelphia on August 21, but the next day, instead of arriving in the "City of Brotherly Love," Jackson was back in Greenville, much to the angst of Stouch, Mack, and everyone else who had supported Joe along the way.[42]

Anxious, overwhelmed, and unwilling to leave home, Jackson was apparently resolved to remain on the outskirts of Major League Baseball. He didn't understand that refusing to report was a one-way ticket to a suspension from all of Organized Baseball. A few days later, after some prodding by Athletics ambassador "Socks" Seybold, Joe again got on a train and successfully made it to Philadelphia. On August 25, 1908, he performed in his inaugural big-league game against Cleveland, and scored a run in his first at-bat with a single to left field. A writer for the *Philadelphia Inquirer* stated that Joe carried himself "both at the bat and in the field with the air of a veteran," and onlookers were convinced that he possessed the necessary tools to play at that level.[43] It was all good news and the Philadelphia press featured lengthy pieces on the new outfielder, relishing in his acquisition.

Everyone but Jackson was happy. His assimilation didn't come easy, and his teammates—many of whom were older, well-traveled Northerners—kidded and joshed the South Carolinian, much like they did any other rookie. It was simple hazing, but for the immature, emotional Jackson, he didn't want to be involved. On August 28, Joe found himself back in Greenville again, this time having left Philadelphia with Mack's permission on a four-day pass to tend to a sick uncle.[44] Needless to say, the four days came and went, and Jackson remained home. It was more than a week before he returned to Philly, and Mack immediately inserted Joe into the lineup on September 8 and 9, and for a doubleheader on the 11th.[45] Altogether, in his five big-league games, Joe went 3-for-23 and had a .130 batting average, considerably lower than his league leading .346 in the Carolina Association. For Jackson, those five games were enough.

By September 14, he was back home in Greenville and his mind was made up. He was done with Philadelphia, a city he despised, and wanted no part of Major League Baseball.

It was later revealed that homesickness was the true reason behind his actions.[46] But, at the time, he was lambasted by critics for his unruly disposition, know-it-all attitude, and lack of overall discipline. It is interesting to note that Mack tried to alter Jackson's batting style during his stay in Philadelphia, even hiding his black bats on him in an effort to break his old habits.[47] Nobody realized it at the time, but adjusting Joe's natural methods might have crippled his game for life. Thankfully, for his own sake, Joe possessed the old Jackson stubbornness and nixed that idea. Of course, since his departure wasn't approved by management, Mack suspended him and sent a notice to the Greenville ballclub, informing them of Jackson's blacklisting, which was recognized across Organized Baseball.[48]

A good-hearted soul, Connie Mack didn't want the irresponsibility of a young player to destroy his entire future, and he gave Jackson another chance. Early in January 1909, Joe responded positively to the gesture, signing his Philadelphia contract with a letter pledging to "be good" in the new season.[49] Obviously having taken the holidays to think things over, Jackson was reconciled with the potential of his major league opportunity. Playing ball for thousands of dollars a year instead of less than a hundred a month was life-changing money for his family in Greenville, and, he reported to Philadelphia's spring training camp at New Orleans in March. He was motivated to perform well and stood out among fellow second-stringers and rookies on the Yannigan squad during exhibitions.

Jackson was reportedly pegged for a regular spot on the Athletics, but a strange episode at the Philadelphia train station altered the course of history. As the tale went, Joe was engaged in a private conversation with Scotty Barr, his ex-Greenville teammate, and griped a bit about the City of Philadelphia, keeping in tune with his previously established sullenness. He mentioned that he'd rather be tied to a tin can headed out of town than remain a moment longer. Connie Mack just so happened to be within earshot of Joe and heard his unenthusiastic remarks. He was less than pleased, and decided Jackson needed another season of experience and maturity in the minors.[50] Within a short time, Joe was sent to Savannah, Georgia, to play with a South Atlantic League franchise managed by Mack's friend, Bob Gilks.[51]

The demotion was handled surprisingly well. Savannah was a little over 250 miles from Greenville, and Joe liked the city immensely. Gilks, a forty-four-year-old baseball veteran, possessed a great mind for the game and was another significant mentor for Jackson. But despite competent leadership and a slugger like Jackson in the lineup, the Savannah Indians were a mediocre club and fell to the bottom of the eight-team Sally League before the end of April 1909. The team faced a number of crucial injuries and Gilks needed replacements to maintain any hope of competitiveness. Jackson, much like his time in the Carolina Association, darted right to the top of league in batting and his steadiness against all types of pitchers made him a dangerous hitter in any situation. His central deficiency at the plate was making contact with low balls and, with plenty of work, he strengthened this weakness measurably during his time in Savannah.[52]

On May 12, Savannah was on the road facing the first-place Chattanooga Lookouts, a club undefeated at home. Headed into the ninth inning, the score favored the latter, 3–2, but Red Murch singled his way on base and Jackson followed with a towering home run over the left-field fence. The Indians held its lead and won a satisfying 4–3 victory.[53] But by May 25, they'd established an embarrassing 8–23 record, while Chattanooga was exactly the opposite at 23–8. Gilks resigned that same week and was replaced by outfielder Ernie Howard. Jackson's individual numbers were more than impressive, and he was up over .400 for parts of May. At Macon on June 10, he again homered en route to a 3–1 victory, and a local writer, in commenting on the intensity of the blast, wrote: "We honestly believe that ball is traveling yet. It's sad but true."[54] With several new additions to the roster and good pitching by future major leaguer Al Demaree, Savannah fought its way out of the basement and settled into fourth place.

Sally League directors called a halt to the first half of the 1909 season on July 3, and kicked off the second half a short time later.[55] Jackson's .342 average in 64 games was way out in front of his contemporaries and his .965 fielding percentage was a stark improvement over the .931 he established in 1908. In dealing with his routine mastery, witty sportswriters in circuit towns liked to formalize his first name in their columns, calling him "Josiah," "Josephus," and other variations. They even touted him as a "villain" at times, emphasizing the damage he was single-handedly doing to their hometown clubs. But when Joe was good, these pundits couldn't help but compliment him. After one particularly good showing, a Columbus journalist declared: "[A] feature was the home run by Jackson, the brilliant rightfielder of the Indians. He is, without a doubt, the star of the Savannah team, and his work in right-field has been little short of marvelous."[56]

The Indians started the second half slowly, again dropping to the tail end of the league before staging a comeback. They achieved third place by early August, situated behind Augusta and Chattanooga, and were continuing to advance up the leaderboard. In the American League, Connie Mack's Philadelphia Athletics were engaged in a similarly heated pennant race, and were trying to gain an advantage over the Detroit Tigers. With the deadline approaching to recall minor leaguers, Mack had to decide whether or not he felt any of his rookie upstarts had the potential of aiding his team down the stretch. Since Jackson was a known commodity, Mack concluded that Joe, along with center fielder Amos Struck (who had been farmed out to Milwaukee), would be valuable additions. After the August 31, 1909, game at Macon, a contest the Indians won 9–3, Jackson returned to Savannah to pack his gear.[57] This time he was making the trek to Philadelphia willingly.

On his way out of town, The *Savannah Morning News* proclaimed: "Jackson is one of the greatest natural ball players who ever performed in this section, and did greater work than even the mighty Tyrus Cobb."[58] It was an incredible compliment.

Four years earlier, Cobb batted .326 for the Augusta Tourists in the Sally League. Now here was Jackson, having hit .358 in 118 games and headed straight for the majors with greater confidence, maturity, and refined ability. Was he the second coming of Cobb? Nobody knew, but Mack certainly wanted the opportunity to find out for himself. Jackson arrived in Philadelphia on the evening of September 6, and was starting in center field against the New York Highlanders the following afternoon. It was an abrupt adjustment—akin to being thrown to the lions—but Joe did his best, garnering a single in an 8–6 loss. However, on one play, he was caught flatfooted on a long drive by New York first baseman Hal Chase and the latter raced around the bases for an inside-the-park home run. A writer for the *Philadelphia Inquirer* believed Chase might've been held to a double if Jackson "moved over the green at a faster clip."[59]

Over the season's final weeks, Joe wasn't called upon by Mack to contribute anything on the field, and was apparently going through a phase in which it was more important to watch and observe than to play an active role. In following the games, he was undoubtedly influenced by the professionalism of his teammates, particularly twenty-two-year-old second baseman Eddie Collins. While Mack himself was a true baseball genius, Joe likely felt disappointed by his benchwarmer status. After all, he was a competitor at heart. For fans of the Philadelphia Athletics, they watched the pennant slip from the fingers of their favorite team, and a pair of losses to the Chicago White Sox on September 30, 1909, gave Detroit absolute claim to the league championship.

Jackson played in both games, but his confidence was clearly weakened by the long hiatus on the bench. In the seventh inning of the first game, he erred trying to catch Billy Purtell's fly, allowing two runners to score. Another runner reached home the next inning on a ball that should have been caught by either Jackson or center fielder Rube Oldring. For Joe, it was an all-around dismal display. The Sox went on to win, 8–3. In the second game, Joe managed to get on base when catcher Yip Owens couldn't handle a dribbler in front of the plate. He'd eventually score, but Chicago closed out the game with a 6–4 victory. Jackson also played in the final two games of the season, a doubleheader against Washington on October 2 and, between them, went 1-for-9. Philadelphia finished the season in second place with a 95–58 record, while the Detroit Tigers went to the World Series to face the Pittsburgh Pirates, though they lost in seven games.

The season ended on a sour note, and Jackson was underwhelming in his limited appearances.[60] In Joe's mind, his tenure in Philadelphia was over for good, and rumors circulated that he'd be with Atlanta of the Southern Association in 1910.[61] Atlanta suited him fine. But before he was officially sent elsewhere, Jackson was ordered to report for Philadelphia's spring training in early March, to which he responded dutifully.[62] Within a day, the decision was made to send Joe to New Orleans instead, and Jackson was anything but happy. Mack, nevertheless, spoke highly about the young athlete, telling a reporter: "Jackson should be one of the greatest ball players the game has ever known. If he will just hustle a little and take the major leagues more seriously he will go as high in the profession as any young man I know of."[63]

In addition to Jackson's wandering mind and moodiness, he was banged up a bit during the spring of 1910, allegedly stemming from being hit by a pitch. There were claims of kidney problems and broken ribs, which might have contributed to his swift transfer to New Orleans. Surprisingly, though, Mack relinquished all rights to Jackson in the process. He essentially gave the outfielder to manager Charlie Frank for free, despite Frank's offer of $1,500.[64] Mack didn't want the money from his friend because he knew Frank was getting a physically injured athlete with plenty of baggage. A few days later, Jackson turned up in New Orleans to have his ribs examined and, on March 9, participated in a light morning practice.[65] His health and conditioning improved quite rapidly, and the fact that he had friends in the league was helpful to his mental state. In fact, his Savannah teammate and pal, Frank Manush, was also signed by New Orleans for the 1910 campaign.

Popular from the start, Jackson was back performing his on-field stunts in no time. His mere presence was enough to boost local enthusiasm, and along with the other personnel changes Frank made, the New Orleans Pelicans were seen as the team to beat in the Southern Association. Their high level of play was demonstrated in several exhibitions against the Cleveland Naps of the American League later in March, and Jackson's power hitting was a real eye-opener for those in attendance. The Pelicans took several wins from their major league counterparts, and Joe's work was usually responsible. His hitting success was so common that it became expected, and sportswriters casually remarked that he achieved his "daily" triple in their postgame columns. "Jackson has hit nearly every pitcher who has faced New Orleans this spring," a writer for the *New Orleans Item* remarked. "That he will prove the batting sensation of the Southern League is a foregone conclusion."[66]

The predictions were accurate. He hit .339 during spring training exhibitions and planned to at least equal that figure during the regular season. But he was still prone to mistakes in the field, including misjudging flies and failing to anticipate bad hops. Manager Charlie Frank was patient with him. He realized that Joe's obvious contributions far outweighed his occasional blunders and was willing to overlook his eccentricities as well, as Jackson definitely had his quirks. One of them was his opposition to having his photograph taken. It was an inane superstition that he firmly believed and, for that reason, he tried to evade them as much as possible.[67] From an outside perspective, it might have seemed like Jackson was presenting unnecessary difficulties, but it was just Joe being Joe.

As the Southern Association season progressed, Jackson's average pushed up over .370, and a writer for the *New Orleans Item* called him the "Ty Cobb of the Minors."[68] Many people felt his return to the majors was inevitable but, on the other hand, there were skeptics who didn't know if Jackson had the stomach for the big leagues. Stories of his multiple disappearances from Philadelphia were well known, and any teams considering him were gambling to a certain extent. He was physically able—perhaps well beyond the normal capabilities of a major leaguer—but his stubborn mind, uneducated and unsophisticated, created a gigantic question mark that couldn't be avoided. Connie Mack was witness to these problems and released Jackson, freeing himself of the worry. But Joe Jackson was going to get another chance, and the fans of Major League Baseball were soon going to see for themselves whether the stories of his extraordinary slugging were true or just a lot of hot air.

2

BOUND FOR THE BIG SHOW

The American League was celebrating its tenth year as the junior organization of the major leagues in 1910, and several teams planned to punctuate the decennial with yet another enrapturing pennant fight. By June, both the Detroit Tigers and New York Highlanders were nipping at the heels of the first-place Philadelphia Athletics, and the Boston Red Sox weren't far behind. At just under the .500 mark, in fifth place, sat the Cleveland Naps, a club seemingly ill-equipped for the continuous pressure of high-level competition. The latter's poor showing shocked rooters, who felt the team should've been faring much better under the leadership of Napoleon Lajoie, Bill Bradley, Elmer Flick, and other well-known stars. But injuries and poor offensive work silenced any serious contention fairly early on in Cleveland's 1910 campaign.

Team executives were anything but heartened by the overwhelming weaknesses shown by their club, and were looking for an immediate improvement. That left manager Jim "Deacon" McGuire, a veteran of more than twenty years of big-league ball, in the difficult position of extracting life from a mostly lackluster outfit. He initiated personnel changes, altered the lineup, and benched players searching for the elusive cohesion Cleveland needed to win. The outfield was routinely in crisis, and despite the availability of a half-dozen athletes, McGuire couldn't nail down a winning combination.[1] The team was also considerably weakened by the overall diminishment of forty-three-year-old legend Cy Young and the arm problems of Addie Joss, which limited him to just 13 appearances.

These problems, of course, resulted in dwindling attendance and indifference among the baseball-going public. Such a decline might have been endurable (based on the circumstances)[2], to some extent, but the Naps had only months before ushering in a new concrete and steel stadium at a cost of $300,000.[3] With seating capacity for 21,000, management needed a winner on the field to begin recouping their investment. However, principal owners Charles W. Somers and John F. Kilfoyle were looking at a significant monetary loss. For Somers, it was a dreadful reversal for the once acknowledged "financial angel" of the American League. Needless to say, none of his colleagues had forgotten how he stepped up to personally finance four ballclubs in 1900–01 to the tune of $750,000, more than $18 million in 2015 dollars.[4]

Without Somers's willingness to bankroll his fellow magnates and overall enthusiasm in the expansion of the organization, the league would never have attained solid ground to eventually prosper. For that reason, American League President Ban Johnson expressed his solidarity by keeping a watchful eye over the dismal situation in Cleveland, and conversed with fellow baseball leaders with the intention of offering aid (whether monetary or personnel). Connie Mack in Philadelphia, one of the recipients of Somers's generosity several years before, was certainly keeping tabs on the calamity, while simultaneously examining the shortcomings of his own team. His obvious weak spot was in left field with old-timer Topsy Hartsel batting around .225. Heading into the final stretch of the 1910 season, Mack was eager to strengthen his lineup with a reliable right-handed outfielder, and trade options were on the table.

Positive reports were still streaming in from the Southern League about Joe Jackson, but Mack had given up on the South Carolinian when he released him outright to Charlie Frank of the minor league New Orleans Pelicans earlier in the year. Always a good judge of talent, Mack had serious misgivings about Jackson and wondered if he'd ever live up to his potential away from Southern ball fields, given his predisposition for homesickness. Also, Jackson was a left-handed batter, which was not what he needed at the time. Interestingly enough, Frank was willing to return Jackson to Mack, despite their previous transaction. He treasured his friendship with the Athletics leader and was unwavering in what was, essentially, an unwritten agreement to give Mack first option on Jackson if he played well during the 1910 campaign. He even rejected a record $10,000 offer for Jackson by Chicago Cubs owner Charles Murphy to remain loyal to Mack.[5]

Mack undoubtedly appreciated the sentiment shared by Frank, but instead of recalling Jackson from Philadelphia, he figured out another way to benefit from a potential arrangement. Turning his attention toward

Cleveland, he decided to initiate a trade to reacquire Bristol "Bris" Lord, a member of his Athletics squad from 1905–07. Lord, the kind of right-handed hitting outfielder Mack wanted, had been positioned in a backup-type role in Cleveland, and the Naps had no problem letting him go. Initially, an announcement came on July 23, 1910, that Lord had been sent to the Athletics for second-string third-baseman Morrie Rath in a most unimpressive swap.[6] But the rest of the deal included Mack releasing his hold on Jackson—which was much more important—and his gesture was acknowledged as a payback of sorts to Somers for his kindness years earlier.

Cleveland immediately began discussing terms with New Orleans and, soon thereafter, on July 30, for a reported amount somewhere in the range of $6,000 cash, succeeded in purchasing Jackson.[7] The acquisition was big news, as the Naps had obtained a player they'd wanted for months. In fact, club officials first laid eyes on Jackson during spring training and were riveted by his hitting and speed. Scout Billy Gilks, who managed Jackson in Savannah the year before, and was a personal friend of Naps leader Jim McGuire, also boasted about his natural hitting style. According to Gilks, Jackson was a must for Cleveland and, finally, after a lot of shrewd wheeling and dealing, he was a bona fide member of the team. There was one remaining hang-up, though. Because New Orleans was in the thick of a pennant race for the Southern League title, Frank refused to let Jackson depart before the season closed in September. Cleveland agreed to the stipulation, and Jackson remained in the South a little while longer.[8]

Holding on to first place in early August, New Orleans was outpacing its toughest challengers (Atlanta, Birmingham, and Chattanooga), and Jackson was a key element to the team's success. He continued to lead the league in batting with a .379 average, and his 125 hits in 94 games were far and away the best in the organization.[9] Rarely did he finish a game without getting on base through the power of his own bat, but pitchers would frequently walk him as a matter of strategy. They figured it was safer to put him on first than have him continuously score the runners ahead of him with long drives to the outfield. *New Orleans Item* sports editor Will R. Hamilton commented that pitchers had "quit feeding him strikes," and noticed how Jackson was extending his arms to swing at balls wide of the plate with some success. It was a bit unorthodox, but was the only way Jackson had a chance for a hit in those situations.[10]

New Orleans was not unconquerable, and Birmingham shut the club out in three straight games through August 10, finding a way to limit

Jackson's bat.[11] The downslide didn't last long, however, and the Pelicans went to work pummeling Montgomery on the road the following day. Although Jackson was the center attraction, he wasn't superhuman. He had his off days, just like anyone else, and there were plenty of instances where he just couldn't connect at the plate. Additionally, from time to time, overt mental lapses in the field displayed his inexperience. Against Birmingham, the twenty-three-year-old was apparently daydreaming while standing at first and neglected to catch sight of a ball hit by teammate Bill Lindsay to right field. Hearing the vociferous yelling from his bench, he broke for second base, unaware that they were screaming for him to return to first since the ball had been caught. He was easily doubled up.[12]

Such an occasion couldn't elicit anything but embarrassment for Jackson, and he learned the importance of staying on his toes, particularly when on the basepaths. Even so, management could deal with many of his limitations when balanced against his consistent offensive production. In winning both games of a doubleheader against Mobile on August 20, 1910, Jackson went 2-for-6 and rushed across the plate for the lone run of the second contest, a seven-inning no-hitter by Pat Paige.[13] Six days later, he went 3-for-4 against Nashville, and added another safe drive the next day with Senator Murphy J. Foster and Congressman Robert F. Broussard of Louisiana looking on. Noted sportswriter Grantland Rice, based on Jackson's clear dominance of the league, named the outfielder to his All-Southern team.[14]

Besides his keen eye and strong bat, Jackson was also known for playing hard and often demonstrating his grit. During the thirteenth inning of a game against the Atlanta Crackers on August 30, Jackson, who had been hitless on the day, bunted on pitcher Tom Fisher and the latter quickly nabbed the ball. Fisher made a move toward third, hoping to catch a runner off base, but the fielder, obviously not expecting Jackson to bunt, was out of position. Fisher instead spun around, chucking the ball toward first in a hurry. The ball was off its mark and collided with the back of Jackson's head, sending him hard to the dirt, and allowing the man at third to score. At first glance, it appeared that Jackson was seriously injured and officials sought to remove him from the game. His grogginess was only temporary, and he regained his composure enough to wave off a pinch runner. Jackson proceeded to steal second, and then scored the winning run on a base hit by Bill Lindsay. These efforts, combined with a spectacular catch earlier in the afternoon, once again had all of the New Orleans sports community talking about Joe Jackson.[15]

Advised to sit out the next game to ensure a full recovery, Jackson didn't adjourn to the grandstand, but tried his hand at coaching the base-runners. He turned in a career day on September 3 against the Chattanooga Lookouts, smashing a double, two triples, and scoring three times. He drove in two others in a 6–2 victory, and a nearly impossible running catch rounded out his stellar performance.[16] Jackson, as the final games of the season were played, was comparatively subdued, but his individual results had no effect on the pennant race. On September 11, 1910, the *New Orleans Item* announced that the Pelicans were the winners of the Southern League championship.[17] That afternoon, Jackson went 0-for-3 in his last game with the club, but New Orleans came around to defeat Atlanta, 1–0. Enthusiastic supporters marked the occasion by giving their heroes solid gold watch fobs as a gift honoring their achievement.[18]

Back in Cleveland, things remained sour for the Naps ballclub despite a number of changes. Management placed a heightened emphasis on obtaining younger and faster players, and began cutting loose some of the team's older veterans.[19] Longtime stars Elmer Flick and Bill Bradley were dismissed from the team, and it seemed that none of the other aged athletes were safe, with an exception of Nap Lajoie (35) and Cy Young (43). The changes were classified as a reorganization of the entire franchise, with big money being poured into recruits without any semblance of hesitation. The outward expenses for up-and-comers were stunning in light of the major financial losses, estimated to be upwards of $50,000.[20] Naps President Charles W. Somers, who'd bought out partner John F. Kilfoyl in July 1910, was more motivated than ever to have a first-class aggregation representing Cleveland.[21]

A commentator in *The Sporting News* backed up that claim, insisting that if Somers had $5 million in the bank, he'd be willing to spend four of it to capture an American League pennant.[22] The forty-one-year-old Somers was that serious, and being a third-generation coal magnate with extensive holdings, he had the resources to make a legitimate impact. His spirited views of baseball elicited confidence in his administration, and with Jim McGuire sharing the same passion as the manager, big things were expected. The arrival of Joe Jackson was considered a momentous step in the right direction, but bearing in mind the previous failures of Connie Mack to indoctrinate him into the majors, there was plenty to be concerned about. That left the number one question from both the team, media, and fans: Could Jackson adapt to life on the American League circuit without an all-encompassing and uncontrollable urge to return to Dixie?

"It is said that Jackson prefers to play in the south and be a big fish in a little pond," one New Orleans writer explained.[23] Minor leaguer Leo Huber of New Orleans, a friend of Jackson, also seemed to think Joe was more interested in remaining with the Pelicans than breaking into the big leagues.[24] Neither belief was very positive for the outlook of Jackson as a member of the Naps, especially if he was going into the journey with preconceived notions of what life would be like in the North. An errant episode could end up similar to his experience in Philadelphia, and find him back in South Carolina before anyone ever realized. In that respect, his time in Cleveland would be completely harmful and diminish the positivity management was striving for.

The opportunity for Major League Baseball was presenting itself once again to Jackson, and it was up to him to seize the moment without reservations. The fears and angst he bowed to previously had needed to be something of the past if he expected to earn the grandiose paychecks offered in the big show. By 1910, Jackson was indeed older and wiser. His behavior on and off the field was shaped by a calm coolness that derived from within. Confidence was certainly a factor, and being able to rely on his natural baseball instincts was comforting. After his marriage to Katie, he was inspired to strengthen his intellect and, although he was never going to be an academic, any small gains in the areas of reading and writing were important.[25] Later in the year, a reporter stated that Jackson was "now able to pen his name," plus "read the papers, and even bits of Shakespeare, Milton, and Browning, and understand most everything."[26]

While such a claim might have been a stretch, there is no doubt that Jackson was making an effort to progress in areas that didn't come to him as naturally as baseball. There is little doubt that he, probably in discussions with his wife, realized that entering the majors would offer the opportunity to make serious money from playing baseball. Toughing out the challenges of big city living and proving to the world that he was of major league caliber was the only way to really improve their lot in life. He was embracing the risky leap of faith to a certain degree, and the support of his wife was instrumental, but the involvement of Billy Gilks as an agent for the Naps was ideal. Gilks, a trusted and influential mentor, was there to bridge the gap between the two entities and ensure that Jackson safely ventured to his new Cleveland home.

Purported to have departed his Carrollton Avenue home in New Orleans on the evening of September 11, Jackson was expected in Cleveland two days later. However, an excitable journalist, apparently tipped off that Jackson wasn't on the Pullman as believed, jumped the gun and released a report insisting that the ballplayer "quit" the trip northward and was headed back to the Carolinas.[27] It wasn't true. The Jacksons, accompanied by Gilks, were running a little late and a missed connection at Cincinnati also delayed their journey. Their train pulled into Cleveland at 3 p.m. on the afternoon of September 15, and Joe was slated to make his debut for the Naps at League Park the following day.[28]

For Jackson, it was critical that he not be overwhelmed by the weight placed on his shoulders in terms of having to achieve otherworldly results right off the bat. Cleveland reporters had touted his skills, and fans were optimistically awaiting the arrival of the next Ty Cobb. That kind of buildup was unfair, but since Jackson had finished his Southern League season with a leading .354 average, it was hard not to anticipate big things for him. Personally, he needed to take things in stride; from dealing with the aesthetics of the major league ball parks, the bustling life in various metropolises, and being surrounded by massive crowds everywhere he went. Adjusting to the styles and cleverness of major league pitchers was one of his biggest hurdles and, in time, would determine whether he was truly fit to be among the best ballplayers in the world.

On September 16, Jackson ran out to center field before the commencement of the first inning, and joined a defensive lineup alongside right fielder Ted Easterly—who normally played behind the plate—and rookie left fielder Dave Callahan. In front of him, manning the infield, were rookies Eddie Hohnhorst at first and Roger Peckinpaugh at short. Terry Turner was situated at the hot corner and Nap Lajoie was acting as the on-field general at second base. Willie Mitchell was on the mound and Grover Land was serving in the backstop role. Their opponents were the Washington Senators, and Jackson, batting third, matched up against right-hander Dixie Walker in the first inning. Anxious to the core, he swung at the first pitch and crushed a liner to right fielder Bill Cunningham for an out. Unfortunately, Cunningham tossed the ball to second to double up Callahan.[29]

Jackson walked in the third inning, but managed a single in the eighth with a blast over second base and later scored. Henry P. Edwards of the *Cleveland Plain Dealer* commended Jackson's work in the outfield, describing a picturesque catch he made in the seventh off Bob Unglaub. Edwards called it a "most spectacular shoestring catch," stopping what might have been an inside-the-park home run, and the audience appreciated his fine effort.[30] Interestingly, Dave Callahan, Cleveland's new left fielder, was talked up as the team's budding star. In fact, Washington manager Jimmy McAleer believed Callahan, and not Jackson, was the "best outfielder Cleveland had got hold of in ten years," according to the *Plain Dealer*.[31] Despite the positive press, Callahan failed to live up to expectations, as he only played in 19 total games of major league ball over two seasons.

After sweeping Washington, Cleveland welcomed Philadelphia to town, and Jackson had a chance to face off against Connie Mack and his ex-teammates on September 19. During the contest, Jackson displayed his speed by stretching a double into a triple, pulling a move only Ty Cobb would've attempted and, in addition to scoring a run, logged five putouts in the outfield. The Naps took the victory, their fourth straight, by a score of 5–4. Topsy Hartsel of the Athletics, following the game, told a reporter, "Jackson does not look like the same player he did with us. He has improved a thousand per cent." Another observer, San Antonio manager George Leidy, who witnessed some of Jackson's miraculous feats in the minors, said, "Joe has not struck his gait, yet. Just wait until he gets over his nervousness and begins to hit them out."[32]

A couple days later, the South Carolinian looked like the All-Star Leidy remembered, going 4-for-4 against the New York Highlanders, and Henry P. Edwards wrote, "Joe Jackson has all the natural qualifications of a big leaguer."[33] That declaration, made less than two weeks into Jackson's time in Cleveland, was a significant boost to Jackson, and represented the wider appreciation for his game play. He was hitting, running, and fielding in a superb manner, and the insider tricks he didn't yet know would soon be taught to him. Of their recruits, there was no more doubting that Jackson was Cleveland's foremost up-and-comer. At Chicago on October 1, he again went 4-for-4, and owner Charles Somers, who attended the game, was mighty proud to see his Southern import live up to his promise.[34]

Jackson got his first look at Ty Cobb in American League competition when the Naps traveled to Detroit for a doubleheader on October 5, 1910. In the initial contest, Joe achieved two hits, the first a bounding missile into center field in the fifth, which Cobb misjudged, and two runs scored on his error.

Jackson also singled in the five-run tenth, helping Cleveland to an 8–3 victory. Detroit rebounded to take the second game, 4–2.[35] With the team guaranteed to finish in fifth place, Cleveland fans held on to hope that Nap Lajoie would top Cobb for the batting title, and the season-ending doubleheader at St. Louis on October 9 was crucial to the final numbers. Lajoie had an uphill fight on his hands, but by forcing a number of bunts toward a deep-playing third baseman, he managed to go 8-for-8 on the day. The league statistician figured Cobb still held an advantage, .385 to .384, and Ty won both the 1910 crown and a Chalmers automobile.[36]

St. Louis pitchers didn't exactly face a pushover with Jackson at the plate during the doubleheader finale. He went 4-for-8 and finished the season with a .387 average. Even though the *Cleveland Plain Dealer* acknowledged him as the "nominal" batting champion, his 20 games were far below the league minimum to qualify for the running.[37] Jackson did admirable work in his limited time, attaining 29 hits, 15 runs, 11 RBIs, five triples, two doubles, and one home run. He continued to bat solidly against Cincinnati in the postseason Ohio State championship series, an interleague competition between the Naps and Reds, but had his moments of shame as well. In the sixth inning of the opening contest at Cincinnati on October 11, he miscalculated a sturdy-hit ball by Dode Paskert and watched it go over his head. He tried to readjust, but it was already too late as the ball rolled back to the bleachers. By the time Jackson got to the ball and made a throw, Paskert was dashing in for a home run.[38] Cleveland fought to a seventh game, dropping the finale on October 18, 8–5.[39]

Nevertheless, Jackson batted .357 with 10 hits and six runs. Pocketing a little extra money, each of the Naps players broke for their homesteads and, almost immediately, the rumor mill spun a web of stories, exaggerations, and light-hearted tales to keep the baseball fan busy during the winter. Jackson, surprisingly, was targeted in some of the bitter commentary, and it appeared that many of those who were willing to speak negatively about him on the record had some kind of agenda.

One of the underlying theories by pundits since Jackson had joined Cleveland was that he possessed a prevailing flaw that Connie Mack recognized, which was the reason why the latter let him go. It was assumed that because Mack was such a tremendous judge of talent, he passed on the South Carolinian for this obscured imperfection, which he believed would eventually derail his chances in the big leagues.[40] The *Wilkes-Barre Times-Leader* responded to the speculation by stating, "The only thing that Jackson seems to be lacking in is thought, and he will not need much of this if he can continue to line the ball out as he did last fall."[41] Other critics went out of their way to invalidate his successful batting average by claiming that pitchers weren't trying their hardest against him given that Cleveland was already eliminated from the pennant race—as were their opponents.

A considerable amount of the pessimism originated in Detroit, apparently from loyalists of Ty Cobb.[42] Tigers pitcher George Mullin was wholly unimpressed by Jackson, despite the fact that Joe and the Naps went 2–4 against him in their only meeting. He bluntly predicted that the slugger wouldn't hit north of .250 in 1911.[43] A Detroit writer went a step further, calling him a "flash in the pan," and felt Jackson wouldn't even be in the majors by the end of the year.[44] These prophecies weren't based on legitimate scouting reports or insider "dope," and the original intentions of the various psychics—other than trying to get inside the head of Jackson and disrupt his positive momentum—was unclear. Pitchers had tried to figure out his weaknesses, presuming balls on the inside of the plate would possibly silence his bat.

But umpire Billy Evans, in a syndicated column, described a structured attempt by the St. Louis Browns to solve Jackson at the plate late in the season. He explained that multiple attempts were made, with varied attacks, but each proved to be failures.[45] Charlie Smith, a pitcher for the Boston Red Sox, came to the same conclusion. He had scouted Jackson in advance of a pitching engagement in Cleveland, watching him intently, and informed a friend, "That fellow would be fooled on a slow ball." He later told a reporter: "I thought I had Jackson's measure, and was tickled when Patsy Donovan had me work against the Naps a couple of days later. I gave Jackson two fast wide ones to make him anxious, and then put up a floater. Jackson swung with all his might, and, say I never saw a ball hit so hard in my life. It went over the field on a line. I ducked just in time to save my head being knocked off."[46]

Cleveland catcher Grover Land offered more support for Jackson. "They say this New Orleans recruit might take a tumble next season when the pitchers get next to his weakness. Well, take it from me; they've got another guess coming. He hasn't any weakness. Usually a free swinger like Jackson is bothered by a low curve around the knees. Well, last fall when Jackson had made a name for himself with his batting in the American League, Jim McGuire told Cy Young to give him everything he had. This was during batting practice. Cy started with a fast one on the inside and Joe put it to the fence. Then he curved one at his knees, and that boy laid on it and winged it over the center fielder's head. Now, Cy has a lot of stuff and he used every bit of it, but he never fooled Jackson. He's certain to be the best batter in the world; maybe not next year, for he's still a little green, but mighty soon after."[47]

Being a rookie, Jackson was obviously prey for the more irritating vocal veterans; guys who enjoyed tormenting and unnerving newcomers. In truth, one of the enduring beliefs about Joe was that he was easily susceptible to teasing and could be thrown off his game by any sort of razzing.[48] His lack of sophistication furthered the notion that he was an easy target for poking and prodding. However, the real effectiveness of any psychological methods was still up in the air.

In terms of genuine physical and playing limitations, the youthful Jackson was thought to have a few. His work in the outfield was largely applauded, but he was prone to mental mistakes and his accuracy was less than desired. Teammate Cy Young had a more brutal opinion of Joe's "outer garden" efforts, saying in 1952: "Jackson was one of the weakest fielders I ever saw in all my years in baseball. He couldn't field a lick. I tried to coach him but he couldn't or wouldn't learn. He had a strong throwing arm but lacked accuracy and too often threw to the wrong base."[49] Another area in need of improvement was Jackson's ability to read a situation and follow through with the correct play. It wasn't all slugging for individual numbers, but oftentimes a smallish contribution to advance runners or just to get on base. He also needed to tone back attempts to grab extra bases in risky situations, meaning he was to avoid trying to duplicate the impossible feats made by Ty Cobb.

While many were expecting Jackson's next season to be a flop, there was a sizable quantity of complimentary press surrounding him as well. Clark Griffith, manager of the Cincinnati Reds, told a reporter that Jackson was "going to be the best in the business," and that he shined "in every department of the game. I wish I had him."[50] Chicago Cubs owner Charles Murphy once again made a play for Jackson, offering Cleveland upwards of $15,000 at the end of the 1910 season. Charles Somers replied to the proposal, saying: "We are trying to build up a ballclub, not tear it down. Fifteen thousand dollars would look very sweet, but where could we play the money?"[51] *The Sporting News* featured a prominent photo of Jackson on the front page of its issue on December 28, 1910, and a news service declared that he had a lifetime professional batting average of better than .380 since his professional debut in 1908.[52]

Optimism was renewed in Cleveland and, naturally, local sportswriters proclaimed that the Naps had gotten the better of the Jackson-Harry Lord deal.[53] While Lord was a key instrument in Connie Mack's World Series–winning franchise, Jackson was an unparalleled prospect and was an invaluable asset. The naysayers were chomping at the bit to slay into the young man, but discerning magnates knew he was cut from an entirely different cloth than the everyday recruit. During the recent Series, Charles Murphy of the Cubs asked Philadelphia Athletics co-owner Benjamin Shibe, "How did you ever let Jackson get away from you?" Shibe replied, "Well, Charley, I guess [Cleveland Vice President Ernest] Barnard must have hypnotized Connie."[54]

Undaunted by the printed comments, good or bad, Jackson considered returning to Cleveland over the winter to invest in a pool hall, but the down-home luxuries of Greenville, South Carolina, kept him close to his family.[55] Nearing the end of February 1911, he ventured to New Orleans to enjoy Mardi Gras. An inquisitive journalist caught up with him, and Jackson mentioned his goal of being in the upper stratosphere of league batters, competing alongside Ty Cobb and teammate Nap Lajoie. It was a bold statement, but otherwise, he was quite unassuming. "I hit 'em and start running," he explained. "If they get me, I have no kick coming, for I'm doing the best I can."[56] Many subsequent reports indicated a more confident tenor to Jackson's expectations, including alleged boastfulness about winning the title over his more experienced rivals.[57] "I wish him all the luck in the world," Cobb said in response to the hubbub. "I hope he hits .400 for that matter, for if he does I am going to try and top him [by] a point or two."[58]

Mingling with old colleagues and friends, Jackson decided to give fans a treat by rejoining the New Orleans Pelicans on March 5, 1911, in an exhibition against the Chicago Cubs. He went 3-for-4 with a run and four putouts in a rousing 5–2 victory.[59] The next day, he made the trip northwest to Alexandria, Louisiana, and met his Cleveland teammates to begin spring training. Although he was said to be in "perfect condition," Jackson was in for a bumpy month, both physically and mentally.[60] It started with an errant pitch by Harry Fanwell to his ankle, causing a painful bruise, and was followed by a minor leg injury a few days later. To top it off, he accidentally smashed into the outfield fence, cutting his finger.[61] Unfortunately for him, this wasn't the end of his poor luck. Not only was he hit in the back of the neck by another stray pitch, but caught a cold and was briefly bedridden.

Finally, to make matters even worse, he received news from Louisville that the stockpile of "Joe Jackson model" baseball bats at the J. F. Hillerich & Son plant had been destroyed, along with many others, in a devastating fire the previous December. The company revealed the sorrowful information after receiving Jackson's bat order for the season, and the latter needed to send one of his existing pieces of timber so that duplicates could be made to specification. Around that same time, keeping with the gloomy nature of things that spring, he managed to break his choice bat during batting practice, and that was the one he mailed to Louisville.[62]

Putting things into the proper perspective, the small injuries and forgettable moments of the spring were nothing compared to the tragic demise of Cleveland pitcher Addie Joss. Well-liked by everyone who he came in contact with, Joss was rebounding from a 1910 arm injury and his leadership and abilities were paramount to Cleveland's success. Becoming ill during a training stop in Chattanooga early in April 1911, he went home to Toledo for medical attention. Two days into the season, on April 14, his teammates were notified in St. Louis that the thirty-one-year-old had passed away from tubercular meningitis. Words almost failed to capture the weight of his death on his friends, and the importance of baseball was shelved to properly mourn.

Cleveland players were adamant about attending Joss's funeral services in Toledo on April 17, and officials discussed postponing a scheduled game that afternoon at Detroit to allow that to occur. Strangely, American League President Ban Johnson at first blocked an attempt to reschedule the game, but was moved to change his mind when players threatened to strike in protest.[63] Unsympathetic league rules were not going to prevent a full showing of respect at the funeral, and on April 17, "the Cleveland team, consisting of twenty-five members," trekked to Toledo to honor their fallen comrade, according to the *New York Times*.[64] Conversely, a report in the *Cleveland Plain Dealer* indicated that only "Eighteen" Naps players went to the funeral, and Jackson wasn't one of them.[65] Understanding the importance of Joss and how he related to rookies and veterans alike with a personal style all his own, there is no clear understanding why Jackson wouldn't have attended his services, if that was indeed the case.

The trivialities of baseball soon took center stage again, and all eyes were on Jackson each and every time he stepped up to the plate. He was, after all, beginning his first full season in the majors. In spite of the various calamities, Joe had a successful spring and was in good shape. His sharpness was demonstrated during an exhibition series against New Orleans, and his confidence increased measurably. Ted Breitenstein, a former Pelican teammate, told a reporter in jest, "We know [Jackson's] weakness: Throw the ball behind him and he'll never get a hit."[66]

Getting tips and instruction from his older peers, particularly in how to use his speed more to his advantage, Jackson was evolving into a more balanced athlete. The care in which manager Jim McGuire handled him was effective, and first baseman George Stovall was so concerned about his development that he became Joe's roommate on the road.[67] This kind of mentorship was crucial as Jackson continued to adjust to his new life.

Nap Lajoie was asked if he thought Jackson was the kind of player who'd endure in the big leagues or if the youngster was just a bunch of hype. "There is not one chance in ten that he will fail to stick," Lajoie answered confidently. "Jackson is a natural ball player. He is a natural batter, a natural fielder and thrower, and such players don't explode. There is no luck about Jackson's success. He has come to the top because he cannot help being a star player. And he is going to stick."[68] The enthusiastic support from one of baseball's undeniable superstars was inspiring, and the relationship between Jackson and Lajoie was without jealousy or acrimony. After being told of Jackson's desire to win the batting title, Lajoie said, "More power to you, old boy. Get on as often as you can and I will try to send you home."[69] With the lumber of Jackson and Lajoie cracking them out, Cleveland fans were greatly encouraged, and the 1911 season promised to be one for the ages.

3

"THAT GUY AIN'T HUMAN"

In the days leading up to the first pitched ball of the new season, experts across the baseball spectrum stepped forward with their official predictions, denoting the supposed winners and losers in the upcoming pennant race. Their comments were entertaining to say the least, and readers were provided with quality insight into what could be anticipated from each major league team. New York–based sportswriter Wilton S. Farnsworth delivered his authoritative "dope" in a syndicated column in April 1911. He liked the chances of Philadelphia repeating as American League champions, and estimated that New York, Chicago, Detroit, and Boston were in the fight for a spot among the top-four clubs. Cleveland too, he figured, had an outside possibility to show well, but it really hinged on whether Addie Joss regained his pitching arm. The emergence of Joe Jackson was also going to be a critical factor if the team planned to reach its full potential.[1]

Joss's sudden death cast a noticeable shadow over the statements of prognosticators and pundits while lessening expectations for the Naps as their season opened at St. Louis on April 12, 1911. The Browns exploited the apparent fragility of Cleveland, winning the initial game 12–3, mostly because of the seven errors the latter committed. Jackson went 1-for-4 on the day, scoring a run and contributing a folly when he bobbled a ball hit to center field.[2] Right from the jump, Jackson displayed an extraordinary consistency at the plate, and it was rare that he didn't rebound after failing to make contact from one at-bat to the next.[3] Batting third in the lineup behind outfielder Jack Graney and third baseman Terry Turner and benefitting from the protection of having Nap Lajoie behind him, Jackson posed a serious challenge to pitchers.

During Cleveland's home opener on April 20 before over 14,000 fans, Jackson earned a standing ovation—not for a safe blast to the outfield—but for his defensive prowess. In the fourth inning he snagged a difficult liner by Frank LaPorte and then hurled a bullet to catcher Syd Smith to get Jimmy Austin who was dashing for the plate. The *Cleveland Plain Dealer* referred to Austin as one of the fastest players in the league, but noted that Joe's perfect throw got him by "two feet or more." Adding a single and a triple, a stolen base, and a run, made Jackson the team's sole highlight in spite of another heartbreaking loss to St. Louis. This time, the Browns managed to score three runs in the ninth inning and one in the 10th to win the ballgame, 4–3.[4] The next day, Jackson demonstrated his immense power by slamming out a 386-foot home run, the longest at the reconstructed League Park in Cleveland. The awe-inspiring ball hit into right-center sailed clear out of the structure and across Lexington Avenue.[5]

Fans marveled at his back-to-back showings and admired his rounded skills. Critics ate the story up as well, and Jackson was propelled into the headlines. In his early performances, he struggled a bit against spitballers Jack Lively of Detroit and Ed Walsh of Chicago, but with an average of better than .360, his successes were already far outweighing his failures. Again, versus St. Louis on May 7, he achieved an inside-the-park grand slam, helping the Naps win 6–2 in 12 innings.[6]

On May 10, he displayed his relentless ferocity in the sixth inning against Boston after slapping a grounder into the mitt of shortstop Steve Yerkes. The latter tossed it cleanly to first baseman Rip Williams for what should have been an easy out. Jackson, however, in his haste, knocked into Williams, causing the ball to roll free and safely attained first. It was arguably a case of interference, but the umpire didn't call it. The hard-nosed maneuver was usually reserved for the more experienced veterans, not a player in his very first full season.[7]

The confidence that was budding in Jackson was not shared by members of the Cleveland Naps as a whole. In fact, things couldn't have been much worse. Shortly after the campaign began, the team sank to the bottom of the standings and manager Jim McGuire was appropriately concerned. (The team was 6–11 after their loss on May 1, which put them in seventh place. They were only behind the 4–11 Browns, who earned three of their four victories against the Naps.) The play of Jackson and left-handed rookie sensation Vean Gregg, who'd pitch his way to a 23–7 record in 1911, were about the only encouraging elements of the club. Despite numerous efforts, McGuire was unable to effect a quick turnaround and he resigned as manager before the team's game on May 3.[8] First baseman George Stovall, his replacement, battled the same impediments and Cleveland didn't win its tenth game until May 13. Injuries to Nap Lajoie and others were persistently a detriment and, considering all of the odd negativity surrounding the team, it seemed to be just a matter of time before Jackson was, in some way, derailed.

Naysayers were eagerly waiting for Jackson's collapse, while other adversaries continued their mission to shatter his resolve. Umpire Billy Evans wrote that he didn't believe that "any ballplayer ever started a season under less auspicious circumstances than did Joe Jackson in 1911." The hardship stemmed from the fact that he was "forced to face a volley of criticism" on a regular basis from hostile players on the field. These specific tormenters believed he was mentally weak and, if pestered enough, was primed to flee the majors for his home as he'd done earlier in his career. "Well Joe, I see you haven't gone home yet," Evans quoted one of his bullies as saying. Another said: "A couple of more days without any hits and it will be back to the Sunny South for Joe."[9] But Jackson wasn't a quitter. He was a different person than he was in 1908–09, and he *was* mentally equipped to not only handle the barbs, but big city living and big-league pitching.

Unfortunately for Jackson, misfortune did catch up with him during a contest with Philadelphia on May 22, 1911. Swinging at the first ball pitched to him by Cy Morgan in the second inning, he cracked a bone in his right forefinger and it was predicted that he'd miss up to three weeks of action.[10] He fought through the pain and returned five days later, still firing on all cylinders. In early June, he broached the .400 mark and was hot on the trail of Ty Cobb for league batting honors. Around the same time, Jackson was moved from center field to right to make way for Joe Birmingham, who George Stovall hoped would provide leadership in the outfield for Joe and Jack Graney.[11] The Naps went eastward with their revised combination and, at Washington on June 6, Jackson had everyone talking after his first inning three-run homer was launched out of Griffith Stadium. Impressed by his clouting, *Washington Times* sportswriter Bob Thayer wrote, "No ball, high or low, in or out, appears to worry this batting wonder."[12]

During the season, Jackson displayed immense heart by playing through injuries to his lower back and heel. He wasn't one to show his physical vulnerabilities and always wanted to stay in the game. When directed to the sidelines by a physician, he did so under protest and immediately wanted back in.

Toughness and resiliency would become synonymous with Jackson in major league circles, and the claims that he was an emotionally fragile athlete were rapidly dismissed. Generally passive, he was willing to ignore trash talking, but if he felt wrongdoing had occurred during a play he didn't hesitate to let the offender know. Considering his size and the obvious natural strength he possessed from years at the mill, he was an imposing presence both on and off the field.

Few men in baseball could hammer the ball the way he had so far in 1911, and reporters often compared him to slugger extraordinaire Sam Crawford of the Detroit Tigers. The similar manner in which they powered drives out for doubles, triples, and homers were unlike their counterparts. On the Naps' June road trip, Eastern cities were exposed to the depth of Jackson's capabilities, and witnesses to his feats now understood why he was up among the league leaders in nearly all offensive categories. Overall, the tour was disastrous for the Naps, as the team went 5–10, including a rough five-game losing streak at New York and Boston. Jackson, in addition, saw his batting average drop to .383.

Back in Cleveland on June 28, Jackson pulled down a difficult hit by Chicago's Ping Bodie. The following day, a frustrated Bodie told the press: "I hope I live long enough to rob Joe Jackson of a home run just to get even for that catch he made off me against the right-field wall yesterday."[13] In making the splendid play, Jackson made hard contact with the barrier and narrowly evaded injury.

He recorded his 100th hit—a home run versus St. Louis—on July 4, 1911, and was the second American Leaguer to reach the century mark for the season; Ty Cobb being the first.[14] Cobb, incidentally, was playing remarkably well. He enjoyed a 40-game hit streak and was batting better than .440 by the middle of July, more than 60 points higher than Jackson. Eddie Collins, Sam Crawford, and Nap Lajoie (in that order) made up the rest of the league's top five hitters, but Cobb's advantage was pretty sizable at that time.

The Naps, under the efficient direction of George Stovall, won 22 of 30 contests and edged into fourth place on July 17.[15] A week later, All-Stars from across the American League turned up in Cleveland to participate in the Addie Joss benefit game. Ty Cobb, Tris Speaker, and Walter Johnson were among the contingent of league celebrities set to play the Naps, and 15,281 spectators attended the League Park affair. Sharing the right-field spot with his former New Orleans teammate, Hank Butcher, Jackson went 0-for-2 and Cleveland was defeated by the score of 5–3.[16] The next day, the Naps went east again and endured a tour only slightly improved over their previous one, winning six games and losing nine. They slipped in the standings and were fighting to keep out of sixth place. Jackson, throughout, was increasing his average a little at a time, inching back toward the .400 mark.

Thirty-six-year-old Napoleon "Nap" Lajoie, in his sixteenth year of big-league service, returned to Cleveland's regular lineup in early August after a sustained absence. The big infielder was badly needed and his comeback from injury was expected to have many positive effects on the play of the squad. For Jackson, the influence of Lajoie was significantly important to his game. His poise on the field, at bat, and in the clubhouse made him a surefire idol, and Joe watched him closely for suggestions on how to develop his game. After all, Lajoie was a multi-time league batting titleholder and the last man to bat better than .400 (.426 in 1901). In terms of his methodology rubbing off on Jackson, Lajoie had a routine of drinking a gallon of buttermilk each day, claiming that it helped strengthen his eyes at the plate. It wasn't long before Jackson was also consuming the beverage, eager for the same results.[17]

"I like to play next to [Nap] in the batting order better than with any other man I know," Jackson explained. "When that fellow gives you the sign for something, you can go ahead dead sure that he will do his part. It isn't often that the play don't go through with [Nap] at bat. I guess he likes to have a fast man ahead of him on the bases. Anyway, he never comes up when I am on without handing out a sign for something or other. That's the kind of a man I like to play with."[18]

The batting race in the American League tightened and newspapers were updating readers on a daily basis to the work of both Cobb and Jackson. Expressing his views, Joe displayed an extraordinary amount of confidence when he told a journalist that he anticipated a .390 average, at least, when the season concluded. "It will be more than that, quite a good deal more, I think," he boldly stated, "but even if it is only .390 I think it will top all the rest with the exception, of course, of [Nap]. He is hitting in grand form now. I'll tell you why I think I'll finish with a better percentage than .390. There'll be a lot of new pitchers coming into the league and they will not know what to pitch to me, will they? I ought to knock down the fences when these young twirlers come along."[19]

Nevertheless, Jackson remained the underdog against Cobb for the batting title. But if you talked to him, he was ever the optimist. In a separate interview, he explained that he had a "good chance" to win over his Detroit rival, saying: "I have it figured out that I must make 55 more hits to take down an average of .414, and I've a hunch that .414 will take off the prize. You see, I hit better in the east than I do in the west and if I don't have any hard luck getting hurt, I'll just about make two hits a game in all those games in the east. I just figure that I've got a little on Ty this way. The other clubs will send their best pitchers against Detroit if the Tigers are still in the race, but they are likely to send some of their new pitchers against us, and I just love those new boys."[20]

Even though he was technically a rookie himself, Joe was already in a position to recognize the benefits of hitting greenhorn recruits brought up for trials late in the season. Much like his admiration for Lajoie, Jackson had great respect for Cobb, and their shared Southern background bonded them almost immediately. The distance from his Greenville home to Cobb's Royston, Georgia, residence was approximately 66 miles, and they had traversed many of the same areas. Their commonality was unique, and sportswriters loved comparing the two. But in regards to their individual batting style, they were very different. Cobb applied the principals of the old slogan "hit 'em where they ain't," capitalizing on defensive weaknesses and utilizing his speed. He had muscle behind his hits when he wanted to, but Cobb was the kind of player who was well thought out in his on-field actions. He, more often than not, made the right play at the right time.

Where Cobb was deliberate, Jackson was impulsive. He swung freely, occasionally taking cues from the bench, a base coach, or teammates. His raw techniques were highly successful and, had he been willing to fashion a scientific approach, some people believed he would have been an even greater threat. Such a transition was wholly avoided. As runners, both were in the upper tier of league stars, but Cobb was considered superior in the way he broke away from the plate to first base after making contact with the ball. The *Washington Times* actually claimed Jackson was among "the poorest of starters."[21] Consequently, Cobb was also a better base-stealer, again, employing a quick motion away from the base. Lastly, and something that couldn't be overlooked, Cobb was exceedingly more spirited in his play than Jackson.[22] It wasn't that Joe was apathetic in any way, but Cobb's everyday passion was unparalleled, arguably, in the history of baseball.

In a personal sense, Jackson and Cobb formed a friendly relationship in 1911, and the latter went out of his way to teach Joe his famous hook slide, which enhanced his chances on the basepaths.[23] Cobb was a shrewd operator and his mind was always developing ways to obtain the upper hand during games. He searched for intelligence on rival players, akin to his own personal scouting reports, and took advantage of the information he found. With Jackson, he spotted his insecurities early on and knew that his Carolinian neighbor idolized him to a certain degree. That was just the insight he needed.

Jackson unquestionably marveled at Cobb's all-around abilities and later called him the "greatest ball player of the age."[24] Their friendship opened the door for a postseason financial opportunity, and Cobb, along with theatrical maestro Vaughan Glaser, enlisted Jackson to join an adaptation of the famous play *The College Widow.* The story, originally written by George Ade with a football theme, was transformed into a baseball saga, and the two major leaguers were to act as the heroes of the production. In the role of "Silent Murphy," Joe was purportedly going to be "short on talk, but long on action," according to a story in the *Charlotte Observer.* Earning upwards of $2,000 for two months, they'd perform the show in league cities and across the South.[25] A conscious decision to limit Jackson's speaking time surely made the offer more attractive to Joe. It was understandable, realizing the job was completely foreign to him, and he didn't want to be seen as foolish in the case he struggled with his lines.

In spite of their cordialness, Cobb watched the batting statistics in the American League with a discerning eye and a touch of concern. He felt the upsurge of pressure from Jackson and concocted a plan to unbalance his friendly foe. The psychological ploy was multifaceted. At times, Cobb purposefully ignored Joe, causing Jackson to wonder what he'd done wrong, if anything, to turn his buddy against him. Additionally, he reverted to over-the-top sarcasm and edgy banter.[26] The mental strain on Jackson was overbearing, and Cobb believed it had a monumental effect on the batting race down the stretch.[27]

Even with Cobb's mind games, Jackson seemed impervious to outside influence and appeared nearly unconquerable at the plate. He batted successfully in 36 of 38 games, including a 27-game hitting streak, and amassed 68 hits in July and August.[28] Propelling his average over .400, he was the logical man to beat Cobb, and if the Tigers outfielder endured a slump of even a fraction, it seemed likely to occur.

Jackson played steadily and, for the most part, confidently, for the last month of the season. However, when the final games were played, the chase for the batting title ended with Ty in possession of a .420 average compared to Jackson's .408. His remarkable achievement set a rookie record for batting average that still stands today.[29] Another benchmark was established by his 233 hits, which remained the pinnacle for all rookies for ninety years, ultimately being broken by Ichiro Suzuki in 2001 (242). Jackson also led the league in on-base percentage (.468), finished second in slugging percentage to Cobb (.590), to go along with 45 doubles and 41 stolen bases.

Cleveland demonstrated some real heart as a club under Stovall. They entered August 30 in sixth place and won their next 10-straight games, including six victories over the Chicago White Sox.[30] Their winning efforts eventually moved them up to fourth and then third and, when the season ended on October 8, that's where the Naps proudly stood with an 80–73 record, silencing critics who panned them earlier in the year. Only the soon-to-be World Series champion Philadelphia Athletics and Detroit Tigers stood ahead of them in the standings. During the postseason Ohio championship series, Stovall's men were stifled by the Cincinnati Reds, losing four games to two.[31] Jackson was embarrassed by two costly defensive errors in the third game, but never stopped hitting.[32] His work, however, was not enough to turn the tides in the series. Earning in the neighborhood of $80 for their battle with the Reds, Jackson and his teammates broke for their individual homes and began the winter offseason.[33]

Looking at Jackson's extraordinary numbers, it was clear the predictions of George Mullin and other sportswriters were highly inaccurate.[34] Guys like pitcher Jack Coombs, winner of 28 games for Philadelphia in 1911, thought they knew the secret to his so-called fleeting talents, but were all proven wrong.[35] "That guy ain't human," said Washington Senators pitcher Tom Hughes after a particularly difficult day against Jackson.[36] His attempts, along with his brethren across the league, had failed to suppress Joe's batting prowess, and all that remained was a straight-up acceptance that Jackson was the real deal and in the league to stay.

Notably, Ty Cobb came forth with public praise for his Southern competitor, telling a reporter, "Joe certainly is a grand ball player and one who will get better and better. There is no denying that he is a better ball player his first year in the big league than anyone else ever was. I know when I was in my first season at Detroit, I could not compare with Joe. He is a wonder and there is no denying it."[37] The adulation for Jackson continued. One sportswriter acknowledged him as the "Crown Prince of Baseball," while another classified him as the "greatest outfielder in the world," of course, next to Cobb.[38] The Chalmers voting committee, made up of sportswriters in league cities, voted him fourth in what was essentially an MVP poll. Cobb was victorious in the balloting with Chicago White Sox pitcher Ed Walsh and Philadelphia Athletics second baseman Eddie Collins, occupying the second and third positions.[39]

The press was sold on the idea of Jackson and Cobb touring together as thespians following the 1911 season. A photographer captured the two hovering over a script for *The College Widow* at Cleveland in September, and anticipation was building for the upcoming show.[40] But Jackson began to have second thoughts and, with a little help from his wife Katie, decided against the venture.[41] While Cobb carried on with the plan and had a successful winter on stage, Jackson went home to Greenville and was celebrated by his townsfolk. He participated in exhibition baseball in the area, collecting around $700 for his appearances, and locals were awed by his maturity since leaving the Carolina Association three years earlier.[42] For recreation, Jackson spent his time hunting; using a single-barreled weapon to target his prey. He told a reporter, "I can shoot much better with a single barrel, and I don't care much about killing the rabbit outright. I would rather wound it and then run it down myself just to keep in condition to circle the bases."[43]

Jackson was utterly consumed by his outdoor pursuit of wild animals in the Greenville region. "I've got about everything within ten miles of this town," he explained to a journalist in February 1912, "and that makes me take long hikes before I can pick up anything." He wrote a letter to his new manager Harry Davis, a replacement for George Stovall, and informed him of his good health heading into spring training.[44] However, in the midst of his workouts, Jackson maintained a steady eating regimen to ensure weight gain. He concentrated on strengthening his legs and arms, and by early March was 10 pounds heavier than he had been during the previous campaign. The added muscle was part of his strategy to develop his all-around game.[45] In interviews, he revealed his true objectives of winning the batting title and outshining Ty Cobb.

"Ty Cobb is a great ball player, but I believe I can make more hits and score more runs than he. He may steal more bases than I will, but I will give him a battle for that honor too."[46] Introspectively, Jackson reviewed his flaws as a hitter and, with a little outside input from coaches and friends, concluded that he was pulling the ball far too much to right field. It was to the point that he was becoming known as a "right-field hitter," and he made it a preseason priority to adjust his style. He told a reporter, "I am going to mix 'em up this year and hit to left field as much as to right. Now and then, I will sandwich in one to center."[47] His comments about prevailing over Cobb and becoming the second man in history to hit .400 in back-to-back seasons, placing his name alongside Jesse Burkett, who accomplished the feat in 1895–96 for the Cleveland Spiders, appeared conceited in some quarters.[48] Bob Dunbar of the *Boston Journal* wrote that Jackson seemed to be "badly swelled up," based on his reported quotes in recent publications.[49]

Prior to meeting up with teammates at spring camp in Mobile, Alabama, Jackson enjoyed Mardi Gras in New Orleans for the second straight year. He mingled with old friends and joined a squad of "All-Stars" for an exhibition against a local aggregation on February 25, 1912. It was his first action on a diamond in several months and, interestingly, he was asked to purposefully strike out his initial time at bat by the rival manager. His deed, the coach believed, would give his young pitcher, Eddie Johnston, some much needed confidence by whiffing one of baseball's best. According to the *Cleveland Leader*, Jackson "willingly fanned." As Joe himself explained it, "I sure did try hard to whale the ball out of the lot [the next time up], but that boy had my measure. I just couldn't locate it."[50] The result was a second straight strikeout by Johnston. Jackson, playing shortstop, went 1-for-3 in the exhibition, and the All-Stars were defeated by the Galiano team, 7–1.[51] Journalists, naturally, highlighted his two strikeouts by a relative amateur.

Traveling over to Mobile with longtime friend Hyder Barr, Jackson was eager to get to work. New Cleveland Naps manager Harry Davis welcomed the enthusiasm. A recent arrival from the Philadelphia Athletics, Davis was an on-field leader and understudy of managerial legend Connie Mack for years. A pro since 1895, he was an important cog in the world championship clubs of 1910 and 1911, and was considered one of the smartest men in the game. Davis had the distinction of playing with Jackson when he first broke into the majors in 1908 and could see how far he'd come. But his challenge as leader of the Naps was sizable. In fact, writers were picking Philadelphia to again repeat as World Series champs, while Cleveland was a middle of the pack club. Davis was facing an uphill battle, and owner Charles Somers was spending serious money to bolster the club with promising rookies. He even went so far as to upgrade his scouts and sought out the best ballplayers the minors had to offer.[52]

Throughout the South, crowds multiplied with Jackson present, and his animated nature was a thrill for onlookers. He was running with vigor, displaying his power at bat and, under the guidance of Davis, improving in his areas of weakness. Jackson's speed was impressive and Davis decided to shift him from right field to center going forward to get more out of his quickness on the defensive end. Pacific Coast League veteran Buddy Ryan, in his rookie year in the majors, would play right. The gusto shown by Jackson in training was generally lacking elsewhere in the ranks, and Davis shared his frustrations after the club moved over to New Orleans toward the middle of March 1912. He intensified the workouts and jumped into a uniform himself to help lead by example.[53] Jackson was as energetic as ever. Under his own volition, he even went to the mound and began practicing as a pitcher in his off time, seemingly fulfilling a personal desire.[54]

Exhibitions during spring training in the Deadball Era usually consisted of games against college and minor league clubs, and this gave Jackson the opportunity to flash his great power against ineffectual pitchers. In the spring of 1912, home run hitting became a normal occurrence for Joe, and fans loved it. Against Louisiana State University at Baton Rouge on April 5, he contributed two of the five homers on the afternoon in a 13–0 rout. As the Naps were making their way northward, they happened to journey into Memphis at the time of a dangerous flood, and the hazardous journey put the team at risk when railroad tracks were overtaken by cresting water. The squad was waterlogged and poor field conditions caused additional worries during a 12-inning game versus the Memphis Chickasaws of the Southern Association on April 7. Jackson joined several teammates on a flat-bottomed boat ride along Main Street, but expressed his concern about the perilous situation. He wasn't a fan of the extreme weather, and admitted that he was "ready to swim" for safety if things got any worse.[55]

The members of the club survived the ordeal and team harmony was reportedly high for the season opener at Cleveland on April 11, 1912. Sporting a younger team and surrounded by public optimism, the Naps won their initial contest over Detroit in 11 innings by the score of 3–2.[56] Jackson went 3-for-5 with over 19,000 spectators looking on. One of those individuals on hand was his wife, Katie, who was in the grandstand beaming with contentment.[57] Before the end of April, Jackson was battling a "severe" illness, but the *Cleveland Plain Dealer* noted that the only way to get him to sit out was "by hiding his uniform."[58] With his average strangely beneath the .300 mark, he told a reporter, "My cold has prevented me from batting very good in the last few games, but as quick as we get a few warm days, I'll get started again."[59] To make matters worse, on April 21, he was hit by a pitch at Detroit and suffered a torn ligament in his right arm.

Once more, Jackson's iron constitution was acknowledged after he refused to spend any length of time on the bench. Sportswriter Henry P. Edwards wrote, "You have got to cut off one of Joe's legs to keep him out."[60] He simply wouldn't surrender to the pain and continued to play. Manager Harry Davis was untroubled by the hardships faced by his center fielder, and despite Jackson's uncharacteristically mediocre average, had nothing but good things to say about him. "In Lajoie and Jackson I have the two greatest batsmen who ever broke into the game," Davis explained. "Jackson hits the ball harder than Cobb and then he is a player who never sulks. Joe can play behind the other fellow all year in the averages and never lose his head and worry. He may trail Cobb all year and then win out in the finish."[61]

The Jackson-Cobb batting rivalry hadn't lost any of its intrigue in the press or on the field. Newspaper stories about their daily efforts were unrelenting, and all eyes remained glued to their every move. In on the drama, Jackson's teammates instigated Cobb from the dugout during an early series against Detroit, rattling his cage. "Better get your eye on the ball or Jackson will leave you at the post," Ted Easterly shouted. Another player yelled, "Run it out, you swell head," after Cobb leisurely trotted to first after hitting a pop fly.[62] The taunts, meant to discourage Cobb, had an opposite effect as Ty was more motivated to show up his opponents when angry. Many players and managers around the American League learned it was wiser to leave him alone.

In addition to his problems in finding a groove at the plate, Jackson was unsteady in the field as well. At Washington, DC, on May 13, he lost his balance trying to make a routine catch of a low fly hit by Clyde Milan. The ball dropped and rolled to the fence, allowing two runners and Milan to score.

Washington won the game, 9–6, and those three runs on Jackson's blunder were the difference.[63] But Joe managed to break the negative spell here and there, and often came up with a timely hit or fielding masterpiece that reminded everyone of his genuine abilities. The Hilltop Park crowd in New York saw some of his magic on May 18 when he made a nearly impossible running catch of a ball hit by Hack Simmons, then hurled the ball in perfectly to nail Bert Daniels racing home.[64] Altogether, though, Cleveland's trip to Eastern cities was a disaster for Jackson. He went 6-for-38 during the trip, and one journalist remarked that it was the "poorest work" of his American League career.[65]

Jackson's hitting improved in late May as his average topped .310. He was shifted back to right field to allow the experienced Joe Birmingham to play center, and his overall game steadily improved. Highlanders pitcher Jack Quinn was so worried about Jackson as a threat that he deliberately walked him on June 5, preferring to pitch against Nap Lajoie, a career .338 hitter and future Hall of Famer. Lajoie proceeded to score three runs in a 7–0 win.[66] Jackson was undeniably a menacing force, and considering he'd already blasted a single and triple against New York that day, Quinn was right in feeling anxious in pitching to him again. But that's what made the Jackson-Lajoie combination so dangerous. If it wasn't Joe doing the damage, it was Nap (and vice versa). And if they both were on their game, Cleveland was terrifically hard to beat.

Ankle trouble and a severe charley horse bothered Jackson into the first half of June, but his offensive work was largely unaffected and, after 50 games, he possessed a .369 average.[67] The Naps, however, struggled during the same period by dropping eight in a row from June 9–18, and manager Harry Davis was losing his cool. He was furious at the lack of hustle and promised roster changes. His boss, owner Charles Somers, was equally sickened. "Candidly I never saw such disgusting work in my life," he said. "Some of those fellows are actually stealing their money. That's all."[68] As custom, writers blamed internal discord and claimed a segment of the team was actively working against Davis and his policies, which tended to be exceedingly strict. Other reports turned up complaints by a segment of the club who were angry at Davis for naming Ivy Olson as the team's captain and not the more popular and longer-tenured Joe Birmingham.

Starting to recover physically, Jackson pulled off a rarity against Detroit on June 27, 1912. It was a situation that Ty Cobb usually negotiated, but this time around, "Shoeless Joe" was the one generating pure excitement on the basepaths, and his primary victim was none other than Cobb himself. The happening occurred in the third inning of a scoreless game. With men on second and third, Jackson slapped an ordinary single into center directly at Cobb. The latter, realizing he had to make a quick throw to the plate to stop a run from scoring, bungled the ball, while at the same time, Jackson was running at full speed past the first base bag to second. Jackson didn't slow for even a millisecond, rushing from second to third as the two runners ahead of him scored. Cobb's relay to Donie Bush was too late to nab Jackson at third as he had already rounded the corner and was headed for home. Fearing nothing, Joe landed at the plate equal to the throw, but catcher Oscar Stanage mishandled the ball and Jackson was called safe.[69]

The exhibition of speed, smarts, and daring were indeed eye-popping. A few days later, he returned to the .400 class of hitters and was in a three-way fight for league honors with Cobb and Tris Speaker of the Boston Red Sox. In the second game of a doubleheader against St. Louis on June 30, he went 4-for-6 with three triples in a 15–1 squash. The pendulum of good fortune swung the other way in July, which saw Jackson slump again. His average dropped upwards of 25 points during the month, but he remained within striking distance of the league leaders. On July 16, 1912, in Philadelphia, Jackson suffered a hip injury sliding into second base and had to be helped from the field.[70] In a different game in August, he received a gash to his knuckle, and in another, saw his thumbnail nearly torn from his hand. He occasionally went to the bench to mend his wounds, leaving the active contest, but was back in the lineup the very next day.

Considering these incidents and the adversity he'd faced earlier in the year, Jackson was proving indestructible. By season's end, he would be among the league leaders for games played with 154, and it was apparent that his mind, body, and soul were deeply devoted to the diamond. His legacy was not yet written, but enthusiasts and experts alike agreed that "Shoeless Joe" Jackson was going to be an integral force in baseball circles well into the future. In fact, if he continued the way he was going, he'd not only be forever mentioned among the greats of the Deadball Era, but of all-time. And with Jackson and Cobb leading baseball's hit parade, it was an extraordinary time to be a fan of the national pastime.

4

THE PERENNIAL RUNNER-UP

The vivid descriptions and animated commentary of baseball writers was a feature of newspapers in each major league city during the 1910s. Colorful imagery portrayed the top players as something beyond superstars, and columnists loved to bestow the virtues of their local heroes. In some cases, the journalists themselves became famous, and their unique eccentricities were exposed on the pages of their daily editorials. Some weren't afraid to lash out and criticize rival teams, singular players, or even hometown athletes who failed to live up to expectations. The various observations were occasionally cruel, and Joe Jackson interpreted many of the remarks made by journalists in Philadelphia to be that way in 1908, when he first appeared in the big leagues. He didn't appreciate references to his reported small-town mentality, stories of his shoeless ball playing, and yarns of him being overcome by the bright lights and tall buildings.

As a result, Jackson became rather hesitant around writers. In early 1911, he told a journalist doing a piece on him to "go light on that mill talk," meaning that he limit any condescending statements about his background.[1] Though wary of writers during his first few years in the league, he stepped out of his comfort zone and gave a lengthy interview to J. A. Fitzgerald of the *New York Herald* in August 1912, which was considered quite revealing. In playful banter he discussed his family and hometown of Greenville. After being asked how old he was, he replied, "four hundred and ten," drawing a confused retort by Fitzgerald. "Gee, I muffed that one," Jackson said in response. "I was thinking of my batting average. I'm continually getting it mixed up with my age, weight, and the size of my hat and shoes. When you're up in that rarefied atmosphere you can't keep it off your mind. I had twenty-five candles [on] my last birthday cake."[2]

The two chatted about Jackson's early baseball experiences, batting abilities, and accomplishments. Fitzgerald asked if he finally was going to catch Cobb in the batting race, and Jackson answered, "I'm going to try my best, but what are you going to do with a player that rips off seven hits out of nine times at bat twice in the same week? Guess we'll have to pull the Sherman Anti-Trust law on Tyrus."[3] Displaying a sense of humor and a pleasant, humble perspective, Jackson opened up to the writer. While Jackson appreciated Fitzgerald's pleasant demeanor during the interview, which put him at ease, readers undoubtedly appreciated the inner glimpse of a ballplayer they'd grown to love. These were nuggets of information not to be found in a box score, and to diehard enthusiasts the interview provided precious insight into the young athlete. As the 1912 season continued, Jackson overcame bumps and bruises, plus a midsummer slump to maintain an average over .375. He had four-hit games twice in August, but the Naps as a whole were playing worse than ever. An Eastern road trip was disastrous, and the team won only two games of sixteen with one tie.

Unable to contain his own frustrations, Jackson had several run-ins with umpires during this time frame, including a confrontation with umpire Fred Westervelt in Philadelphia and another with umpire Joe O'Brien in New York. The latter was instigated by a high called strike that Jackson protested by throwing his bat. He was not only ejected from the game, which was the first of a doubleheader, but was disallowed from participating in the second as well.[4] The anxieties and aggravations of Cleveland players continued to sabotage the club, and the internal dissension was causing things to rapidly deteriorate. The breaking point was reached just days after manager Harry Davis claimed there was "perfect harmony among the players and between the players and myself."[5] On the morning of September 2, 1912, Davis handed in his resignation and the popular Joe Birmingham took the reins.

Team cohesion improved almost immediately. Birmingham, utilizing his superior knowledge of the strengths and weaknesses of the players, began making effective changes that positively impacted the club.[6] He placed an emphasis on speed and rearranged the batting order with Doc Johnston leading off, followed by rookie shortstop Ray Chapman, Terry Turner, Jackson, and then Lajoie. Under Birmingham's leadership, Cleveland went 21–7 and finished the season in fifth place with a 75–78 record. In *The Sporting News,* Henry P. Edwards offered the fanciful notion that "The World's Series might have been staged in Cleveland had Harry Davis been convinced earlier that it was time for him to quit."[7] In the end, the Boston Red Sox (105–47), managed by Jake Stahl, captured the pennant and beat the New York Giants for the World Series title, four games to three.

For the second straight year, Jackson was runner-up in the batting race with a .395 average, 14 points behind Cobb (.409). He tied Cobb for the major league lead in hits with 226 and was second in the American League in on-base percentage (.458), slugging percentage (.579), doubles (44), and extra base hits (73), while leading in total bases (331) and triples (26). He garnered 16 votes in the Chalmers balloting, but was far below winner Tris Speaker, who received 59 and won the automobile.[8] Nevertheless, a pundit for the *Washington Times* acknowledged Jackson's striking numbers and confirmed that no other player in history hit better than Jackson over the first two full years of their big-league career. Jackson's .402 total average topped Pop Anson, Honus Wagner, and other premier batters and the writer declared, "Jackson probably carries the greatest batting eye ever focused upon a pitched ball."[9]

An interesting abnormality of the closing days of the season occurred during an exhibition at Toledo against the American Association's Mud Hens on September 23, 1912. Jackson participated in what the *Toledo News-Bee* called a "joke battle," and reportedly "provoked wild enthusiasm for his stunts in right and on short and third."[10] His play at three positions, especially in the infield, was exceptionally rare. He readily admitted that even as a boy, he "never" occupied an infield station and gravitated to either right or center field.[11] The game was altogether unimportant, and the Naps were defeated, 6–5.

Following the season's final game on October 6 at St. Louis (an 8–3 victory), Jackson returned to Cleveland to settle his affairs before journeying to South Carolina. On October 29, he joined many of his longtime friends and was led by his old Greenville manager, Tommy Stouch, in a special exhibition game against the Philadelphia Athletics in Charlotte. The Athletics, headed to Cuba for a winter tour, sent star pitchers Eddie Plank and Chief Bender to the mound, but Jackson was still in the zone. He rattled off three hits, including a double and a triple, while stealing a base and scoring a run. Unfortunately, his teammates, consisting of mostly minor leaguers, were unable to produce much at the plate and the Athletics steamrolled them, 12–3.[12] For winter recreation, Jackson went hunting, visited his old haunts in Savannah, and enjoyed motion pictures in Greenville. One of the touted presentations featured Jackson himself on his farm near

Paris Mountain, South Carolina, again displaying a side of his life that was previously unknown to the public.[13]

Back in Cleveland, team owner Charles Somers was dealing with the dreadful financial numbers produced by the Naps in 1912. His club was sixth in the league in home attendance (336,844, almost seventy thousand less than the previous season), and instead of spending thousands more for recruits and a long spring training trip, he wanted retraction.[14] Although financially independent, Somers had money concerns and only so much to invest in his ballclub. Thus, he felt leaving the capable Joe Birmingham to run the squad with only subtle changes was the best bet for a winning aggregation. But there was still a problem relating to his payroll and potential holdouts. November was not yet over when Jackson was mentioned by the press as being dissatisfied with his paycheck, leaving many questions about his status for the 1913 season.

Sportswriter Joe S. Jackson of the *Washington Post* relayed his thoughts on the presumed holdout, insisting that the ballplayer (of no relation) desired a raise and was likely to remain on the sidelines "a long while" if he didn't get a $1,000 raise over what he was tendered. He predicted a multiyear deal would be signed, and assumed Ty Cobb had mentored Jackson in the art of negotiating so that he'd achieve a better financial sum for himself.[15] Making light of the story, a writer for the *Indianapolis Star* indicated that Jackson's demand for more money connected to the high cost of shoes, "baseball shoes, high shoes, low shoes, black shoes, tan shoes and, perhaps, some shoes of smaller size."[16] But legitimately, Jackson did have a high volume of ever-growing expenses. Notably, on the positive side of things, he was able to pay off his farm, plus buy an additional 50 acres of land with "nearly $4,000" earned from the 1912 season.[17]

Greater than all else, Jackson gladly accepted and maintained the majority burden for the financial security of his immediate family. He wanted his parents and siblings happy and healthy, untroubled by monetary worry, and baseball had always been his gateway to being that central provider. The mill and butcher shop back home gave the family day-to-day income, but in terms of the heavy lifting, his money was stretched the furthest. Jackson's parents and sister resided in his home during the summers and Joe joined them with Katie in the winter.[18] The constant company and closeness of his family was comforting, and he endured the hardships of the road with them always at the forefront of his mind. Jackson was also reflective about the big picture and his future as a professional ballplayer.

"I'm not always going to be a star," Jackson told a reporter in Savannah, "and while I'm going good, I intend to reap a fair return at least from the benefits of my labors. Now, if I'm not worth what I've asked of the Cleveland club then I figure I'm not worth anything and am going to get out of the game. That, of course, is easier said than done, but I've thought the thing over a whole lot since the season closed, and it's going to be either what I've asked for or no more ball playing from me."[19] Jackson had alternatives to baseball; however, whether they'd prove as lucrative as his baseball salary was doubtful. First of all, he was invested in a Greenville pool room that catered to sports enthusiasts and his many friends in the area. With regards to his agricultural interests, he was convinced it was a profitable venture. "I have always liked farming," he explained, "and believe I can make as much out of it as I could in baseball."[20]

In another interview, he said: "I have been on the go ever since I was fifteen years old, and although I enjoy traveling with a crowd of ball players such as the Cleveland fellows are, yet I detest city life and will only be too glad when the time does come when my wife and I can evade the bustle and hustle of it all. If I had my ranch now, I would quit the game tomorrow."[21] Such statements did not elicit confidence in Jackson's future major league plans, and the combination of purported financial problems in Cleveland and his dissatisfaction opened the door for journalists to speculate about a possible trade. Out of the winter meetings in December 1912 came talk of a deal between the Naps and Chicago White Sox, with the latter sending outfielder Ping Bodie, first baseman Rollie Zeider, and catcher Walt Kuhn to Cleveland for Jackson's services. *The Sporting News* acknowledged the "fake story," and noted that Somers "would not entertain such a proposition for a second."[22]

The truth of the matter was, despite all the hullabaloo and comments by Jackson himself, there was no official holdout. In fact, Jackson hadn't yet received his 1913 contract. "Cleveland folks have been good to me," he said, "and naturally I am appreciative. I am looking for my contract in a few days, and I am sure when it comes it will be satisfactory."[23] He had received $3,500 in 1912 and simply expected a raise on par with his exemplary work, and his earlier remarks echoed that sentiment.[24] It was also stated that Somers, in 1912, gave Jackson a $1,000 bonus for batting over .350 on the season, which was quite liberal under the circumstances.[25] So it wasn't shocking to learn that Jackson was pleased by the way Somers took care of him at contract time. And with all that said, before the end of January,

Joe had signed and returned the document to the Naps' home office in Cleveland. He was perfectly satisfied with the $4,000 offered him.[26]

Sleeping nine hours a night, spending time with family at his farm, and relishing in the outdoors, Jackson experienced a relatively quiet winter. He was asked to participate in a series of games by the organizers of a semi-pro league at New Orleans in January and February 1913, and would've joined Detroit slugger Sam Crawford on the local Braquet squad, but respectfully declined. By postcard, he notified the Naps that he was eagerly anticipating training camp in Pensacola, Florida, but ironically ended up being more than a week late.[27] He turned up at the San Carlos Hotel on March 6, and scribes gave two separate reasons for his mysterious tardiness. The *Cleveland Leader* claimed Joe was delayed because his wife was in ill health, while the *Cleveland Plain Dealer* cited his stopover in Mobile to visit acquaintances, plus a lag in train availability.[28] Whatever the reason, his failure to appear caused concerns, but were quickly put at ease upon his arrival in camp.

Jackson was feeling good, smashing the first ball pitched to him in camp over Pensacola's right-field fence.[29] On March 18, his towering fourth-inning homer with shortstop Ray Chapman on base helped decide a contest against Toledo, and after seven preseason games, he boasted a .500 average (11-for-22). Seeing the ball spectacularly, Jackson rode into the 1913 season on a cloud of self-assurance, going 3-for-3 with two doubles, a triple, and two runs in the opener against the Chicago White Sox on April 11 (a 3–1 victory).[30] His flawless play was publicized with gusto in American League circles, especially since the reigning king, Ty Cobb, was engaged in a full-fledged monetary holdout against Detroit. In some ways, Jackson was picking up the slack as the organization's primary swatting star, and he didn't want to let his fans down. Before the end of April, he was batting over .350.

On May 2, while in St. Louis, Jackson received a jolting telephone call informing him that his father was near death.[31] He began making plans to return home, but after his father's condition stabilized he remained with the team, although with a heavy heart. The next day, sportswriter Henry P. Edwards complained about Jackson's apparent lack of teamwork, insisting that the player should have sacrificed Ivy Olson to third in the fourth inning instead of swinging away and flying out during their 3–1 victory on May 1. "There are times when even Joe Jackson should think less of base hits," Edwards wrote.[32] It wasn't the first time Edwards had called Jackson out for what he perceived to be individualism, and certainly wouldn't be the last. Ty Cobb, who returned to the game in late April, was regularly lambasted for the same thing, and Edwards claimed Jackson had acted in "overconfidence."[33]

Prior to the season, Edwards dialed back his optimism for the Naps, telling readers that the club had "no chance" of finishing better than third in the standings.[34] The defending champion Boston Red Sox were expected to lead the competition, and on May 7, were in town to face the Naps. The game was lively from the start, but took on another level of excitement in the fourth inning when Jackson attempted to score from third on an infield hit to second baseman Neal Ball. With little effort, Ball threw home and Jackson appeared dead in the water. But Joe didn't slow up and slid hard, spikes first into catcher Bill Carrigan, tearing at his knee pad. Out on the play, he was condemned by the Red Sox for his tactics and, from there, the game spiraled away from regular sportsmanship. By the end of the day, a handful of players entered a wild brawl under the grandstand, venting their frustrations on their opposition. To prevent suspensions, the combatants were sworn to secrecy and it is unknown whether Joe was among the pugilists.[35]

Batting .400 after 21 games, Jackson went on a tear during the first half of May and Tom Terrell of the *Cleveland Leader* observed that his average for a recent six-game stretch was an amazing .714.[36] On May 11, he hit an inside-the-park grand slam against the New York Yankees before 19,000 joyous Clevelanders at League Park and went 4-for-4 on the afternoon. The Naps won 7–2, and were sitting comfortably in second place with a 17–7 record. Philadelphia was in first place, and Joe's ex-manager Connie Mack was wary of Jackson's latest hitting spree. In fact, Mack refused to let Jackson be the linchpin to beating his club, choosing to intentionally walk him five times over the course of a four-game series a few days later.[37] Annoyed, Jackson felt a conspiracy was in the works and made a recommendation to officials: "I think the big leagues ought to pass a rule either forbidding the passing of a batter purposely or to let each runner on the sacks advance a base. That would prevent their passing me with a runner on third."[38]

One sportswriter, after a particularly drab showing by Jackson, jokingly wrote that he'd been intentionally walked so many times he'd "forgotten how to hit."[39] But it was obvious that Joe was ready to unload a barrage of firepower almost at will and, in New York on June 4, he blasted a second-inning home run over the right-field grandstand. With a distance approximated at over 500 feet, the impressive drive caused great furor, and the *Brooklyn Daily Eagle* called it "the longest hit ever recorded [at] the Polo

Grounds."[40] Veterans of the local baseball scene agreed, and the feat added nicely to Jackson's reputation as a must-see attraction. Baseball fans in league cities outside Cleveland were electrified by his slugging. They recognized that, much like Ty Cobb, he brought a unique skill set to the diamond and voiced displeasure when their home team chose to purposefully walk him, thus depriving them of seeing Joe swing away.

Jackson was eccentric, at times, and occasionally the press acknowledged his peculiar on-field behaviors. A journalist in Philadelphia noticed some irregularities in his play during a series against the Athletics in mid-June 1913. According to the report, Jackson was allegedly peeved about being forced to play right field, his normal position, because the sun at Shibe Park was a constant bother (called a "sun field"). As a result, he pouted and lackadaisically allowed a single by Jimmy Walsh to go for a triple. The writer called him, simply, a "lazy performer."[41] However, there was more to the story. Two years before, during a doubleheader in Philadelphia, he narrowly avoided serious injury on two occasions while playing right field.[42] He survived the ordeal with bruises and cuts, but the incidents grated on his memory. Needless to say, he had good reason to have anxiety at Shibe Park.

Jackson's offensive production was turned upside down in Philadelphia as well. Whereas his batting average on the season was better than .430, he went 2-for-15 (.133) at Shibe Park, and the overriding psychological distractions wreaked havoc on his psyche. A few days later, on June 20, he was the victim of an errant throw by Chicago White Sox second baseman Morrie Rath which hit him in the left ear causing slight hearing loss.[43] On June 22, 1913, he uncharacteristically yet aggressively argued a call by umpire Jack "Rip" Egan in the seventh inning of a contest against Detroit. It was a losing fight, and he was quickly ejected for his actions. Jackson was forced to miss the second game of the doubleheader and then was suspended indefinitely by American League President Ban Johnson for his actions.[44]

His use of foul language was to blame, it was reported, but this wasn't the first time he'd had problems with Egan. In fact, a writer for the *Cleveland Plain Dealer* wondered if Egan "entertained a grudge" against the outfielder. Jackson admitted he was caught up in the moment, saying, "I cursed him, but he cursed me first."[45] Regardless, to Gordon Mackay at the *Cleveland Leader*, Jackson was clearly out of line and called his actions "pure foolishness."[46] The ban lasted a few days and as he was returning to the daily grind, major problems in the Cleveland clubhouse were revealed. The situation developed from Joe Birmingham's benching of Nap Lajoie, the venerable star. Lajoie was anything but pleased and began criticizing the unseasoned leader publically.[47] Quickly wising up, Birmingham reinstalled the veteran at second base and the discord, which had potential to crack the foundation of the club, was temporarily quelled.

The first player to 100 hits on the year, Jackson led in the American League batting race by midseason, keeping just ahead of Ty Cobb and Tris Speaker. The competition tightened in late July, and Joe lost ground after suffering finger and wrist injuries, falling under the .400 mark to .394 in early August. Cobb was confident, telling a journalist, "I'll beat him out. If he bats .500, I'll finish the season with .501." Jackson humorously responded, "If Cobb bats .501, I'll go to .502. I'm out to beat him this year, and I will."[48]

Interestingly, Cobb was skeptical about the treatment he was receiving from various league pitchers versus that given Jackson. He actually believed some hurlers were giving away free hits to his Cleveland rival all due to a personal bitterness toward him. Cobb wondered about Senators ace Walter Johnson possibly being among those secretly rooting for Jackson to win batting honors. "Does Johnson pitch as hard against Jackson as he does against me?" Cobb inquired. "I notice that Jackson doesn't have much trouble hitting him this year, and I can't understand it. I don't blame Johnson for this, nor do I charge him with it, but it does seem strange—that's all." Johnson flatly denied it, insisting he pitched equally hard to both. He said: "I don't think any pitcher is giving Jackson anything except the best he has."[49] In his opinion, Jackson was earning every one of his hits.

As Jackson and Cobb traded the lead for the batting title through August, the latter took hold of the top spot by the middle of September. A correspondent for the *Cleveland Leader* suspected, based on appearances, that Jackson had "lost confidence in himself" and was failing to swing up to his usual standard. "He hesitates and seems to worry," the journalist added.[50] Was the pressure of perhaps finally beating Cobb too much to bear? Had Cobb's psychological magic worked on Jackson yet again, derailing what looked to be a winning gait? His shaky disposition was made even worse when he collided with the wall, specifically a wooden advertising sign, at Griffith Stadium in Washington on September 12, 1913, knocking himself unconscious. He was bruised by the accident and limped for several days, but, of course, played the following day.[51]

Pure and simple, Jackson was destined for another runner-up position, and finished the season with a .373 batting average, seventeen points behind champion Cobb. His 197 hits led the majors and although he was a leading candidate for the Chalmers Trophy, he was ousted by Walter Johnson, who posted a 36–7 record and a 1.14 ERA. Johnson received 54 points to Jackson's 43.[52] While there was much to be proud of in terms of personal statistics, Joe let the batting championship slip through his fingers and the title, essentially, was his to lose after months of leading the league. Cobb hadn't necessarily proven to be a better player in 1913, but, in a way, Jackson beat himself down the stretch and ultimately relinquished all rights to the crown.

The downfall of Joe Jackson coincided with the slide of the Naps. The club dropped to third place in the midst of a 6–13 road trip, a disappointing fact considering the team had rested in second since early in the season. And third is where they remained. Injuries and mismanagement were said to be factors in Cleveland's demise, and Larry Woltz touched upon rumors of in-house feuding in a column for *The Sporting News*. "There was absolutely no discipline amongst the players and they were oftentimes fighting almost themselves," he wrote.[53] Manager Joe Birmingham led his players to an 86–66 record, but according to reports, had lost control of the clubhouse. Players, on the other hand, rallied in a postseason series against the Pittsburgh Pirates (a regional series arranged for owners and players to collect a little extra cash), winning in seven games, with Jackson delivering on both offense and defense. The highlight, though, was his game-winning hit in the bottom of the 11th on October 7, 1913.[54]

With an additional $232 and change in his pocket from the Pittsburgh series, Jackson loaded his automobile, dogs, and other personal items onto a train and headed back to South Carolina. His World Series pick proved incorrect as the Philadelphia Athletics thumped the New York Giants four games to one, and the rumors that he planned to act as a Series correspondent (with a ghostwriter) for a syndicated newspaper were just plain gossip.[55] At Charlotte, a team billed as "Joe Jackson's All-Stars" was formed to compete against the Brooklyn Superbas, a National League club touring in advance of a trip to Cuba.[56] Initially slated for October 21, the exhibition was instead shifted to Greenville because of bad weather and held the next day. Garnering three hits, Jackson lived up to expectations, but the Superbas were too much for the local underdogs, winning 3–1.[57]

The Hot Stove League wasn't even burning at full speed when an expert deduced that recent meetings between Naps owner Charley Somers and Charles Comiskey of the White Sox were related to a possible trade for Jackson.[58] Such was the scuttlebutt in December 1912 as well and, like that occasion, officials rapidly denied any deals for their star right fielder. "Not a chance," manager Joe Birmingham said, "My team suits me right now. I'm not giving the best hitter in the business away to a rival."[59] Despite the clubhouse problems, Somers liked what Birmingham had accomplished in Cleveland, and the latter's third-place finish—plus the sizable gate increase—secured his job going into the 1914 season. In fact, the Naps achieved record attendance with a turnout of 541,000 at League Park, third in the league, and averaged over 6,700 a game.

Since Jackson and Lajoie were the only two regulars in the .300 class, Birmingham knew there was plenty of room for improvement. Pitching was a strong suit with two twenty-game winners, Cy Falkenberg (23–10) and Vean Gregg (20–13), and Fred Blanding and Willie Mitchell victorious in 15 and 14 games, respectively. If his entire roster returned for the 1914 campaign, Birmingham was optimistic they'd be in the pennant fight, and he anticipated great things from youngsters Nemo Leibold and Ray Chapman.[60]

Chapman was one of the most talked about up-and-comers in the league, and his friendliness made him an instant hit among teammates. The twenty-two-year-old shortstop was already part of a unique clique on the Naps, a group collectively known as the "Rebs." While it was widely understood that his residence was Herrin, Illinois, in the southern part of the state, Chapman was born in Kentucky and his ancestors fought for the Confederacy in the Civil War.[61] Because of that, he identified with his Southern teammates more than anyone else, which included roommates Joe Jackson and Doc Johnston (Tennessee) and pitchers Willie Mitchell (Mississippi) and Nick Cullop (Virginia). This faction would grow in 1914 with the additions of Arkansan Roy Wood and Jackson's Greenville neighbor, Walter Barbare. Reporter Bozeman Bulger asked Birmingham about the group after seeing them together, and the latter replied, "That's a meeting of the Southern Confederacy, probably laughing at us for putting sugar in our cornbread or something like that. Did you know that my club ought to be called the Rebels or the Survivors of the Lost Cause? They drop so many

Rs at the tables that the waiter has to sweep out the dining room after each meal. It looks as if I'll have to get myself an interpreter."[62] For Jackson, he particularly enjoyed spending his off-time palling around with Johnston and Cullop, joking and telling stories.

The crew took immense pride in their Southern heritage. Jackson was well known for the drawl in his speech, and umpire Billy Evans admitted that he'd occasionally initiate discussions with him "just to listen to him talk in his typical southern manner."[63] In some situations, the transition from life beneath the Mason-Dixon Line to the North was difficult. Georgian Ty Cobb, for instance, not only struggled to adjust to his surroundings, but grappled, sometimes literally, with teammates from opposing backgrounds. Ex-Cincinnati Reds pitcher Jack Rowan offered his perspective on the matter, saying, "Few people realize that a ballplayer has to be an A1 diplomat, politician, and handshaker. If he wasn't, he'd surely get into serious trouble time and again, and the news columns would record lots of rows, riots, and untimely deaths of gentlemanly athletes. He may be Southern-born and yet be playing in a Northern city when the natives are celebrating in honor of Grant or Sherman."[64]

Essentially, there was pressure on players with Southern loyalties to conform to the liberal attitudes and perspectives of the North. It wasn't unreasonable, but was occasionally a jolt to individuals with established viewpoints. Joe Jackson was considered to be a devoted Southerner, but as Gordon Mackay of the *Cleveland Leader* wrote in 1913, he was "accustomed to the north now."[65] As a unit, though, the "Rebs" disliked the designation of the "Federal" League, the upstart outlaw organization vying for a place equal to Organized Baseball. The name itself was somewhat offensive to them, and Nick Cullop told a reporter, "We don't belong to the Federals, no sah."[66]

Developed initially in 1913, the Federal League was an independent organization with six clubs—primarily based in the Midwest—with Pittsburgh being its easternmost franchise. By the end of the year, officials revealed their big aspirations of being on par with the American and National Leagues. That meant a multimillion dollar investment into new stadiums and a war for talent. The promise of superior player treatment and guaranteed salaries greater than what Organized Baseball owners were paying was an intriguing lure, with players and owners alike taking a double-take.

The superstars of Organized Baseball were obviously the most coveted, and the leaders behind the Federal League didn't seem to care about broken contracts. Big-time financiers wanted to instigate jumping from one organization to the other, and tremendous amounts of money were on the table. Players were going to be tempted, while others definitely saw the new league as an opportunity to cash in.

Preying on the alleged team discord and topping salaries by a sizable margin, the Federals wanted to strip the Naps from top to bottom. Of course, Jackson was among several players targeted, but everyone knew he was the real prize. H. T. McDaniel, a writer for *The Sporting News,* noted that Jackson would likely remain faithful to Cleveland if he sought "the advice of responsible parties." However, McDaniel knew Jackson was a "temperamental fellow," and that there might be lingering questions about his frame of mind.[67] That became a legitimate issue after it was reported Jackson was offered a record multiyear deal worth $65,000. It was a life-changing opportunity, much more money than what Charles Somers could possibly offer. But the question remained whether Jackson would throw away everything he'd built in Organized Baseball and with the Naps for the almighty dollar.

5

BASEBALL'S SCANDALOUS THESPIAN

During Joe Jackson's sophomore season of full-time duty in the major leagues, the popular Boston-based publication *Baseball Magazine* ran a feature on his career to date. The article, written by editor F. C. Lane, acknowledged him as the "coming star of the baseball world," and noted that his previous accomplishments were "unparalleled in the annals" of the game. Of course, that was considering his extraordinary minor league slugging, plus his .387 average in 20 games in 1910, as well as his record of .408 as a bona fide rookie in 1911. Lane believed Jackson was the only modern player who could challenge Ty Cobb for individual honors, and perhaps the designation of the "greatest player the game has ever known."[1] Without a doubt, it was a controversial proclamation, chiefly because Jackson was still a relative newcomer to the diamond. His longevity was far from established in comparison to Honus Wagner, Cap Anson, Nap Lajoie, or even Cobb for that matter.

Syndicated sportswriter Frank G. Menke contrasted Jackson with the latter quartet of stars after the 1913 season and figured Joe had a greater batting average for his first four years in the majors than his colleagues. He achieved a remarkable .391—which was beyond impressive—though he had a long way to go before he could be compared to veterans of 10 or 20+ years of experience.[2] Experts had no way to gauge whether his lifetime average would remain among the best in history but, in terms of durability, Jackson had repeatedly shown his toughness by playing through injuries. Nobody regarded him as a flash in the pan by the end of 1913, and greatness seemed assured.

The Federal League was a legitimate threat to Organized Baseball, and Cleveland felt the sting when ace pitcher Cy Falkenberg jumped to the Indianapolis Hoosiers for a higher salary. Three others—Fred Blanding, George Kahler, and Nemo Leibold—were reportedly on the cusp of doing the same, but would return to the Naps fold in 1914. The tempting offer made to Jackson was ultimately rejected, and he told the press: "I hardly considered the offer made me by the Federal League, although $65,000 for three seasons is much in advance of the sum I am to receive from Cleveland. President Somers as well as other officials of the club have been kind to me and I would rather play with that club than any other in the big leagues."[3] Needless to say, the news was a big relief for Somers and Cleveland fans alike.

Ironically, and actually very surprisingly, Jackson took a lot of abuse from wiseacres in the newspaper field in the aftermath of his decision to remain loyal to Organized Baseball. The commentary wasn't so much related to his dedication to the righteous side of the sport, but rather how he had turned down such an obscene amount of money. The *Charlotte Evening Chronicle* editorialized, "Jackson, the baseball slugger, has refused an offer of $65,000 to play with the Federal League. We are now convinced that Joe has no education."[4] Another reporter wrote, "If [Joe] had been offered that much in silver dollars and words of one syllable, he would have swum up Niagara Falls," while Grantland Rice remarked, "If Joe Jackson was ever offered in fact, $65,000 for three years, and then passed it up, no wonder Connie Mack let him go."[5]

These personal slights on his mental faculties had to be demoralizing to Jackson, and the truth is he was unfairly roasted for being honorable when he could've easily jumped ship.

Joe inked his new three-year contract with Cleveland in January 1914, valued at $16,000, including a $2,500 signing bonus. He'd receive $4,500 annually, a raise of $500 over 1913. In addition, the Naps would pay all of his wife's expenses during spring training for the three years and also agreed to nix the contentious 10-day clause, which allowed management to cut players on 10-days' notice.[6] To Jackson these were pleasing stipulations but, monetarily, his deal was far less than the $10,000-a-year some sportswriters publicized he would receive.[7] For years pundits had overinflated the salaries of major leaguers in articles, heaping huge figures on the Wagners and Cobbs of the baseball world. The numbers were rarely given out by people in the know, seldom confirmed, and hardly ever correct.

But there was quite a distance between $4,500 and $10,000, and although Cleveland was in a better position economically, Charles Somers wasn't prepared to pay anywhere near the amounts reported.

The continued illness of his father was a significant concern of Joe in early 1914, and he didn't expect to report to spring camp in Athens, Georgia, on time.[8] He wanted to stay close to family and ensure his father received the best care possible. Doctors stabilized George's condition and the family awaited his recovery. In the meantime, a business opportunity opened up and Joe ventured to Richmond, Virginia, with longtime friend and former Greenville teammate Bill Laval, arriving on February 10, 1914. Laval was a member of the local Virginia League club, and discussed with Joe the possibility of together buying an interest in a Richmond billiard parlor. Jackson liked the idea and the two went northward to make final arrangements.[9] The next day, George passed away and Joe immediately raced back to Greenville.[10] The timing of his trip ended up being inexplicably terrible, but Joe couldn't have known.

The close bond between father and son was never broken, and that was despite the fact Joe played baseball as a career. The elder Jackson didn't see the game as a conduit to earn a living, and loved seeing his son toiling around the family's butcher shop. But it was evident the income derived from baseball was never going to be earned cutting meat or laboring at the town mill. According to Joe's recollection, it was in the fall of 1911 that George first saw him play ball, having traveled to Cleveland for business and ventured out to the stadium. The ambivalence toward his profession didn't seem to bother Joe, and he did all he could to support his parents. As the dependable oldest child, Joe was named the sole heir in his father's will, and managed the funds from the sale of the butcher shop.[11]

Financially, things were going well for Jackson. He purchased a brand new Hudson Six-40, seven-passenger automobile in Greenville and, after taking care of family matters, decided to drive the 100 miles to Athens, Georgia, to begin spring training.[12] Upon arrival on March 3, in a typical showy manner, he proceeded to maneuver his vehicle onto the outfield grass, drawing the attention of all.[13] After properly parking his car, Jackson quickly rushed to the plate and hit a few to the outfield. Proclaiming that his eyes were "all right," he told a nearby reporter, "Just look out for me this year."[14] Back in the saddle, Joe experienced the usual soreness and blisters from early training. Others faced similar problems, but for Ray Chapman, his preseason obstacle was a broken leg after a bad slide.[15] It was a devastating injury to a key player, and the Naps were significantly weakened even before the season had begun.

Considering the close proximity of Athens to Greenville, it was somewhat logical to arrange an exhibition in Jackson's hometown to not only drum up a nice payday at the gate for the team, but to honor Joe with a rousing event. It was a nice idea, but things didn't go exactly as planned. For whatever reason—perhaps the cold weather or a lack of publicity—the people of Greenville didn't shatter local attendance records in a mass show of respect for their local hero, and only around 400 to 500 fans were on hand for the event on March 14, 1914. Nevertheless, Jackson relished playing before family (his wife, mother, sister Gertrude and brother Earle watched the game from an automobile parked along the first baseline), and made the best of the afternoon.[16] The *Cleveland Plain Dealer* called the affair a "burlesque game," and the Naps easily trounced the Furman College squad, 26–4.[17]

Though Jackson had passed on the offer from the Federal League, he was confronted by several of the league's agents in Georgia, with one telling him that regardless of what he was being paid by Cleveland, they were willing to pay "four times" more. Jackson said, in response, "I simply turned on my heel and said goodbye."[18] The *Washington Times* reported that Jackson was offered a $45,000 deal by the rival organization, which Jackson was seriously mulling over, but the story blew over as just another series of rumors.[19]

The batting gods were shining brightly upon Jackson that spring, as he'd gone 32-for-60. Though he was hitting over .500, he was a bit troubled by his remarkable showing. "I would just as soon not hit so well before the season opens," he explained. "As a rule, when I don't hit well on the training trip, I cut loose when the bell rings, but somehow or other, I just can't help hitting this year."[20] During the first week of April, the Naps were in Cincinnati for a series against the Reds, but Jackson became ill with ptomaine poisoning and was laid up at the Havlin Hotel. He didn't depart with the team and remained bedridden with his wife as his primary caregiver for several days. But when the season opened at Chicago on April 14, 1914,

Jackson was in his regular right-field position. He went 1-for-4 in a defeat by the White Sox, and the Naps kick-started a foul losing streak, encompassing the club's first eight games.

Prior to Opening Day, baseball prognosticators levied the "dope" on the likelihood of Cleveland winning the pennant, and the prospects were quite unlikely. Bozeman Bulger of the *New York Evening World* felt the injuries to Ray Chapman and others, plus the loss of Cy Falkenberg to the Federal League, would devastate the club and left the Naps with "little chance."[21] After eight losses in a row to start the season, Bulger's commentary appeared right on the money. The Naps sank to the bottom of the league standings and planted themselves there for the duration of the season. There was nothing Joe Birmingham could do, but he certainly tried a multitude of different lineups, hoping to strike gold somewhere along the way.[22] The outfield became a musical chairs-like situation, and Jackson shifted between right, left, and center field as Birmingham tried to find a balance between Nemo Leibold, Jack Graney, and rookie Roy Wood.

Wood was able to use his bat to keep himself in the lineup, as his average was over .400 in May. For a time, Jackson and Wood were running neck and neck with the former at .405 and the latter .412.[23] The inspired hitting, however, could not be sustained, and the entire team fell into a deep slump. Even Nap Lajoie, the team's focal point, was batting 70 to 100 points less than his usual standard. Henry P. Edwards of the *Cleveland Plain Dealer* complained in May that the team had seven players batting over .300 at the same time in 1913, but only Jackson in 1914. He stated that the Naps were "disgracing themselves and Cleveland" with their horrible play.[24] On the first day of June, Jackson himself sank into the abyss by committing three painful errors in a 10–5 loss to St. Louis.[25] His wild arm and inability to snag a key fly ball were incomprehensible and borderline laughable. Oddly, Jackson homered in the same game, demonstrating a bizarre juxtaposition of his overall poise on the field.

Even with Jackson's bat, the team continued to play poorly. Right-hander Jim Scott of the White Sox shut Cleveland down for nine innings on June 4 in Chicago, but a second-inning single by Jackson prevented a no-hitter in a 2–0 loss.[26] Naps pitchers Allan Collamore and Fred Blanding walked twelve Boston Red Sox batters on June 9 in an embarrassing display, and attendance at home averaged around 1,200 in June, well below Major League standards. Batting around .321, Jackson suffered a left knee injury against Philadelphia in mid-June and missed more than 20 games. He rejoined his teammates on July 8, 1914, at New York, but was hit by a pitch in his shin during practice a few days later, again resulting in a trip to the sidelines.[27] However, he recovered with a vengeance and within a month was leading all American League hitters with an average of over .360.

To fans, a batting championship for Joe as a consolation for Cleveland's inept team play was a fleeting thought. That feeling disappeared in September, as Ty Cobb and Eddie Collins sailed past him in the rankings. The Naps never broke out of eighth place and finished with a dismal 51–102 record. The statistics revealed an utter inability to win, but didn't expose the reasons behind the dramatic failure. Joe Birmingham was blamed by many observers, but Jackson defended him, telling a journalist in late August that he was a "fine manager." Joe added: "I believe that no other manager in the league—McGraw, Mack, Stallings, or Carrigan—could have done any better than Birmingham has this year under the same conditions. Look at the accidents. In my own case, I know that I ought to be hitting about fifty points better, but you see I've been banged up so much."[28]

Still firmly believing that Birmingham was nothing more than a "bush leaguer," a comment he made publicly the year before, Lajoie was joined in his conflict against the team manager by close pals Ivy Olson, Doc Johnston, and several others. "Birmingham is the poorest excuse of a manager in the major league," said Buddy Ryan, who played 166 games for the Naps between 1912 and 1913. "He was so much of a farce that the ballplayers finally threw up their hands in disgust and got along the best they could without listening to him."[29] Philadelphia Athletics pitcher Carroll "Boardwalk" Brown took it a step further by stating that nearly the entire Naps outfit was despised. Late in the 1913 season, he explained, "We'd break a leg rather than have the Naps win the flag. Outside of Nap [Lajoie], not one of them has a friend around the circuit."[30]

Some animosity was directed toward Jackson as well. Bob Thayer, in the *Washington Times*, claimed Jackson overdramatized his actions, specifically playing to the galleries, and cried wolf "so much during a season" that most of his teammates didn't care when he suffered a mishap on the field.[31] Thayer was known for his criticisms of Jackson and whether there was any resentment toward "Shoeless" among his teammates is not well documented by journalists of the period. But the lack of team harmony and dwindling fan support in Cleveland was evident as 355,000 less patrons attended games at League Park in 1914 than they had the previous season. Altogether, it was surmised that owner Charles Somers lost approximately $60,000 over the last year and rumors of the club being on the market were popping up left and right.[32]

The Naps' financial hole and the stress from the Federal League war were only amplified after Somers began to experience personal monetary issues from other business dealings. He was considered a millionaire with extensive holdings, but because of his mounting debt, he found it necessary to make a deal with creditors to aid in his economic rebound.[33] Even with receiving financial aid, the situation was going to tie his hands as far as the Naps were concerned. The first step would be a general downsizing of salaries. He would no longer be able to spend large sums of money to improve the club, and he didn't even bother drafting players in late 1914. Additionally, he planned to send a reduced number of players to spring training and chopped the number of scouts looking for talent. Bearing in mind that Somers was one of the most liberal spending owners in the league only a few years earlier, the turn of events was nothing less than shocking.

With regard to the future of the Naps, Somers and Birmingham devised a plan to revamp the roster by eliminating suspected troublemakers and expendable big contracts. In the span of seven months, Vean Gregg, Ivy Olson, Doc Johnston, Fred Carisch, and Nap Lajoie departed the team either by sale or trade.[34] The departure of Lajoie, the team's franchise player, to the Philadelphia Athletics made headlines, especially since he'd been a superstar with the club since 1902. His .258 batting average in 1914 alerted many to the possibility that his best days were behind him. However, because of his popularity and innate ability to make an exciting play on any given occasion, he'd remain a box office draw in whatever city he played. Cleveland, understandably, would drop the "Naps" from its team designation, electing to instead be known as the "Indians."[35]

Jackson was disappointed to hear about Lajoie's exit, as the two were good friends, and was also saddened by the sale of roommate and pal Doc Johnston.[36] The faction targeted by Birmingham and Somers was made up of Joe's cronies, and it wasn't much of a question that he was on the outside of the collegian clique. That being said, there was an outside chance Jackson would be added to the growing list of Clevelanders playing elsewhere in 1915. Talks were purportedly held on the subject midway through the 1914 campaign, and New York Yankees boss Frank J. Farrell was excited about bringing Joe to the "Big Apple."[37] Jackson had his own preference, though. "I have always liked Washington," he explained, "and nothing would please me better than to either be sold or traded to the club that is managed by [Clark] Griffith."[38]

Neither Somers nor Birmingham could bring themselves to deal away their biggest attraction and surest hitter to an American League rival. But officials were aware of Jackson's decline in offensive production in 1914. His .338 batting average was the lowest since 1909, while most of his other stats were his worst in five years. Jackson's bread and butter, slugging, was decidedly inferior compared to previous seasons, and he wasn't even included in the top ten for doubles (22) whereas he was usually among the leaders. His 13 triples were half of his 1912 total and he struck out 34 times, the most since 1911. The odds were likely he'd rebound at the plate if he remained healthy, and if Birmingham could restore the club's cooperative spirit, Cleveland was in a significantly better spot going forward.

Following the season and final payouts, Jackson quickly ventured home accompanied by teammate and fellow Greenville native, Walter Barbare. Joe was an enthusiastic traveler, desirous for his tranquil homestead, his pet chickens, and to reacquaint himself with family. By November 1914, he was ready to diversify his interests and purchased a cigar shop in Greenville, to be managed with his brother, Dave. According to *The Sporting News*, the operation was dubbed, simply, "The Smoker."[39] Combined with his pool hall and investments in real estate, Jackson was proving his worth as an entrepreneur, and Greenville cotton mogul Thomas A. Miller affirmed his status, telling a reporter, "It is not generally known that Joe is a very thrifty and businesslike individual."[40]

To the condescending folk who seemed to take great thrill in harping on Joe's lack of education, Miller's comments were most likely a bombshell. Joe was certainly an industrialist, though on a small scale. His investments usually involved the type of places he himself was partial to hang out, and billiard parlors and cigar stores were right up his alley. He loved to sit back with a cigar and a beer while laughing with the boys about nonsensical things and telling people about his life in baseball. In that environment, Jackson was socially adept and could entertain a crowd of likeminded pals, some of whom were undoubtedly glossy-eyed by being regaled by the famous slugger. His businesses were not overly successful but, even so, he always kept his eyes open for opportunities outside of baseball.

In January 1915, Jackson was presented with a unique set of circumstances and leapt at a chance to enter the theatrical field with a half interest in a comedy act.[41] Utilizing his famous name, the production was billed as

Joe Jackson's Baseball Girls where, in each performance, Joe would take the stage with a brief monologue. Speaking before an audience of theater-goers was a little different than joshing with pals in a smoke-filled pool hall, but Jackson was building his confidence to endure the task. Deep down he loved all the histrionics, whether it was on the stage or the field. He enjoyed watching movies and minstrel shows, and personally enjoyed making people smile and laugh. The theatrical effort mixed comedy, song, and dance, and featured a throng of attractive female entertainers. Among the colorful programs they offered were *When Twins Marry, The Unlucky King,* and *Two Fools There Were.*

An old baseball town from Jackson's earliest days on the diamond, Greer, South Carolina, a suburb of Greenville, opened the production in the last week of January. From there, the act went to Atlanta for a week at the Bonita Theatre, where Jackson and his crew drew good crowds.[42] The next stop on the tour was the Palmetto Theatre in Anderson, South Carolina, followed by a run at the Majestic Theatre in Asheville, North Carolina, and the crew ran multiple shows a day. The advance hype into each town was bountiful in newspapers, and the spectacle was received with much curiosity. The *Asheville Citizen* remarked, "With a record for packing houses acquired so far this season, Joseph expects to repeat here and to break the attendance record at the Majestic."[43] After the opening night in Asheville, a reviewer commented that "The Company is a clean, capable one, presenting musical comedy in tabloid [form], attractive chorus girls, and clever comedians."[44] Overall, it was a very pleasurable experience for spectators.

Jackson was eating up the positivity from audiences and was thoroughly enthralled by the footlights.[45] He was enthusiastic, but remained instinctively nervous. Words didn't come easy to him when on the spot, and a columnist described Joe's verbal skills by saying: "While the Carolina Demon can punch the pill for an average of well over .300 when he gets out on a baseball diamond, in the Conversational league his batting average is about .029."[46] As a comic, Joe did his best. "I have given Cobb several hard races in my time, but as yet I haven't been able to Ty Cobb," he told a receptive crowd. "I once told my wife that I never thought I would be an actor. She said: 'Don't worry, Joe, you never will.' The only hit I ever made with my wife was when I asked her to marry me." And when he was asked "Who settled Philadelphia?" he replied, "The [Boston] Braves, last fall." With a few swings of the bat, Jackson rounded out his stage performance, and ticketholders roared in approval.[47]

In the meantime, the Federal League was still leveraging for players in the bitter baseball war, and Jackson's name continued to be mentioned in rumors. He rejected yet another proposal in August 1914 at Boston, but the outlaws didn't take no for an answer.[48] They approached him again in December at Greenville with a three-year $50,000 deal, but Joe refused to break his contract and turn his back on the Indians.[49] Nobody figured he would but once he was bitten by the stage bug the tenor of Joe's attitude began to change. He apparently informed a journalist in late January 1915, that he was considering leaving baseball altogether to focus only on his theatrical enterprise.[50] A few weeks later, this information corresponded with an announcement that Jackson had been tendered $25,000 from vaudeville agent George B. Greenwood of Atlanta to do just that, essentially walking away from baseball for show business.

A longtime booking agent, Greenwood sank his teeth into Jackson and grandiose promises of incalculable riches from their affiliation were undoubtedly made. On Jackson's behalf, Greenwood notified the press that Joe hadn't obtained an official order to report from the Indians so far that year, and if he didn't receive something by March 8, he was going to sign the vaudeville deal. The Indians, according to *The Sporting News*, did send Jackson a definite reporting date of February 27; however, Joe didn't join the club. Sportswriter Henry P. Edwards and others didn't buy Greenwood's motives and felt he was part of a sly scheme by the Federal League to double-cross Organized Baseball and, apparently, it was working to some degree.[51] Greenwood also boldly offered to purchase Jackson's contract from Cleveland, but owner Charles Somers was in no mood for amateurish humor.

Somers immediately sent team secretary William Blackwood to South Carolina to figure out what was going on, as it was nearly impossible to separate truth from gossip. The latter discussed things over with Jackson and found that while he was deliberating a future in vaudeville, he planned to report in San Antonio for spring training with the Indians as anticipated.[52] "There is no danger of my deserting the ball field for the stage," Jackson explained. "At least I am not going to take up stage work for a good many years unless I have some terribly bad luck. Do I like the stage? Well, in some ways I do, but I feel that my baseball ability is worth more to me than any ability I might develop on the stage. I have only played in cities where I am known from my baseball career and have enjoyed the experiences very much."[53]

Jackson divulged more of what appeared to be a conflicting series of public statements to a Greensboro newspaper. "I do not intend to jump to the Feds, although one club in that circuit offered to allow me to name my own salary, but in case I can't come to terms with Cleveland, I will lay off this year and travel with my troupe."[54] No one was quite sure what conditions were still being discussed with the Indians, as his contract had already been signed, sealed, and delivered. In some ways it seemed as if Jackson was just being difficult and purposefully creating chaos. He later revealed that all the Federal League talk had been "a lot of bunk to advertise the [theatrical] show."[55] Jackson, as it seemed, was savvier than people gave him credit.

Oddly enough, throughout this time-period, there was an underhanded tinge to Jackson's actions, and his strange behavior worried Katie substantially. She followed his road show to Anderson and Winston-Salem, trying to be a watchful and protective wife, but the subtle yet unconfirmed signs of marital infidelity were emerging a little at a time. The *Twin-City Daily Sentinel* of Winston-Salem, North Carolina, didn't avoid remarking about his perceived suspicious conduct on March 8, 1915. It stated that Joe, three days earlier, snuck off on an early morning train for a mysterious location, and noted that a particular girl from his theatrical group, Irene Rene, was on the same Pullman. No word was received from either until Joe turned up in Greensboro on March 7, the newspaper reported. Katie believed he was headed back to Greenville to handle some type of business, but never ended up speaking with him. The newspaper added, "The affair created much talk among those who knew the circumstances."[56]

Not much was known about Rene. She was described as a "pretty" vaudevillian by the *Wilmington Morning Star* the previous July, but her background and general relationship with Jackson was unclear.[57] The press didn't have proof of any wrongdoing, but speculation was rampant and Katie was rightfully concerned. For Jackson, he realized it was time to head west to Texas, perhaps to dodge any questions about his personal life. On the evening of March 13, he arrived in San Antonio—far out of shape, but ready to begin camp. The following afternoon, in an exhibition against the St. Louis Cardinals, Joe stepped to the plate for the first time and singled. He would also score in a 10-inning, 7–7 tie, but manager Joe Birmingham pulled him after two plate appearances, hoping to start his physical training process slow to prevent injury.[58]

The Indians were rusty in early exhibitions, dropping a game to San Antonio on March 16, but Jackson's batting eye strengthened rapidly. In fact, his power hitting was in fine form, as he homered at Waco and Palestine, and twice at Beaumont, Texas. On March 28, he hit a timely single in the 10th inning to assist the Indians in beating New Orleans, 3–2.[59]

Jackson, though, was a bit more eccentric than usual, seemingly affected by his theatrical opulence. An observer in New Orleans spotted him wearing expensive jewelry to an early practice session, including a couple diamond rings.[60] The flashiness of his ornaments wasn't entirely unnecessary for the ball field, but Joe felt comfortable showing off his pricy gear for one reason or another. Continuing with the abnormal theme of the spring, Jackson suddenly departed the club in early April because his brother was ill, receiving permission from Birmingham.[61]

Joe never made it to Greenville—at least not initially. His family there was somewhat surprised to hear he wasn't still with the Indians playing ball, and it was reported that, instead, he "spent thirty-six hours in Atlanta." Of course, his unaccounted time was extraordinarily mysterious.[62] Jackson blamed it on a missed train connection, but things just didn't add up. The *Washington Times* indicated that "trouble with his wife" was the reason behind Jackson's vanishing act, and whether he was again off with Irene Rene remained an appropriate question.[63]

From there the story got stranger and stranger. A sheriff from Greenville County said to be acting on a warrant prompted by Katie, began hunting Joe in Atlanta. He diligently located the ballplayer and began to drag Jackson to the train station for the journey back to South Carolina. Joe decided he didn't need to be hauled anywhere by the man in uniform, knocked him out with a swift punch, and went to Greenville on his own accord to post bail on the original charges.[64]

A Greenville newspaper cited the story as being "entirely erroneous," and Sheriff Hendrix Rector added: "It's all a lie. Who ever heard of such an outrageous thing? Why I haven't been out of Greenville County in ten days. And as far as I know no other officer has been to Atlanta to arrest Jackson. If there is even a warrant here against him, I know nothing of it." Rector affirmed that the problems in the Jackson marriage were of a personal nature. For that reason, Katie and Joe's brother Dave journeyed to Atlanta themselves to figure out what was really going on. She told a writer that she never went to the sheriff to press charges on her husband, but it was obvious she was confused by the turn of events.[65] Around the same time, it was revealed that Katie was contemplating a divorce action against Joe for cavorting with Rene, and if anything could bring Jackson back to his senses her genuine threat was the one to do it.[66]

Turning the drama away from his marital problems and back to baseball, sportswriters centered on two aspects. One was that Jackson was said to be disgruntled about his salary with Cleveland, and the other was his supposed rift with manager Joe Birmingham, which Jackson later denied. However, the latter did want to be traded.[67] With additional anxieties from his cigar shop going out of business, Jackson was facing a depression in nearly all areas of his life; his marriage, his business, and the future of his baseball career in Cleveland were all up in the air.[68] For the Indians, it was a poor time for Joe to be making waves. They needed stability and leadership from him in the clubhouse and on the field. They absolutely required his big bat in the lineup winning games. What they didn't need was a cloud of controversy and scandal by a part-time ballplayer and thespian. Birmingham wanted nothing more than to reunite the team and fight toward a pennant. But he needed Jackson on board—mind, body, and spirit.

Katie Jackson was a forgiving woman and wasn't going to let the recent problems destroy their marriage without ample time to properly discuss everything that had occurred. Once Joe decided to return to the club, she expected to soon leave Greenville herself to rejoin him on the road and talk things over. "I'm just waiting to hear from Joe," she revealed. "I got a telegram yesterday from Secretary Blackwood of the Cleveland team, stating that Joe had joined the club at Chattanooga and said he would let me hear from him right away." The newspaper indicated that Katie had become reconciled, and it was true.[69] She wanted to put the entire mess to bed forever.

The painful reality of the situation caused Joe to lose between 15 to 20 pounds in a 10-day span, and the *Cleveland Plain Dealer* called it a "nervous collapse."[70] But with his sights retrained on the baseball diamond and Katie venturing northward, his condition was gradually improving. Before long he was back to making spectacular plays in the field and being the awe-inspiring hitter people had come to know. Before the opening game of the 1915 season at Detroit on April 14, Jackson joined Ty Cobb for a lengthy discussion, and a Cleveland journalist jokingly hinted that the two were discussing the finer points of operating a "burlesque show."[71] Joe respected Ty, and a conversation with one of the most focused players in the game was a good way to strengthen his resolve to get back to the business of playing championship-caliber ball. That afternoon, he went 1-for-4 at the plate in a 5–1 victory over Detroit.

By early May, Jackson was hitting over .330 and well within reach of league leaders. He successfully rebounded from his several-month ordeal and his body snapped back into shape for the long campaign ahead. If he avoided any on-the-field mishaps, there was no reason why he couldn't challenge for the batting championship again by season's end. But 1915 was a year of unpredictability and, although he was wearing a Cleveland Indians uniform in May, there was no telling where he'd be by midseason. In fact, teams across the American League were still beckoning for his services. If the Indians continued to underperform at the box office, owner Charles Somers would have no other choice but to assess the value of his players—not only for the current season, but for the years ahead. That meant perhaps Jackson was expendable, of course for the right combination of talent and cash.

6

THE $65,000 MAN

Entering his eighth major league season in 1915, Joe Jackson was a battle-tested veteran with the scars to prove it. He'd been around the circuit, faced off with the best pitchers in the game, and owned remarkable statistics. In his quest for eternal glory on the diamond, Jackson became known for his extraordinary slugging with many games being decided by his powerful drives to all corners of the field. Fans watched intently each and every time he stepped to the plate and wondered with heightened anticipation what he'd do next. They were drawn by his magnetism; his intriguing approach to baseball which provided great fascination, from the style of bat he used to the atypical way he stood at the plate. Joe's methodology was unique, and his idiosyncratic ways were further developed and strengthened through the years. No one handled themselves quite like Jackson, and for that reason, he was even more interesting.

Jackson was quirky from top to bottom. He referred to his baseball bats as his "babies," and cultivated a personal bond with them, recognizing their individual importance.[1] To him, as a premier hitter in the game, they weren't just wooden sticks to be used and discarded, but terrifically significant tools of the trade. He felt that by taking care of them, they'd do the same for him when he stepped up to the plate. So he gave them names, forbid anyone else from touching them, and ensured they were always protected. For instance, after the 1913 season, Joe took special time to enclose his bats in protective casing for the trip back to South Carolina, deciding it wasn't smart to leave them in the North. "Climate up in Cleveland is too cold for them bats," he explained. "Bats are like ball players, you know. They like the warm weather, not too warm, but just warm enough. Wouldn't think of leaving those pets up here."[2]

His comments weren't part of an elaborate act to be funny, either. In fact, he couldn't have been more genuine, as it was another case of Joe simply being Joe. "Now, there's 'Old Ginril,'" Jackson said, naming off his bats for reporters. "Not for a minute would I leave him here. 'Ginril' was the one that hit the ball the time I knocked it over the stands at the Polo Grounds. Now here's 'Old Caroliny.' She's one of the sweetest bats I have, but lately she's kind of balked on me. Don't know what's the matter. I could always call on her for a hit in June or July, but when the weather got cooler, she got cranky and, well, she wouldn't produce. When she went back on me, I tried out this baby—'Big Jim.' Say now, isn't he a peach? Just keep your eye on 'Big Jim' next spring and watch me drive 'em to the bench. But 'Old Ginril' and 'Old Caroliny' will be the pair to get your bets down on next summer. They're my hot weather clubs."[3]

"Black Betsy" would become the most famous of his offensive weapons but, during his career, he went through countless bats. Most of them were of the same color (black) and approximate length (35–36 inches) and weight (48–50 ounces). Compared to a number of his contemporaries, his bats were gigantic in size. Tom Terrell of the *Cleveland Leader* once noted that Jackson's bat looked like a "telegraph pole," and, to Ty Cobb, it appeared Joe was lugging a whole tree with him to the plate.[4] A 1910 report confirmed that Jackson, then still a rookie, carried the largest bat in the American League.[5] However, two National Leaguers—Chief Meyers and Larry Doyle of the New York Giants—topped him by several ounces.[6] But the heavier bats were Jackson's preference and, because of the challenge of meeting a major league pitched ball with such a weighted club, he couldn't necessarily afford to be sluggish during a swing, needing to put his entire body and abundance of natural strength into making contact.

And when he did make contact, the ball was typically blasted out of the infield—at the very least. Scorching line drives were commonplace with Jackson at the plate, and infielders were wise to pay attention at all times when he was awaiting a pitch. To managers and coaches, Jackson's affinity for heavy bats and his trademark stance were not exactly the recommended formula. The legendary Connie Mack immediately wanted him to make adjustments and couldn't see him being successful without a severe modification. "When I joined the Athletics in 1908, Manager Mack told me I would become a great batter if I went about it a different way," Jackson explained. "He told me to quit pulling away from the plate and he hid my black bats with which I had been knocking down fences in the South.

He had me use Harry Davis's bats. I didn't hit nearly as well, and made up my mind then and there that I would continue to bat as I had before."[7]

Jackson's system of "pulling away" was highly frowned upon by baseball purists and meant he shifted his right foot from the vicinity of the plate, wide toward first base on every pitch—wide meaning an amazing two to four feet.[8] He used his long arms to reach across the plate at the same time, pulling the ball with immense power. Pitchers initially thought his actions were due to some kind of internal fear, but quickly realized that theory was wrong. Jackson was definitely not afraid. It was simply that the form he'd developed worked well for him, and he had no reason to completely amend his style to better conform to the methods of ordinary players or textbook recommendations. Managers learned to leave him to his own devices. Detroit Tigers pitcher George Mullin insisted in 1911 that "A player who pulls away from the plate as Jackson does isn't a real hitter."[9] Jackson batted .408 that season.

The next year, writer Grantland Rice described a Jackson at-bat by saying, "Shoeless Joe looks to be anything but an alert, concentrated actor at the platter, with his bludgeon swung loosely and aimlessly below the waistline. But when the correct moment comes, the coil tightens, the springs flip back into place, and Jackson at the second of his swing is the genteel acme of litheness and poise."[10]

Regardless of any criticism about his intellect or unorthodox approach, Jackson became a practical genius at bat; oftentimes seeming to control his own destiny by learning from his mistakes through trial and error. Going into the 1912 season, he decided he wanted to hit more consistently to left field, and spent hours practicing to ensure he'd do just that.[11] He also knew the opportune time to crowd the plate, to step wider, or to purposefully take a pitch. Jackson didn't have the mental acumen of many of his fellow players, but his instincts during a game were usually right on the mark.

With regard to his black bats, Jackson preferred to use them, and only didn't in rare instances where he didn't have a choice. For example, after breaking his three dark-colored models in 1911, he was forced to use a regular light brown version until a new shipment arrived.[12] Legend has it that his bat's black color was created by tobacco juice, but that was a fallacy (at least for those clubs created by J. F. Hillerich & Son of Louisville, Kentucky, which became Hillerich & Bradsby in 1916). "Jackson insisted that every one of his bats must be black," recalled Henry Morrow, a longtime agent for Hillerich in 1943. "We didn't paint the bats, but colored them by burning them over a flame." Without a doubt, in his several decades of employment with the company, Morrow figured Jackson's demand to be at the top of the most peculiar he'd ever received.[13]

But that was Jackson. He liked things his own way and had personal beliefs about every phase of baseball. In preparing for a season, he paid particular attention to strengthening his eyes for future plate appearances. For one, he felt billiards and pool were excellent tools to sharpening eyesight, but only if the games were played in direct sunlight.[14] Trapshooting was another venture he liked for its benefits, and Jackson once said, "Next to baseball, give me a shotgun. In the field or at the traps I find great enjoyment in its use."[15] Through the years, innumerable reporters and commentators have mentioned Joe's practice of closing one eye and staring at a candle to improve his batting eye. Considering his affection for such idiosyncrasies, it is completely conceivable. Jackson also disavowed movies and driving automobiles fast because he believed of their potential to strain his vision.

Undoubtedly, he employed his array of tactics prior to the 1915 season, and by mid-May, was batting just over .350. While his methods seemed to garner results, the Cleveland Indians weren't as lucky. The team was failing to turn things around and remained several games under .500 while bouncing between fifth and sixth place. After 28 games (12–16), it was apparent to owner Charles Somers that Joe Birmingham was not cutting it as manager. The two had disagreed over several strategic moves, the most specific being the shift of Jackson from the outfield to first base (per Somers's request), a position he wasn't skilled at—nor one he'd ever played on a professional level). But, nevertheless, Somers wanted Jackson standing at first with upstart Elmer Smith in right field, whereas Birmingham didn't want to risk his best hitter getting hurt. Birmingham purposefully delayed the move until May 19 against Boston and, that afternoon, Jackson made an auspicious debut at first, going 2-for-4 with two triples in a 5–2 victory, which snapped the team's four-game losing streak. The *Cleveland Plain Dealer* even lauded his work in the infield.[16]

Birmingham was fired from his post two days later, and Indians coach Lee Fohl was promoted to manager.[17] As for Jackson, he remained at first base through June and had his ups and downs. Sportswriter Henry P. Edwards, who was always willing to equally commend and condemn Joe's on-the-field work, made no attempt to hide his feelings on June 2, 1915, after a poor showing by Jackson in a 2–1 loss to St. Louis the day before. Edwards pointed out that in the fourth inning, with a man on base, Jackson "preferred" to raise his batting average rather than sacrifice the runner, and hit into a double play. And in a one-run game, it was a costly mistake—Edwards felt—as Jack Graney soon doubled and, had there been a man on base, he would have scored. In the sixth, Jackson was tallied with an error for a poor throw, leading to what ultimately became the winning run for the Browns. "Joe Jackson was the most important reason why the Indians did not win," Edwards proclaimed.[18]

The erroneous throw was a consequence of a rapidly deteriorating right arm, stemming from his move to first base. Joe retired to the bench after the game with what was suspected to be torn ligaments from playing out of his natural position. Jackson was using different parts of his arm muscles than normal, and the soreness was seriously hampering his ability to do the simplest of things.[19] His injury was exactly what Birmingham warned Somers about, but the skipper's words were ultimately ignored. Jackson was later sent for X-rays, where a chipped bone was found.[20] Joe was spirited enough to return almost immediately, but a doctor kept him out for six full games (though he was allowed to pinch hit in two of those games). He rejoined his teammates at Boston on June 14, 1915, and was all too ready to reassert himself, achieving three hits—including a triple—in a 4–1 loss to the Red Sox.

Through his early struggles at first, Jackson eventually displayed his versatility and had many fine moments. But there was still much criticism. Louis A. Dougher of the *Washington Times* straightforwardly declared, "Joe Jackson is no first baseman," and cited a recent game between the Senators and Indians in which Jackson nearly injured second baseman Ray Morgan with a rough tag during a slide into first. Dougher said Joe performed clumsily and Morgan, angry about the occurrence, verbally grumbled about the incident at the time. "There are any number of players in this league who will spike Jackson at the first opportunity," the writer added, stating that Jackson still had a lot to learn. "The difficulty he will have, though, will be to cut out his circus stuff and escape risk of injury. It is doubtful if a man of his nature can very well do that."[21]

With all the criticism, Jackson was doing his best under the circumstances. On June 24, he made 24 putouts at first in the longest game to date at League Park, a 19-inning affair that went to the White Sox, 5–4. Altogether, he'd start 29 games at first, complete 284 putouts, contribute to 12 double plays, and have 15 assists. He also made seven errors, finishing his tour of duty with a .977 fielding average. Jackson concluded his run at first base on July 5, 1915, and returned to right field the next day. Since mid-June, his batting average had dropped around 30 points, and the status of the Cleveland club had not significantly improved under manager Lee Fohl. According to Henry P. Edwards, the Indians were "rapidly becoming [the] joke of the big leagues." In the 16 games played between June 20 and July 6, the club had lost all but four and were averaging less than 2,100 fans at home.[22]

Edwards, who was highly influential between his daily reporting for the *Plain Dealer* and as a correspondent for *The Sporting News*, indicated that it might make sense to trade or sell Jackson, Ray Chapman, or Guy Morton to aid in the club's rebuilding.[23] Talk of Jackson being dealt away had prevailed most of the year. In February, he was mentioned in a possible deal with the New York Yankees and manager Bill Donovan told a reporter, "We'd be tickled to death to have a man like Jackson in our outfield."[24] Then, in May, there were rumors of a swap with Washington involving shortstop George McBride. Senators manager Clark Griffith was all for the idea but, like the situation with the Yankees, Charles Somers backed away from letting Jackson go.[25] But the reasoning of Edwards in early July, referencing the club's heavy financial loss, seemed to resonate with the public and his departure seemed like an inevitability.

Aside from with all the talk of trades and potential deals, tragedy almost struck for Jackson on July 7, which could have easily cost him his career. That afternoon, a scheduled game against Detroit was washed out when League Park was oversaturated. Once the weather cleared up, Joe decided to take his wife and sister-in-law on a leisurely and scenic ride along Lake Shore Boulevard, northeast of Cleveland proper. During the trip, Joe began to hear an odd noise emanating from the engine compartment but, instead of pulling over, decided to take a peek while the car remained in motion. His wife controlled the wheel as he stepped onto the side board of the car, extending his body in an attempt to see what was wrong. The car had slowed, but none of the three occupants took into account vehicles passing them at a high rate of speed. At the exact moment Joe was extended outside his auto, a fast-moving horse-drawn wagon rushed by and sideswiped the dangling ballplayer.[26]

Jackson lost his grip and was thrown hard to the ground. Suffering a tremendously bruised left arm and cuts to his arms, legs, and face, Joe was badly hurt in the mishap. He was rushed to Glenville Hospital in nearby Euclid, Ohio, where they immediately patched him up, knowing how the accident could have been a lot worse.[27] Luckily for Joe and the Indians, no bones were broken, but the star would still miss 22 games. While he didn't return to the club in a full-time role until July 30, he was able to appear for an exhibition at Scranton, Pennsylvania, on July 26, and went 2-for-2. The next day, he fulfilled a pinch hit role at Washington, going 0-for-1. During his absence, though, Lee Fohl realized that it was indeed possible for the Indians to survive without their superstar by using a mishmash of lesser-caliber athletes. While it wasn't ideal, it was indeed manageable, and speculation about Jackson's departure began to once again grab headlines.

The Federal League smelled blood, and wanted the upper hand in any possible negotiations. Joe Tinker, manager of the Chicago Whales, ventured to Cleveland, with the intention to meet with several local players.[28] Tinker was a pitchman; selling the ideals of the fledgling outlaws and, in doing so, promised both hefty contracts and freedom from the ills of Organized Baseball. Jackson was at the top of a short list of targets, and on Sunday, August 15, the latter turned up at Joe's residence ready with an eye-popping proposal. The terms were in the neighborhood of $10,000 to $15,000 a year, for three years, plus a $10,000 bonus. Additionally, a correspondent for *The Sporting News* noted that if Jackson was tied up legally and unable to play for the Feds, he'd still be paid his salary.[29] All Tinker wanted was Joe's signature to betray the Cleveland Indians, the American League, and the entire realm of OB.

Tinker's smooth talking sent Jackson's head into a fog. It wasn't before long that Joe was buying into what the manager was selling, envisioning life as a big-money player in Chicago. Tinker was a veteran of the baseball world, having begun his major league career in 1902, and certainly knew how to raise questions in the mind of an athlete, especially when it pertained to club management.[30] By the end of their conversation, Jackson was livid at the way Cleveland had treated him, just as Tinker hoped. Joe's ire revolved around his mid-month pay, which was supposed to be doled out on the 15th, but was going to be paid on the 16th because the 15th was a Sunday. Tinker's clever scheme to turn Joe against the Indians worked like a charm, and the next day Jackson announced: "I claim my contract has not been lived up to by the Cleveland club."[31]

The proclamation appeared to be a tactical maneuver by Jackson to wiggle out of his agreement with the Indians on a technicality, thus freeing him up to sign with Tinker. Charles Somers was completely aware of the situation. In fact, team secretary Bill Blackwood heard of Tinker's visit while it was going on, and hastily rushed to the Jackson home to interfere. Once there, he instructed Joe not to sign and explained that if he wanted to play for another team, a discussion could be held to figure out a course of action.[32] But crossing Organized Baseball was the last thing he'd recommend. Jackson listened, and still chose to play his cards on Monday, claiming his contract was violated by a failure to remit his mid-month check. The *Cleveland Plain Dealer* called it a move of "financial shrewdness," and Somers was prompted to hold an emergency meeting with Jackson in an attempt to work things out peacefully.[33]

Early that week, maybe even that same Monday, Jackson and Somers discussed matters and came to the mutual decision to part ways. It made sense for both parties, as Somers needed money and players and Jackson wanted a fresh start elsewhere. Before they figured out the details of a possible trade or sale, the two decided to ink a new contract for 1917 and 1918, locking in terms beneficial to Joe, including a $6,000 base salary with the ten-day clause eliminated.[34]

This contract would be carried forward wherever Jackson was sent and protected his interests to a certain degree. With that out of the way, Somers went ahead and started to size up potential deals, particularly those from Clark Griffith of the Washington Senators and Charles Comiskey of the Chicago White Sox. The former reportedly stepped up with a $20,000 offer, but Comiskey, widely known as "The Old Roman" of the baseball world, was not ready to be outbid.[35]

Comiskey sent his most trusted assistant, Harry Grabiner, to Cleveland with the orders: "Watch the bidding for Jackson, raise the highest one made by any club until they all drop out."[36] No other owner in the league had a chance; Jackson was destined for the White Sox. Comiskey later said: "Somers and I are old friends. You know we started business together when the American League didn't mean as much as it does today. Perhaps the memory of old times had something to do with it, perhaps the knowledge that I was anxious to build up my club and spend any necessary amount of money for that purpose. At any rate, when Somers decided to dispose of Jackson, he wired me informing me of the prospect. I made him a good offer and he accepted. It looked like a good investment. Jackson has been a wonderful player. His record has declined for two years and the owner always take a gamble in buying a star. If Jackson plays that brand of ball which I know he can deliver, he will be worth a great deal to our club."[37]

In terms of public relations, specific information was released in newspapers to curb any possible negative backlash. For instance, following Tinker's attempted "raid" of the Indians, it was said that Jackson flatly rejected the Federal League offer to remain loyal to Cleveland. Joe was quoted as saying how satisfied he was with the treatment provided by Somers and how he planned to remain in Cleveland through the end of his current contract.[38] But that quotation obviously didn't reflect the hardball he was playing behind the scenes. For Somers, he blamed Tinker's influence on his decision-making, telling a reporter: "I did not intend to sell Joe Jackson, but when the Federal League got after him I knew that I could not compete against them when it came to a matter of money. I could not afford to pay Jackson any more than I was paying him. Since I couldn't hold Jackson and was likely to lose him to the Federal League, the only thing left me to do was to dispose of him for as much as I could get."[39]

The announcement of Jackson's acquisition by the White Sox was made on the evening of August 20, 1915, and the story was widely featured in newspapers the next morning. In exchange, Chicago was to give Cleveland three players and a "cash consideration," which *Baseball Magazine* declared was $31,500.[40] Sportswriter Henry P. Edwards immediately went to the defense of Somers against those critical of the transaction. To some fans, there was no logic in dealing away a superstar of Jackson's magnitude, but Edwards reminded readers of Joe's individualistic streak and failure to play for team interests. Citing poor attendance, he acknowledged the inability of Jackson to draw crowds and didn't want people censuring Somers for doing what he had to do, not only for himself but for the entire franchise.[41] Edwards was an unyielding supporter of the Indians and would never have admitted it was a bum deal, at least at the time. From his perspective, it was just what the team needed.

Jackson was content as well. A St. Louis reporter claimed Joe had previously expressed a burning desire to play in Chicago and had gotten exactly what he wanted by being sent to the White Sox.[42] Interestingly, Chales Weeghman, owner of the Federal League's Chicago Whales, hinted that Joe received a $5,000 bonus (from the money Comiskey paid Somers) for agreeing to the deal.[43] If true, Joe had more than enough reasons to be happy. He admitted he was in a "rut" in Cleveland, and felt his game play was going to improve in a different uniform. While his salary terms of $6,000 a year were going with him to Chicago, Jackson was still quite optimistic about making greater monetary sums. He told a journalist that he stood a better chance of "getting into some sweet World's Series money" now that he was out of Cleveland.[44]

The players going to Cleveland in exchange for Jackson were not initially known, but Edwards accurately predicted two of them: utility man Bobby "Braggo" Roth and pitcher Ed Klepfer. Among the others said to be in contention for the third spot were catcher Tom Daly and the twenty-three-year-old outfielder Oscar "Happy" Felsch.[45] The latter was a skilled fielder, and the Indians would have benefitted from his slugging in ensuing years. But neither Felsch nor Daly was sent to Cleveland. Instead, the choice was Larry Chappell, an $18,000 purchase by Comiskey in 1913, bumping the total value of the Jackson transaction up to $65,500—the most costly deal in major league history to date. Ultimately, Roth became the biggest success of the trio, ending his career with a .284 lifetime batting average in eight years of big-league play. Klepfer pitched six years with a 22–17 record, and Chappell's career was cut short by injury and military service, then passing away from influenza in 1918.

Charles Comiskey was a liberal spender when it came to buying talent. His purchase of Jackson broke his own record, set the December before when he gave Philadelphia $50,000 for second baseman Eddie Collins. Through the years, he purchased the rights to an endless stream of minor leaguers, and his acquisitions weren't second raters but rather players leading their various leagues in batting and pitching. He sought the cream of the crop and often outbid his counterparts, only to be disappointed later by inadequate performances. The White Sox had worn the designation of "Hitless Wonders" since the 1900s, and Comiskey wanted nothing more than to put a lineup of real sluggers on the field. Finally, he decided to buy proven talent instead of recruits, and raided the American League. In addition to Jackson and Collins, he spent another $18,000 to obtain Nemo Leibold from Cleveland and Eddie Murphy from Philadelphia, meaning he splurged upwards of $95,000 in cash to revamp his roster.[46]

"I'm glad to spend the money," Comiskey explained.[47] "My ambition, in brief, is to give the people of Chicago, who have supported me so loyally all these years, the best club I can gather together. They have come to my park and paid to see my team when it wasn't as good a team as I should have liked to own. They have stood by me when times were hard and I shall stand by them. They have given me their money when I didn't have a winner. Now I am trying as hard as I can and sparing no expense to give them a winner.

That is the reason I bought Joe Jackson."[48] The truth of the matter was that Comiskey had admired Jackson for several years and had made a handful of overtures to Somers about a possible trade. He also wanted premier shortstop Ray Chapman, but that's where Somers drew the line. Chapman was Cleveland's franchise player and wasn't going anywhere.

The increased motivation for Comiskey to bolster his club during the summer of 1915 was due to the fact that the White Sox were the strongest they'd been in almost a decade and a sincere contender for the league pennant. His push for radical change started in December, when he announced Clarence "Pants" Rowland as the new Sox manager. Rowland, two months shy of his thirty-sixth birthday, had no major league experience and was a veteran of the Three-I League, a minor organization based in Iowa, Illinois, and Indiana. The decision to propel Rowland to the leadership position was panned, and Rowland was negatively referred to as a "bush leaguer." But Comiskey didn't lose any sleep over his choice and was fully confident in Rowland's ability, even if others—including the fans—were not.

Rowland surprised many of his detractors by leading Chicago to first place before the end of May. For sixty-six days his club sat atop the American League, but it soon became apparent that the Sox were far from a well-oiled machine. The team struggled at the plate, and Rowland flipped his lineup more than thirty times over the course of the season in search for the right synergy. Of his regulars, only Eddie Collins and Jack Fournier were hitting above .300, while most others were far below par. The team went 13–14 in July, and fell to third place on August 4 in the midst of a six-game losing streak. Already panicking, Sox management rushed the Jackson deal after first basemen Jack Fournier went down with a serious arm injury in an attempt to retain a chance for the pennant. But the Detroit Tigers and Boston Red Sox were setting a difficult pace, and Chicago had very little time to ward off growing pains if they wanted to remain in the hunt.

On August 21, 1915, at Comiskey Park, Jackson made his debut for the Sox in a doubleheader against New York, receiving a nice reception from the local faithful. He was given the center-field assignment alongside Eddie Murphy in right and Happy Felsch in left. Having played mostly right field and first base for Cleveland so far that year, Joe adjusted to the new position, as it wasn't completely foreign. The season before, he participated in 30 games in center and compiled a .971 fielding average. Versus the Yankees, Jackson didn't make much of an initial impression, but Sox fans certainly knew what he was capable of. The closest he got to a hit was a drive at second baseman Luke Boone, which got away from the latter after a bad hop and although the *Chicago Daily Tribune* recorded it as a single, most scorers gave Boone an error. That same paper also proclaimed, the "$15,000 star doesn't shine," because the only other time Jackson was on base during the doubleheader was as a result of a base on balls.[49]

The Sox split the two games with the Yankees, and then went on to win their next four (three against New York and one versus Washington). Jackson achieved his first official hit for his new club in his third game on August 22, and his first extra base hit the next afternoon with a triple against New York's Bob Shawkey. His timely smash occurred in the bottom of the 11th and scored the winning run in heroic fashion, topping the Yanks 4–3. The *Chicago Daily Tribune* noted that his hit "justified the cost of his acquisition," and South Side fans couldn't have been more pleased with their new idol.[50] However, the Sox again began to slump, going 4–8 between August 25 and September 5, and in most cases the players were beating themselves by poor decision-making, errors, and a lack of will to win. Their shortage of enthusiasm was palpable against Philadelphia's rookie pitcher Tom Knowlson on August 28. Chicago was handed eight walks, had one player hit by a pitch, and made seven safe drives, but could only manage two runs while leaving nine on base in a 4–2 defeat.[51]

Even with a solid lead, Rowland's warriors were routinely capable of collapsing under pressure. On September 7, the Sox were ahead 10–1 in the bottom of the sixth against Detroit, but quickly fell apart when they gave up three runs in the seventh and four in the eighth. Pitcher Jim Scott was called upon to enter the fracas for Reb Russell, who lost any semblance of control, and won the game for the Sox, 10–8.[52] Following a blown game at New York on September 17, sportswriter I. E. Sanborn wrote, "All the Rowlands need nowadays is a little help and they will lose any ball game."[53] Despite the club's deep-rooted troubles, Jackson was ego-free among his new teammates and did what he was told by the manager. He upped his small-ball game, sacrificing and bunting, and played the percentages to score runs rather than improving his individual numbers. He was doing the tiny yet important things that writers in Cleveland complained he neglected, and his rounded play was critical for the Sox to win close games.

While paying attention to the little things, Joe still occasionally made inopportune errors and displayed his mental laxity. At New York on September 20, he lifted a ball to left fielder Roy Hartzell. It appeared an easy out, so Jackson slowed on his path to first. But Hartzell dropped the ball, and Jackson suddenly turned on his speed, trying for second, where he was tossed out.[54] Had he been running hard the entire time, there was no doubt of his safety, and Rowland likely pulled him aside afterwards for a chat. But as easy as it was to occasionally make a mistake like any other player, Jackson was able to leave his personal imprint on a ballgame through his extraordinary hitting. On September 27 in Philadelphia, he exploded on the ball, lifting his fifth and final home run of the season over the wall in right center, a shot acknowledged as the longest of the season at Shibe Park.[55] In the *Chicago Daily Tribune*, I. E. Sanborn joked that a fire engulfing a nearby shop was caused by the detonation of Jackson's powerful drive.[56]

The Sox pulled things together and won their final 11 games of the schedule, from September 23 to October 3. Though they finished strong, it didn't stop pundits from lamenting about the overall failure of the team to legitimately contend for the championship. George S. Robbins, a Chicago-based correspondent for *The Sporting News*, summarized his thoughts by stating: "The White Sox [were] outclassed by the Tigers and Red Sox for the simple reason that Comiskey's team has been an ever-changing team, lacking unity of purpose and team play."[57] An absence of stamina down the stretch was also said to be a factor, and of course, players placed the blame elsewhere. They cited Comiskey's extended preseason exhibition schedule as the primary reason for their endurance problems.[58] When things were all said and done, Chicago finished the season with a 93–61 record, third in the American League behind Boston and Detroit. The Red Sox would go on to beat the Philadelphia Phillies in the World Series, four games to one, for the title.

Jackson and his brethren missed out on the Series jackpot, but were in line to earn a little extra money from the postseason City Series against the Chicago Cubs. The Sox were riding the high of their winning streak and demonstrated great confidence on the field; much better than they had in August and a majority of September. They refused to be denied victory and topped their North-Side rivals, four games to one, to capture the local championship. Joe did his part, lifting spirits in the third game when he drove a liner down the left-field line, scoring two runs and aiding his team's 5–2 win.[59] He batted .316 in the series, going 6-for-19, and made about $420 for the five bonus contests. Afterwards, some players griped about missing out on a mammoth Sunday box office gate, feeling that owners had predictably manipulated the schedule to ensure they garnered the bigger share.[60]

The sentiment of major leaguers with regard to the supposed greed of club owners was one of the most common threads across the sport. Those who bought into the idea felt magnates were in a place to rack up incredible sums of money off their hard work, and believed they continuously received the short end of the stick during salary negotiations. Any hint of unfairness drudged up a reaction, and the 1915 City Series in Chicago was no different. "Leave it to the big bosses to cop all the dough," an unnamed member of the Sox told a reporter after the series finale.[61] Like other big-league moguls, perceived for their insatiability for wealth, Charles Comiskey's actions were negatively construed, and money was the bottom line. The facade was falling off the sport of baseball and it was rapidly becoming apparent to fans that playing for the love of the game was steadily disappearing. Owners and players were thoroughly commercialized, and both sides wanted nothing more than steeper profits and greater gain.

7

THE JACKSON OF OLD

The reported dalliances of Joe Jackson in 1915 were an aberration in an otherwise straight and narrow existence. He was a bighearted family man with immense love for his wife, parents, and siblings. Nothing meant more to him than his family and securing their future. Although he traveled extensively during the summer, Greenville remained the center of his world. It was known that he would have traded all the skyscrapers, the hustle and bustle, and even baseball itself for a quieter life back home. For whatever reason, Joe was captivated by the promises of fame and fortune directed at him by cunning theatrical manipulators, and then, to make matters worse, made perhaps the worst decision of his life by spending time with vaudeville performer Irene Rene. These suspicious, disloyal actions were not made by the man his family knew and loved, but by someone obviously thinking out of character. His deviation from normalcy lasted only a few months, but it was a few months far too long for his wife Katie.

About six years younger than Joe, Katie was just a teenager when she first joined her husband on his path to the majors in 1910. At that time, Joe needed her to ward off his perpetual homesickness, which often haunted him and almost derailed his potential career.[1] The couple was usually inseparable; they never missed an opportunity to see a movie or enjoy a nice meal. Katie simply adored him and his idiosyncratic ways. She displayed her respect for Joe in an old Southern manner, referring to him as "Mister Jackson" in public.[2] In Cleveland, she was able to see many of his games, but Katie was relatively inconspicuous compared to other wives and appeared like any other young rooter—though her cheers for Jackson were the loudest. Following one game, those seated around her were shocked when she ran down the stadium's stairs and planted a big kiss on the popular outfielder. They had no idea—based on her youthful looks—that she was his wife.

Katie loved baseball. Wanting to ensure Joe's diet was well rounded she would leave every game early—around the seventh inning—so that she could prepare dinner. It helped monitor his eating habits and afforded her the opportunity in giving him the many delicacies reminiscent of home that he desired.[3] When they were in Greenville, they reveled in spending time together on their farm doing the various chores, and Joe maintained a flock of prized chickens. The fresh air was cleansing and helped both of them decompress from the craziness of the previous season. "All ball players like farm life," Jackson told a reporter in 1913. "The boys I know on the diamond tell me it is their ambition to own a winter place in California. But I tell you, old Carolina is good enough for me. And the only reason those other fellows like California best is because they don't know the South Carolina hills and old Paris Mountain."[4]

As much as Katie doted on Joe, he wanted her happy just the same which made the 1915 occurrences that much more painful. Indicative of their profound love, the fractures between them quickly healed, and they decided to go forward with a clearer perspective of what was really important: their marriage and happiness together, regardless of the challenges they faced. Over the years, Joe tried to be the picturesque husband, supporting his wife's decisions and purchasing her material items that elevated their quality of life. Other times he bought her pricy gifts for the sake of doing so. In one instance, during the summer of 1913, he spent around $1,000 for a Hupmobile Model 32, just for Katie's private use. He taught her how to drive and tailored his purchase to ensure she had one of the safest automobiles available.[5]

Joe was protective of his family and always spoke highly of his brother Dave, who was five years younger and also an athlete of note. In fact, his athletic skills were such that Joe actually believed he was the better ballplayer. After taking up with the Cleveland Naps, Joe tried to convince Dave to join him, figuring the Jackson Brothers were a formidable combination for major league pitchers. But instead, Dave got married and resigned himself to mill work and regional baseball.[6] "He can do everything I do," Joe explained in 1911. "I think he hits the ball harder. He likes the south, and I don't think he will leave, no matter how much money they offer him. I don't pose as a judge of ball players, but Dave is a better player than I am, and the club that can coax him away from home will land a wonder."[7]

Unfortunately, Dave suffered a badly broken arm in a mill accident a short time later, and *The Sporting News* reported that he was partially "paralyzed."[8]

By 1914, Dave was back in uniform and seemed to be completely recovered, grabbing headlines in the Piedmont League. Not before long, he advanced to the North Carolina State League and patrolled the outfield for the Greensboro Patriots. Joe continued to cheerlead for his brother, telling a reporter in August that he believed New York Giants manager John McGraw was scouting him.[9] Any club owner would have been foolish not to give Dave at least a look based on who his brother was, but, in all honesty, the latter had few similarities. A journalist in Asheville, North Carolina, stated that Dave did resemble Joe, "but his batting eye did not even faintly approach that of the 'shoeless' one."[10] Expecting Dave to be the second coming of his famous brother was a little out of the realm of possibilities, but it was fair enough to suppose the mill accident he experienced severely damaged any hope of major league competition.

The turbulence of 1915 wreaked havoc on Joe's statistics. His combined batting average with Cleveland and Chicago was .308, which was a full 30 points less than the prior season and by far the lowest of his career. In his 45 games with the Sox, he batted just .272, a mighty disappointing figure considering the amount of money paid for him. But Jackson was clearly affected by the depressing state of affairs in Cleveland, and his own personal tribulations complicated matters on and off the field. Being on a new team offered a chance for a fresh start, and as Joe adjusted to his surroundings, his teammates, and the management style, there was little doubt he'd be back among the league leaders. However, rumors sprouted up that owner Charles Comiskey and manager Clarence Rowland were already tired of Jackson and that he was headed out the door as soon as a deal could be finalized.

Another story surfaced claiming Jackson was going to be riding the bench during the next series as a result of his poor showing. The news completely unsettled Joe, and he ventured to Chicago in January 1916 on a specific mission to see Comiskey and Rowland about the reports. According to James Crusinberry's outline in the *Chicago Daily Tribune*, Jackson promised great things for the upcoming season, even touting a run at Ty Cobb for the league batting championship.[11] Neither Comiskey nor Rowland had made a decision to bench Jackson, but the possibility of a trade was still lingering. By mid-February, prior to the American League's meeting in New York, the rumor mill was active once again. This time around, the gossip was a little more specific.

Just days before owners gathered at the Wolcott Hotel, the Yankees purchased the rights to third baseman Home Run Baker from the Philadelphia Athletics, a famed member of its $100,000 infield. The purchase was expected to relegate Fritz Maisel to a utility role. To Comiskey and Rowland, Maisel was the perfect man to fill their third base hole. To obtain Maisel, Jackson was reportedly being dangled to the Yanks as trade bait.[12] No one from the Sox would admit the negotiations, but eventually all talks ceased without a transaction, meaning Jackson was staying put. All the whispering about a trade would normally have created a somewhat contentious environment but, for Jackson, he turned it into a positive. He used it as motivation, working extra hard to prove his value to the club. There was no more skating by on his previous reputation. He had to demonstrate his worth to club management, his teammates, and enthusiasts alike.

Equally important, Jackson had to dispel the suspicion that he played for average at the expense of his team, a criticism which had followed him from Cleveland. Rowland was fully aware of the stories and watched Joe closely, looking for any evidence of selfishness. There was no room on the Sox for bigger-than-life personalities and expansive egos, and Rowland wasn't going to let any of his highly touted stars dismantle the synergy he was striving to build. As for the wavering confidence of Jackson, Rowland spent his time boosting his self-image rather than focusing on his inconsistent play and harping on mistakes.[13] He wasn't presumptuous enough to believe he could fix Joe's weaknesses like Joe Birmingham had in Cleveland, but smartly understood that any man who could hit .408 in the big leagues had a pretty good idea as to what worked and what didn't. Rowland simply told Jackson he was a great ballplayer and gave him the freedom to regain his form on his own.

It all circled back to psychology. Joe was easily—almost too easily—affected by exterior happenings. For instance, a rowdy spectator taking him to task about a misplay could crack his confidence in a split second. He was sensitive in nature and reveled in the cheers of the crowd. Any negative outpouring, regardless of how insignificant it might have seemed, had the ability to turn his stomach and cross his eyes at the plate. Rowland encouraged Jackson, offering uplifting words of praise, and was credited with bringing out the best in the outfielder. One Chicago sportswriter went as far as to acknowledge Rowland for restoring Joe's "old aggressiveness."[14] Rowland extended the same type of finesse to the entire roster, and the manager's mild-mannered approach was popular with players as he wasn't an overbearing disciplinarian. He also didn't embarrass his players by way of verbal tirades. Rowland relied upon diplomacy and, slowly but surely, his statesmanship was uniting the team's many off-beat characters.[15]

Of course, there was little question of the talent in Chicago. At the top of the list was future Hall of Famer Eddie Collins, a Columbia University graduate, who transferred to the Sox in 1915 after nine years with Philadelphia. Collins was an understudy of the great tactician Connie Mack while with the Athletics, and his forward-thinking mind created many opportunities that would have been missed by a lesser-caliber athlete. He was a standout as a leader on and off the field, and the kind of clean-cut idol that represented baseball extremely well. Rowland certainly admired his play, telling a reporter in 1915 he believed Collins was the most valuable player in the majors.[16] Years later, Ty Cobb gave Collins the ultimate compliment by calling him the best of all-time. Who could argue with Cobb? But as a member of the Sox in the mid-1910s, Eddie was expected to hit well over .300, provide leadership as team captain, and act as sort of a middleman between management and players.

Comiskey and Rowland, additionally, hoped his professionalism would funnel down to his teammates who would be influenced by his all-around efficiency. Catcher Ray Schalk was cut from the same cloth as Collins—not because of his shared textbook education but for the depth of his baseball knowledge and leadership. Having joined Chicago in 1912 at nineteen years of age, Schalk was schooled in hard-knocks baseball and demonstrated over and over that he was tough to the core. He was more than willing to face down any runners approaching the plate, especially those much bigger than his 5-foot-9, 165-pound frame, and held his ground when collisions were an obligatory part of the game. He caught trick pitches from Ed Walsh, Jim Scott, Eddie Cicotte, "Doc" White, and many others, and regularly reined in pitchers of much greater experience with his wisdom. Sportswriters, managers, and fellow players had no trouble admitting Schalk was perhaps the best catcher in the game.

The combination of Collins and Schalk was more than formidable, providing the Sox with two above average on-field leaders. It's likely that the Sox players took more cues from this pair than Rowland during the season, but when things went south during a game, it was difficult for both men to suppress their aggravations. Without question, Collins and Schalk played to win every second of a ballgame, and Collins, in Philadelphia, proved his winning mentality beyond dispute. He was a consequential cog on three World Series championship teams (1910, 1911, and 1913), and won the league's Chalmers Award for most valuable player in 1914. But when he watched the Sox boot away game after game because of simple mental mistakes, he was blinded by frustration. However, like Rowland and Schalk, he restrained himself and played the diplomatic card to extract better results the next time around. Nothing was to be gained by maniacal outbursts.

The left side of the infield was stabilized by the striking defense of George "Buck" Weaver, a personable young shortstop from the small town of Pottstown, Pennsylvania. Affiliated with the Sox since 1912, he was improving every year. Although his numbers didn't always reflect his complete value to the team, Weaver was without question a major asset. Harry Daniel in the *Chicago Inter Ocean* wrote of Weaver, "In addition to his wonderful mechanical skill, he is a youth possessed of a keen brain, supreme self-confidence, without egotism, and a marvelous eagerness to learn more."[17] And with Collins next to him on the field, Weaver was able to learn from the best. "If he does not become one of the greatest of ball players it will not be because he is not ambitious, studious, and alert," Daniel added.[18]

Weaver appeared destined for baseball immortality, but the frequency of his hitting needed to improve. After batting .272 in 1913, he dropped 26 points the following year, only to bat to .268 in 1915. But with Rowland in charge, Buck's sacrifice hitting improved from 10 in 1914 to 42 in 1915, tying him with three others for the major league lead.[19] Rowland wanted Weaver to advance runners with more consistency, and the latter was responding in a big way. Jack Fournier was among those to benefit from Buck's fine sacrificing. The powerful first baseman and outfielder from the Pacific Northwest was in the .300 class in both 1914 and '15, and there was great optimism for his continued success as a slugger in the future. There was one problem, though. His work at first base was not major league caliber, as he committed 25 agonizing errors at the position in 1914, and another 10 in 1915.

Rowland did his best to get improved results in the field but, in looking for the best possible lineup, he ended up weakening the club tremendously. For example, four different first basemen were tried in 1915, with four others being placed at third base and nine players tested in left field.

These positional uncertainties had a negative effect, and fans didn't know what kind of a lineup they'd see on any given day. Jackson was finally established as the team's regular left fielder, putting an end to that revolving door (while also settling on Oscar "Happy" Felsch in center). Felsch, in his early twenties, was a product of Milwaukee and had graduated from the American Association after hitting 19 home runs for the Brewers in 1914. He was a hard worker with amazing athletic versatility in chasing down fly balls. He also possessed a potent arm, and the opposition quickly became aware of just how precise he could be after a few bullets were thrown from the deep recesses of Comiskey Park. "[Felsch] is of a type which, were there more like him, would make the game a better spectacle for all concerned," sportswriter Mark Shields wrote.[20]

The Sox had two capable outfielders on the bench in Eddie Murphy and Nemo Leibold, both obtained by Comiskey just prior to the acquisition of Jackson. Leibold was actually Joe's teammate in Cleveland and was not only a talented outfielder but a solid leadoff man. The only problem was his batting average, to that point in his career, was never better than .264. Murphy was a weaker fielder but a better offensive weapon, hitting .315 in 70 games for Chicago in 1915. He was also a member of Philadelphia's 1913 World Series team.

A different "Collins," John Collins, better known as "Shano," was another outfielder for the Sox and would become the primary right fielder in 1916. Like Leibold, he was a standout when it came to defensive work, but struggled as a hitter. His best year was in 1912 when he put together a .290 average, but dropped to .239 in 1913 and .257 in 1915.[21]

The pitching rotation centered on five individuals in 1915, including second-year man Red Faber from Cascade, Iowa, who went 24–14 with a 2.55 ERA in 50 games. Jim Scott, a year older than Faber at twenty-seven, also won 24 games, while Joe Benz went 15–11 and Reb Russell 11–10. Thirty-one-year-old Eddie Cicotte, the oldest of the quintet, attained a record of 13–12 during the 1915 season. Known as a shine ball expert, Cicotte, originally from Michigan, had been a major leaguer since 1905. His previous employment in Boston flashed moments of greatness, and posted a record of 14–5 in 1909. But Eddie's consistency was a problem at times, and a change of environment from Boston to Chicago allowed him to rebound in 1913, going 18–11 with a 1.58 ERA.[22] His 1914 results were again lackluster (11–16), but he was seemingly headed for greater things. In fact, nobody knew at the time, but Cicotte's wide variety of pitches—plus his excellent accuracy—was going to vault him into an elite class of league stars before the decade was over.

Stemming from the wide criticisms about Chicago's failure to retain conditioning throughout a full season, Charles Comiskey scaled back the preseason schedule going into the 1916 season. The team departed for spring camp at Mineral Wells, Texas, three weeks later than usual and booked "about one-fourth" as many exhibition games as in years past.[23] It was considered a wise move, and players were enthusiastic about the change in plans. They were easily rounded up and into uniforms just hours after arriving at their Texas headquarters on March 14.[24] Jackson arrived the next day and was just as enthusiastic, rushing out for afternoon practice ahead of his peers. Rowland ordered players to take things slow at first, and gave them the option of how they wanted to exercise for the first couple days. Training began to ramp up and soon they were engaging in intra-squad games. On March 29, Jackson flexed his muscles, powering out two homers in stunning fashion, but strained his back in the process.[25]

The injury wasn't serious, and Jackson returned to practice within a few short days. As a whole, the Sox looked promising. They were playing as a collective unit, fluid in their actions, and looked motivated to win. I. E. Sanborn of the *Chicago Daily Tribune* sized up the club and felt they were definite contenders. He liked the placement of rookie Zeb Terry at shortstop and the shift of Buck Weaver over to third. Regarding Jackson, he wrote, "[Joe] has acquired the White Sox spirit and is not only going after the batting championship with confidence but believes he is on a team of champions at last."[26] Jackson had forgotten any previous talk of being traded and was in the right state of mind to help Chicago any way he could. Fans in the "Windy City" were immensely excited about their South Side franchise, and an estimated 31,000 people attended the Sox opener on April 12, 1916. But, unfortunately, Detroit's Harry Coveleski put a damper on things, handing Rowland's men a 4–0 loss.[27]

Baseball was about to endure a boom period in Chicago. The end of the costly Federal League war (which occurred in December 1915) couldn't have come at a better time, and people wanted to see good, competitive baseball. They didn't want to hear about salary disputes or read about players jumping from league to league. It was back to clean, hard-nosed baseball.

The excitement of spectators was palpable at Comiskey Park, but noisy crowds couldn't compel the Sox to win games. The team lacked consistency at the plate, and although Jackson managed to hit successfully in the first seven games, he was batting a miserable .237 by the second week of the season. He was still making poor decisions, too. On April 16 against St. Louis, he had an opportunity to ride out an at-bat against a wild pitcher who had walked four men in the ninth inning. But with two outs and a 2–1 count, Jackson decided to swing away and grounded out, ending the game with St. Louis the victor, 6–5.[28]

For a time, Ray Schalk was the only .300 hitter, while Eddie Collins and others were playing well below par. Errors were costing them close games, and the Sox were doing everything possible to contradict reports claiming they were a potential pennant winner. Jack Fournier and Zeb Terry were benched and Weaver, batting just over .215, was moved back to shortstop. Yet another rookie, Fred McMullin, a product of Southern California, was inserted at third base. Rowland tried an endless number of lineup configurations and was searching for any signs of life. Jackson soon established himself as the only steady batter, pushing his average over .350 by mid-June. Over the course of two days (June 16–17), he went 6-for-6 with two hit-by-pitches and a walk in nine plate appearances against Boston. Three of his hits were made off the sensational twenty-one-year-old Babe Ruth, who would ultimately lead Red Sox pitchers with 23 wins and a 1.75 ERA.[29]

Tempers flared against Joe's old team on June 25, and several fights were stomped out by attentive umpires. James Crusinberry believed the Indians were trying to injure players with the intent of knocking the Sox out of the pennant race. "Never in history has Cleveland showed such rough tactics in baseball," he wrote in the *Chicago Daily Tribune*.[30] But the Sox showed heart in the way they fought fire with fire, battling back and never giving an inch. They refused to lose against Cleveland that afternoon, and took the game by the score of 4–3. The team clearly wasn't hitting at a normal clip, but their intensity to win was more and more evident as the season unfolded. Rowland had them doing everything possible to outwit and outplay opponents, and the cunning pitching of rookie Lefty Williams was a delightful surprise.

Chicago edged into third place before the end of June. A few days later, Jackson logged his name into the history books and into the consciousness of all Sox fans with a gallant performance. His heroics on July 4 were recounted in the introduction, and helped cement Joe as a local legend.

Winning over the fans went a long way to boost his confidence even more, and the left-field bleacher section at Comiskey Park cheered just about everything he did during a game.[31] Jackson, around the same time, took the lead in the American League batting race with a .382 average, edging past Tris Speaker who had been dealt from the Red Sox to Cleveland earlier in the year. George E. Phair of the *Chicago Examiner*, in acknowledging the history of "Hitless Wonders" on the South Side, comically wrote: "Joe Jackson has shown that a man can hit in spite of the fact that he is a member of the White Sox."[32]

The Sox were fast becoming the talk of the league and went 13–3 between July 23 and August 4, launching them into first place. The turnaround from the club's wretched play early on in the season to topping the standings was nothing short of amazing. And again, it was being done without tremendous hitting from the entire lineup. Had Eddie Collins, Buck Weaver, and Happy Felsch been pulling their weight at bat, the White Sox might have run away with the pennant. But as it was, the race was a three-way fight between Chicago, Boston, and Detroit . . . and the competition was steep. Rowland's players were alone atop the standings for less than a week, and needed to maintain a Herculean gait to remain within reach of first.

With the pressure mounting, playing the way they did on August 13, 1916, left them little chance to win the title, at least as far as Crusinberry saw it. "The White Sox made a sorry mess of their final game with Detroit yesterday," he declared, and described a number of flawed actions, including three double play pickoffs from the outfield by the Tigers defense. These incomprehensible mistakes and "half-hearted fielding" were not representative of a pennant winner, and Chicago sportswriters routinely called out similar blunders as the reason for losses.[33] An unfavorable road trip east later in August didn't exactly help their cause, but it didn't destroy their chances either. The Sox fought back to second place on September 20, but Boston had just enough juice in its tanks to maintain first for the remainder of the season.[34] In the end, the Red Sox would beat the Brooklyn Robins (Dodgers) for the World Series championship in five games.

According to his statistics on the year, the Jackson of old had returned with a vengeance. A majority of his numbers were his best since 1912–13, particularly his batting average of .341, his 202 hits, and 40 doubles. He led the majors in triples (21), total bases (293), and extra base hits (64), while setting a personal best in sacrifices with 16. However, Tris Speaker walked away with the league batting championship, sporting a .386 average with

Cobb being the runner-up (.371) and Jackson finishing third. It was obvious Jackson was still developing as a ballplayer, and the lessons learned from Rowland and his teammates in Chicago were immensely valuable. He was adjusting to a unique lineup and playing his role, while at the same time batting for average. No one could criticize his efforts, but the Sox, as a whole, still had some growing to do. The synergy just wasn't quite there, and based on the fact that Chicago scored 116 less runs in 1916 than the year before, the offense wasn't as sharp as it could be.

The postseason City Series against the Chicago Cubs was a quick and painless endeavor, as the Sox won four straight games and took the title, capturing their sixth straight local pennant. In the final game, Jackson homered to center field and was involved in driving in most of his club's runs in a 6–3 win. "The class of the south-siders stood out in every one of the four games," a writer for the *Chicago Daily Tribune* noted. And most remarkably, each pitcher put in a complete game, while the Sox lineup remained the same for all four contests.[35] Many people were surprised that some kind of secret conspiracy wasn't in the works to allow the Cubs to win the fourth game on Saturday, October 7, to provide for a Sunday game. Sundays, as it was known, was usually the largest crowd of the week. That meant a huge gate for owners, but it was not to be. "Joe Jackson is a rude, wicked person. He hit the ball so hard that he knocked the management out of a Sunday crowd," wrote George E. Phair in the *Chicago Examiner*.[36]

Once released from his baseball commitments, Jackson returned home. While he loved the Greenville area of South Carolina, he had considered purchasing a new home for some time. A friend had previously talked up the Richmond, Virginia, area and Jackson visited the city in 1914 to give it a look.[37] But he also had fond memories of Savannah, Georgia, from his days in the Sally League, and examined the possibilities of living there. Just prior to leaving for spring camp in 1916, he and Katie found a suitable property in the latter locale, and made the $7,000 purchase.[38] In making the decision, Joe thought of his family's needs above everything else, and believed it would make a nice residence for his mother as well. The home was constructed at a total cost of $15,000, and was completed around the close of the 1916 season.[39]

Jackson met his family in Savannah, and almost immediately began weighing two different opportunities during his offseason. One was as a baseball coach for the University of South Carolina, and the other was playing winter ball in Cuba.[40] Apparently, the offers were less than he desired or he found home life a little too comforting, because Joe decided instead to stay put. After all, he had the challenges of a new abode before him and that was enough to keep him busy all winter. With a guaranteed salary of $6,000 expected for 1917 and the controversial 10-day clause eliminated from his contract, he had little to be concerned about. But in the sphere of baseball's powerbrokers, there were innumerable concerns about the state of the game. The recent World Series exposed flaws in the system that had everyone talking, and many of the discussions were going to impact players not only in the coming season, but for the future of the sport.

First and foremost, it must be recognized that baseball experienced dramatic growth in 1916. Over a million more tickets were sold in the American League compared to the prior year, and *The Sporting News* denoted two specific reasons for the increase: a hotly contested pennant fight and the cessation of the Federal League.[41] Fans were energized, and their support for high-class baseball was demonstrated across both leagues. However, during the World Series, enthusiasts in Brooklyn were greatly dismayed by the hike of ticket prices and Ebbets Field did not sell to capacity for either game played between the local Robins and Boston Red Sox. Additionally, H. C. Hamilton of the *United Press* speculated that fans were growing somewhat apathetic in some circles, particularly because the Series had featured East Coast clubs for six straight years.[42]

So, despite the growth, there were evident cracks in the armor of Organized Baseball and club owners were salivating at a new series of preemptive measures, including the possibility of salary cutbacks, supposedly to keep ticket prices down. But owners were going after the players war-time contracts and were using the "protect the fans from being gouged" agenda as the public front to their scheme. They also wanted to rework contracts to ensure the 10-day clause was an available option, as well as strengthening the reserve clause. Sportswriter George S. Robbins wrote that these aspects were "once more giving the magnate the whip hand over the player, enabling him to dispose of players who are set down as dead timber and giving him a chance to sign new blood." In favor of the new maneuver, Robbins felt that the two clauses were going to help bring about a "restoration of the conditions that brought prosperity prior to [the] Federal League."[43]

Another Chicago-based writer, Oscar C. Reichow, added to the perspective, stating: "For three years conditions in baseball have been abnormal, but the time has arrived when they will return to normal, putting the game back on a plane where it can be conducted successfully, properly, and in a sportsmanlike manner."[44] A great percentage of writers were fully on the side of the owners, and one could only guess whether kickbacks or friendships gave way to such interests. But these same scribes lashed out at the players for their selfishness, essentially blaming them for the evolution of baseball into a vast complex of commercialism. Reichow wrote: "Ball players were spoiled by the Federal League. They were offered such enormous salaries and bonuses that they lost sight of the game itself. The conversation on the field . . . was on money, automobiles, or farms. The players had their minds elsewhere instead of on the battle, and as a result the game lost its punch and the interest that made it the finest of all sports."[45]

Cincinnati writer Jack Ryder mentioned a happening at the recent Series whereupon members of the Brooklyn team "thought not of the game [they had just lost], but only of the gate receipts, and even accused the National Commission of holding out a few tickets from the official count." He felt it was a perfect example of the "money-mad disposition," which had infected the player ranks.[46] Additionally, noted New York columnist Joe Vila declared: "The players have squeezed the magnates almost to death. They have been pampered and petted beyond all sense of reason. The players must not be allowed to run baseball, for it would soon run into disaster."[47] With regard to a potential strike from players as a response to the salary cuts, Vila insisted the public would be behind the owners and William A. Rafter of the *Brooklyn Standard-Union* agreed. The latter wrote: "The fans are getting rather tired of hearing the [well-paid] players count themselves among the downtrodden."[48]

Of course, there was an opportunity to balance reasonable salaries with smart ticket prices, but once owners formed a consensus on an issue there was little hope of turning back. In a way, these magnates were angry about being held over the fire for the last couple of years as players held most of the power. If the athletes had wanted a salary increase, all they had to do was threaten a jump to the Federal League and owners were forced to comply or compromise. But now that the Federals were gone, major leaguers were back at the mercy of their original owners, some of whom were not in a generous mood. The divide between club management and the players was widening, and it wasn't limited to any one league city.

Back in Savannah, Joe Jackson rested comfortably far from the intense boardroom arguments and probably only picked up bits and pieces of information from townspeople who wanted to talk baseball. The news didn't directly impact him, at least at the moment, and if the Players'

Fraternity (which had been formed to safeguard the interests of major leaguers) decided to head out on strike, Joe would have to figure out his best option. He was firmly for the players, no doubt, but he wasn't pushing to rock the boat. As far as he was concerned, baseball didn't begin until March of the following year, and he wanted to enjoy the holidays in his new home with family. Everything else was secondary. Life for Jackson was serene in those regards, and any internal debates in the realm of baseball were far from his area of interest. Only time would tell whether he'd be personally drawn into any of the hullabaloo but, going into 1917, he was content with things remaining nice and quiet.

8

WORLD SERIES AND WORLD WAR

Over the course of his career, Joe Jackson found ways to improve his game-play, sharpening his skills and curtailing any bad habits. He was embarrassed by on-field mistakes—never wanting to show any kind of mental slip before the public—and worked extra hard to avoid repeating the same blunders. Hitting always came naturally, but on defense he faced a number of challenges, and no one who watched him, reported his games, or played alongside him would have called Jackson a brilliant outfielder. In fact, a reporter for the *Washington Post* said he was an "ordinary fielder" in 1914, while another journalist referred to him as "mediocre" in *The Sporting News* the same year.[1] More often than not, he was overshadowed by his sensational outfield mates like Joe Birmingham or Happy Felsch, but Jackson was fully capable of creating memorable moments of his own.

He was known to launch pinpoint throws from the outfield to double up a greedy runner, and that included players testing his arm trying to score. Jackson prided himself on his distance throwing and would entertain fans by hurling the ball from around the outfield wall to the plate when there was no direct need to do so. Oftentimes he was just being showy and drawing applause by demonstrating his arm strength.[2] Jackson made smart choices, too, bluffing in certain instances to draw runners into a false sense of security, only to make the out. In 1916, he recorded 17 assists from the outfield—his most in several years—but also knew when to play it safe and avoid potential trouble. While his arm strength was never in question, he was often hindered by the sun when chasing fly balls to a great degree and never really got the hang of it. As a result, Joe was shifted on occasion, depending on the stadium, to give a better versed player rule of the "sun-field."

Chicago manager Clarence Rowland later denied such a practice. "Every one of my regular outfielders is a sun-fielder," he exclaimed in 1917.[3] But across baseball, Jackson's limitations were common knowledge. Playing the left- and right-field lines, Joe did remarkably well and was quick to cut off extra-base hits. He learned to deal with the various heights of stadium walls, some of which were quite short (like Shibe Park in Philadelphia), and handled tricky caroms with increasingly better expertise as the years went by. But in those same years, he came face-to-face with the reality that he just wasn't as fast as he used to be. Whether he was chasing a ball or running the bases, he was a few steps slower and unable to perform many of the feats that had once come easy to him. There was a time, years earlier, when he was considered one of the fastest men in baseball. In 1910, a New Orleans pundit declared Joe was circling the bases at a clip "that no base-runner in America could have beaten."[4]

An eminent sportsman in Cleveland, George Dietrich, who worked at a major horse track and deemed an expert timer, made a few startling proclamations in 1911. After recording Joe's trip from the plate to first in 2.25 seconds, he stated: "If this is not record time, it is precious close to it. I have timed a good many other players over the same route, and I never caught another man under 2.75 seconds. I really believe Jackson to be the fastest man in running out a hit that has ever been seen in baseball. I know he is the fastest man I ever have seen and I have been watching the major league boys more than twenty years."[5] Of course, the outspoken Ty Cobb had something to say to these claims, calling it the "worst kind of buncombe." He said: "I have timed a great many men to first and have never yet seen the feat accomplished in less than 3.4."[6]

Dietrich may indeed have been wrong. Jackson was timed at 4.2 seconds during spring training in 1911, and his former teammate, Fred Blanding, verbalized to a reporter in 1914 what many insiders had already realized.[7] "Jackson isn't a fast man going down to first base," he explained. "He is thrown out on many a hit that any ordinarily swift base runner would beat out. He's a light-footed person after he has turned first; not even Cobb himself [would] make more bases on a long drive. But it takes time for him to get started. By the time he is rounding second base on a trip, say, or a possible homer, Jackson is going just about as fast as any man in the American League can cover ground. But that doesn't help him to any singles. It handicaps him, too, as a base runner. Jackson looks to be a long way off first most of the time and he is. But he's not very often in the right position to steal."[8]

Nevertheless, Jackson did get his steals. He grabbed 41 in 1911 and another 35 the following year, including swiping home twice in the same game against New York on August 11, 1912. (A major league record he still holds to this day, although tied with ten others.) But in the years that followed, his numbers dropped to 26 in 1913, to 22 in 1914, and to 16 in 1915. Proving that he was recharged in Chicago, he stole eight more bags in 1916 than the previous year, but his dwindling speed—or other miscues—led to being caught on the paths 14 times. Going into the 1917 season, opposing pitchers didn't have to worry much about Jackson looking to take an extra base, as his threat to run was clearly not what it had used to be. Clark Griffith, manager of the Washington Senators, simply said that Jackson did "not shine as a base-runner," but had no problem publicly acknowledging his many other attributes.[9]

In the case of the Chicago White Sox, the baseball gods smiled upon its franchise that winter, at least in the opinion of several sportswriters. It was no secret that the team had struggled with stabilizing the first base position for some time, as Clarence Rowland played five different players at the position in 1916. The sizable Jack Fournier, who hit .322 the previous year, was the primary aspirant, but he slumped both at bat and in the field, making 22 errors in 85 games at first and hit a lowly .240. Rookie Jack Ness was also rotated into the spot, but his .267 average and 15 errors were only a shade better than Fournier. The Sox wanted a proven commodity, an experienced battler, and someone who could add an additional punch to their lineup. When Rowland and Charles Comiskey heard that Cleveland was looking to shed some excess after signing a rumored prodigy from the Pacific Coast League, they swooped in and purchased the type of man they were looking for, a six-year veteran of the major leagues.[10]

The player, Arnold Gandil, incidentally, was an ex-member of the Sox, having begun his big-league career with the organization in 1910. At that time, he was a rough-around-the-edges rookie and toiled in vain to meet the cunning deliveries of expert pitchers. Gandil, better known as "Chick," had outward potential, but Comiskey sold him to Montreal of the Eastern League, believing he needed more refinement.[11] The Washington Senators later acquired him and profited from his maturation, as Gandil hit .318 in 1913, and was a critical factor in the club's second-place finish. However, his batting average fell below .300 the following year, and he often butted heads with manager Clark Griffith, occasionally displaying his aggressive personality. These factors made him dispensable, and he was sent to Cleveland prior to the 1916 season. But his discord with management continued there and his lack of significant production (.259 batting average) again weakened his job stability.[12]

Despite all the negative talk about Gandil, Comiskey liked his first base work.[13] He felt the possible benefits outweighed the risks, and "Chick" was purchased in late February 1917 for $3,500.[14] John Alcock in the *Chicago Daily Tribune* was thrilled, telling readers, "Get Your Seat for [the] '17 Series!"[15] He apparently believed the addition was the final piece in the White Sox machine to complete a championship-caliber club. But not all writers agreed with that sentiment. Mark Shields in the *Chicago Day Book* declared that the arrival of Gandil did "not materially change the first base situation." He insisted that "Chick" was "woefully slow," having had "trouble with his legs for two or three years." Shields instead recommended Fred McMullin for first base, stating that the latter had the "ability to make good at any infield position."[16] While it was true that Gandil had previous knee problems and wasn't the nimblest first baseman in the majors, he was being brought in to start for the Sox, regardless of various opinions.

On March 5, 1917, Joe Jackson appeared in Mineral Wells, Texas, with his wife, ready to begin spring training. He was joined the next day by a majority of his teammates, as the special train from Chicago pulled into town.[17] The aforementioned strike being deliberated by the Players' Fraternity fizzled out and everyone but Jack Ness, who decided to retire after receiving a contract for $500 less than he received in 1916, was seemingly satisfied with the money Comiskey offered. Spirits were high, even with the looming threat of American military action in Europe on the horizon. To incorporate a sense of patriotism and discipline into their preseason rituals, the Sox brought along an army sergeant named Walter Smiley to act as a part-time military instructor for the players.[18] Other teams did likewise. The athletes took it in stride and accepted the marching and rifle drills without objection.

The military training worked miracles for the Sox. Not only did it contribute to their physical health, but strengthened their minds and built a remarkable sense of teamwork and camaraderie. The added layer of discipline almost singlehandedly prevented the rise of damaging cliques and kept the men working toward the same goal. Jackson was among those to experience physical gains, and he unloaded a homer during an exhibition in the small town of Smithville, Texas, on March 23.[19] While his body was ready for the upcoming grind, he suffered a bit of bad luck when injuring a tendon in his ankle, and was later cut in nearly the same location by an opposing player's spike.[20] His ailments were serious enough to sideline him, and even though a physician told Joe to rest, it was hard to keep him away from the field.[21] He was back in the thick of things within a few days.

In the press, there was usual support for Jackson in the coming batting race, and syndicated sportswriter Grantland Rice featured a blurb from a supposed correspondent named "Carolina Pete" in a March column. The latter said: "It is Joe Jackson's time to reach the top this season, as he is long overdue. He has an average for five or six years above .360. He came back again last year after a slump, and if he doesn't finish in front of Cobb and Speaker this time, I'll eat his bat."[22] It was obvious that Jackson's loyal fans were ready to see him finally win league honors. Too many years had passed with too many close calls, and aside from his ankle troubles, Joe was believed to be in the right kind of condition to initiate a historic campaign. These hopes remained in place when the Sox opened its season at St. Louis on April 11, 1917, but it was soon apparent that Jackson wasn't himself at the plate. His confidence, and the famous consistency that drove his average above .350 earlier in his career, were both absent.

By May 6, Jackson was batting a mere .217 and some of his teammates—Eddie Collins, Chick Gandil, and Ray Schalk among them—were performing even worse. Swede Risberg, a highly touted rookie from the Pacific Coast League, who did so well during spring training that he earned the starting shortstop spot, was hovering around the .130 mark. None of the poor hitting made sense considering the kind of talent Chicago possessed, but strangely, in spite of the feeble offense, the Sox were still winning. The club won nine of its first 11 games and held first place for most of April. Pitching and overall teamwork, with small contributions from everyone—including utility players—were giving them the edge. When Jackson and Collins failed to hit in a pinch, guys like Eddie Murphy, Nemo Leibold, and Shano Collins stepped up. Buck Weaver and Happy Felsch continued to play their usual roles, and the united effort was producing amazing results.

During the first week of May, Joe was handicapped by illness, missed one game at Cleveland, and was fatigued in at least two others.[23] He certainly recognized his own ineffective play and upped his small-ball game to aid the team. That meant more bunting, sacrificing, and improved base-running. But some of Jackson's ideas were good in concept, though not in execution. For instance, against the Yankees on May 10, he tried to stretch a single into a double against Elmer Miller and was gunned down at second.[24] Two days later, in his enthusiasm, he ran past second a little too far on a tight play, and was thrown out by Home Run Baker before he could return safely to the bag.[25] In yet another game, he was nailed at second trying for a stolen base, but had he resisted the urge, he would have scored when Felsch doubled later in the inning.[26]

The fans in Chicago witnessed some exciting moments in support of their team. On May 24, 1917, the Sox and Washington Senators matched up in what the *Chicago Daily Tribune* called, "one of the most brilliant defensive battles ever at Comiskey Park." The two teams entered the bottom of the 12th without a run on the board, but the Sox were determined to bring things to a satisfactory conclusion. It started when Jackson got himself aboard with a base hit to right field, followed by Felsch sacrificing him over to second. George Dumont, on the mound for the Senators, then threw a wild pitch to Gandil and the ball sailed to the wall behind home plate. Jackson saw nothing but the victory ahead of him and raced around third looking to score. As the voices in the stadium cheered in unison, Joe scraped across the plate by the skin of his teeth and brought home the 1–0 victory.[27]

Although last in the league in hitting, the Sox were still at the top of the standings, which was evidence enough that manager Clarence Rowland and coach Kid Gleason were inspiring their players to pull out all the stops.[28] Jackson boosted his average into the .270–.285 range, and though no one on the club was much over .300, their bats had certainly begun to warm up.

Pitching was a saving grace throughout this period of dismal offense, and thirty-three-year-old Eddie Cicotte was leading the staff with exceptional control. En route to 28 victories for the season, he was one of the most dominant pitchers in 1917, and nearly every team he faced succumbed to the effects of his supposed "shine ball." But the "shine ball" was mythology, according to Cicotte. He claimed it was something he devised along with Happy Felsch. "The idea was to rub the ball in a peculiar way to make the batsman think I was doing something to it. I wasn't really, but others thought I was," he told a reporter.[29]

Cicotte might not have wanted to admit it, but the shine ball was, in fact, very real. He had originally learned it from Dave Danforth, and by 1917 was practicing the pitch with perfection.[30] However, everyone in baseball at the time was confused, unsure if it was real or plain fiction. Some rivals believed it to be an illegal delivery and wanted league president Ban Johnson to investigate. That led to balls being sent to labs for examination, but there was never any evidence of wrongdoing. But that did not stop the rumor mill. Sportswriter Fred Lieb actually heard from members of the Yankees who claimed to have seen a sponge jutting out from Cicotte's pocket and cited the latter's use of talcum powder as part of his trickster repertoire.[31] "Cicotte has been accused of using everything from English breakfast tea to crude petroleum on the ball," wrote Louis Lee Arms in 1917. "Yet those balls which umpires captured have shown nothing. The shine ball is an extra knuckle ball, and that is all there is to it."[32]

New York writer Damon Runyon called Cicotte a "chunky right-hander," and described his pre-pitch motions as first taking the ball to a spot on his knee, then rubbing it on his shirt prior to delivery. He also reminded his readers that nothing was ever found to support the accusations that he was doing anything illegal.[33] But just Cicotte's actions of rubbing the ball were enough to drive opposing batters and managers crazy, even if it was just a ruse when throwing his shine ball. To that degree, it had great psychological effects, and psychology was an important part of Chicago's success beginning in 1917. The smarter baseball men on the team, beginning with Kid Gleason and funneling down to the likes of Cicotte, helped perpetuate a system of coordinated methods to win the mental war during a ballgame. That included the art of trash-talking, a custom Gleason was a master at. But there were many other tricks in his bag.

During a game against Cleveland on August 15, 1917, Cicotte was taking some abuse on the mound and Gleason decided to interject. He appeared from the dugout carrying a mysterious white handkerchief, rushed over to Fred McMullin at third base, handed him the cloth, and returned to the bench. It was a swift maneuver, but everyone, including the Indians, noticed. McMullin then brought it to Cicotte and returned to his spot on the field. Gleason's thought was that the handkerchief would represent a certain "replenishing" of the "dope" Cicotte used to make his pitches so effective. Whether it was some kind of jelly or other foreign substance, Gleason gave it to his pitcher so he could return to his unbeatable self, or at least that was the psychological intention. It was most likely just an ordinary handkerchief, but in this case the ploy didn't work and the Indians continued to beat up on Cicotte. Finally, Jim Scott was called in to win the game for the Sox, which he did in 10 innings, 5–4.[34]

The United States entered World War I on April 6, 1917, and the White Sox were incredibly patriotic all season. Under the guidance of Sergeant Smiley, they continued to reap the rewards of studying the Butts' Manual of Arms, a method of physical training using real Springfield rifles. They learned more complicated drills and began to execute them before games, confident in their abilities before large crowds while donning regulation army khakis. It was hard not to be impressed by their uniformity, and the same teamwork that shined while marching was demonstrated during games. Crowds, rivals, and even military units appreciated their fine work, and when the Sox marched out during Military Day at Comiskey Park on August 23, the fans didn't immediately recognize their baseball heroes, as they looked like a real company of soldiers.[35] Interestingly, a military judge awarded a special $500 prize to the St. Louis Browns as the best American League squad in competitive drill, with the Sox finishing fourth.[36]

On occasion, the Sox performed special exercises for the amusement of audiences. At Philadelphia on June 5, players, from their initial marching stance, bounded into "marine maneuvers," and ran across the diamond, dropping down to the ground into firing positions. According to the *Chicago Daily Tribune*, "the boys finished by marching to the home plate, where they sang 'The Star-Spangled Banner.'"[37] This extraordinary scene was repeated in other cities, and the respectful adulation was the same each time. They were utterly impressed; but that wasn't the only way the Sox were impressive. After a striking victory at Navin Field, a Detroit fan was overheard as saying, "I don't see how any team can beat those fellows out of the pennant. They certainly looked good."[38]

Jackson was plagued by lumbago (a sore lower back) into July and his weakened condition likely contributed to his failure to produce with the bases loaded on two occasions against Detroit on July 5.[39]He delivered a timely home run in the first inning of an important game against the Boston Red Sox on August 1, helping Chicago win, 4–0, and breaking a tie with Boston for first place. From this juncture, the White Sox never surrendered its hold on the top spot.[40] Jackson and his teammates won 17 of 21 games during a homestand between August 17 and September 3, and ran two different strings of nine straight wins in the closing weeks of the season. Boston quickly fell out of contention and, by the end of the season, was nine games behind.

Red Faber, the tall right-hander from Cascade, Iowa, pitched the White Sox to the pennant on September 21, 1917, and had the race been any closer, Fenway Park would have been packed from pillar to post. As it was, less than 5,000 fans cared to see their local team meet Chicago in what was destined to be a pennant-winning contest for opposing Sox. Nevertheless, it was a memorable 10-inning game, and Larry Woltz of the *Chicago Examiner* said it would "always occupy a prominent page in Beantown baseball history." Ironically, an Irishman from Boston, Shano Collins, put Chicago ahead in the top of the 10th. Collins's single scored catcher Ray Schalk, giving the White Sox a 2–1 lead. In the bottom half of the inning, twenty-two-year-old Babe Ruth, who went 24–13 on the mound with only 142 plate appearances on the season, had an opportunity to deliver the game winner for the Red Sox, but grounded into a double play as Chicago captured its first league pennant since 1906.[41]

As the White Sox left Boston for Washington, Jackson remained behind to participate in a special benefit for the family of Tim Murnane, a well-known sportswriter who had passed away in February. Actually, on the whole, it was a way to give Joe a couple days rest. The benefit, in the form of an exhibition match, took place on September 27. Jackson was fired up to play alongside a contingent of American League All-Stars, and stood alongside Ty Cobb and Tris Speaker, which was arguably the strongest outfield combination in baseball history. But Boston proved to be more spirited, giving the fans a good show in a popular 2–0 victory.[42] At one point during the exhibition, Jackson displayed his powerful arm by throwing out Dick Hoblitzell at the plate. This effort, combined with his pregame distance-throwing victory during a series of field events, demonstrated that Joe still maintained one of the greatest arms in baseball.[43]

Jackson rejoined the White Sox in New York for the final three games of the season beginning with a doubleheader on September 29. In the second contest, Chicago won its 100th game, which was a proud milestone for manager Clarence Rowland and the franchise. With an array of substitutes in the lineup, the Sox lost the other two games to the Yankees, and finished the season with a 100–54 record. Notably, the New York press was on hand in full force to see Chicago perform and littered newspapers with columns in succeeding days, contrasting the style of Sox players with that of John McGraw's Giants, the National League champions and their World Series opponents. For at least one of the games, three Giants superstars—third baseman Heinie Zimmerman and outfielders George Burns and Benny Kauff—also scouted the Sox from the crowd.[44] Chicago had the same idea, as Kid Gleason, Eddie Collins, and Eddie Cicotte took in a Giants game at Philadelphia on October 2.[45]

As could be expected, New York pundits were overwhelmingly in favor of the Giants over the Sox. Damon Runyon predicted the latter would win "with comparative ease," and other writers could hardly give Rowland the advantage in terms of strategy over McGraw, winner of six league pennants and one World Series championship (1905).[46] After all, who could really argue? McGraw himself was even confident of victory.[47] But reporter Hugh Fullerton of Chicago, who each year provided in-depth Series analysis for a syndicate of newspapers, believed in the Sox and predicted Rowland's men would win in six games.[48] His pro-Chicago stance was predictable to a certain degree—especially since he was close to club owner Charles Comiskey—but he wasn't always impartial in his player-by-player breakdowns to those wearing Sox uniforms. In fact, he asserted that Eddie Collins had played "sloppy, careless, and at times seemingly indifferent baseball" for most of 1917, and minced no words when it came to Joe Jackson.[49]

To sum it up, Fullerton insisted that Giants left fielder George Burns was more valuable to his club than Jackson was to his, and referred to Joe as the "White Sox fading star." Of course, he made mention of Jackson's lack of mental power, stating Burns could "give Joe two brain revolutions the start and beat him to a given thought." Fullerton, on the other hand, did marvel at Jackson's hitting, and admitted that he was always dangerous at the plate. As far as all-around players went, Burns was simply better, the writer explained, and the statistics did support these claims.[50] However, Oscar C. Reichow, a journalist for the *Chicago Daily News,* wondered if Jackson was going to step up and become the "hero" of the upcoming Series. "Jackson is one of the most important factors on the South Side club because of his tremendous driving power and his hitting will be depended upon in the pinches by the Sox," Reichow explained.[51]

But, overall, the truth couldn't be ignored. Joe wasn't the rabid base-stealing threat, the defensive prodigy, and apparent successor to American League batting champion Ty Cobb that he was earlier in the decade. The comparisons to Cobb had diminished, and although he was fully capable of breaking up a game with his slugging, his looming presence was not what it used to be. At the same time, no manager would ever take him lightly, especially during a critical moment in a game. As far as Joe was concerned, he was sensitive to the criticism, but didn't live and die by what was being printed in the papers like some of his peers. Most of it, perhaps luckily for him, went over his head and didn't weigh on his conscience. He was usually carefree and allowed his natural abilities and extreme might with a bat to do the talking for him. That was his normal reply to the wordy journalists for their sometimes unwarranted disparagement.

To a larger extent, Fullerton attributed the Sox pennant to the fine work of Ray Schalk, Chick Gandil, and Buck Weaver, but there was no denying that the team had come together and won the championship as a unit. They fought hard, backed each other up in tight spots, and supported their pitchers. While they weren't the strategic and intelligent team New York had proven to be, the Sox were able to win a contest in many different ways. They had the slugging, the defense, and even the small-ball game to win a pitcher's duel. And with Eddie Cicotte, Red Faber, and Reb Russell expected to start, with Lefty Williams and Dave Danforth available out of the bullpen, the pitching outfit was not only strong, but physically ready for their National League opponents. The Giants were prepared as well, and the entire sports world was captivated by the first-ever World Series meeting between the two most populated cities in the country.

The Sox left New York after the season ended and ventured to Jackson's old stomping grounds in Cleveland, where a special tune-up exhibition was scheduled to help them limber up for the Series. The willingness of the Indians to aid the Sox was not just a friendly gesture, but stemmed from the fact that Cleveland was owned in part by several members of the Woodland Bards, a famous White Sox rooter organization. The principal owner, James C. Dunn, who bought the club from Charles Somers in 1916, was a longtime supporter of the Sox and a close ally of Charles Comiskey. On top of that, Comiskey and American League President Ban Johnson were silent partners in the purchase of the Cleveland franchise. This somewhat scandalous information was withheld from the public, and later, after the secret was revealed, it was noted that their money was just loans as they did not purchase specific stock in the club.

Fans in Chicago eagerly awaited the arrival of their champions and, following an 8–5 victory over the Indians on October 2, the pennant-winners boarded a train home. For Jackson, he arranged a room for him and his wife at the Great Northern Hotel in the downtown area of Chicago, as did Lefty Williams and his spouse.[52] Jackson and Williams were quickly becoming inseparable friends. They shared ideals and perspectives and, of all his teammates, Joe liked spending time with Williams the most. Born in Southwest Missouri, Lefty grew up in the Springfield area and developed as a pitcher in regional leagues. His productivity increased in 1917 and he closed out the year with a 17–8 record and a 2.97 ERA. No one considered him a primary starter in critical games—at least not yet—but the twenty-four-year-old had come a long way and was definite relief help against New York.

The days just prior to Game One of the World Series were a whirlwind. On October 3, at the Edgewater Beach Hotel, players were regaled by speeches, fed exquisite cuisine, and given hearty congratulations by members of the Woodland Bards and other loyal fans.[53] The next day they were out at Weeghman Park to see the Giants warm up in an exhibition against the Cubs and, finally, on October 5, the team went through its final workouts. Afterwards, they gathered for a special clubhouse meeting to discuss their scouting reports of Giants players and probable strategies. Along with Kid Gleason and Eddie Collins, Clarence Rowland encouraged and motivated his players, preparing them mentally for the challenge ahead. The words of Collins, who was entering his fifth Series, were undoubtedly valuable. When Rowland briefly talked with a reporter on the way out, he boasted: "Just tell the Chicago fans that my ball club is fit and we are going to beat the Giants!"[54]

Jackson and his teammates were greeted by a welcoming audience of more than 32,000 for the initial contest against New York on October 6 at Comiskey Park. It's hard to imagine that Joe wasn't a little overwhelmed by the pomp and circumstance surrounding his first-ever trip to the Series, and, at the plate, he went hitless against the Giants' tall left-hander, Slim Sallee. Though struggling at bat, he executed what Oscar Reichow called, "the most sensational play of the day" with a shoestring catch off Lew McCarty in the seventh inning, likely saving a run. Jackson did it in style, too, turning a somersault in the process which was greeted by a roar from the crowd.[55] Giants second baseman Buck Herzog said the catch was "the turning point of the game," which ended with a 2–1 victory for the Sox. "I know Jackson is a brilliant ball player and I certainly have no desire to rob him of any glory," Herzog later said, "but he may never make another catch like that in his whole career."[56] Happy Felsch's home run in the fourth and the pitching of Eddie Cicotte were also critical reasons why Chicago was able to overcome their National League adversaries.

Jackson's bat came alive in Game Two on October 7, and he singled his way on base in the second, third, and fourth inning. The latter drive to center field scored two baserunners, and his 3–3 performance was rounded out by a walk in the sixth inning. The Sox were assisted on the mound by Red Faber's masterful throwing and won the game, 7–2. Notably, aside from his pitching, Faber went above the call of duty when he dubiously tried to steal third in the fifth inning with Buck Weaver already standing on the base. "What are you coming down here for?" Weaver asked, according to reporter George S. Robbins. "Search me," Faber replied. "Guess I've pulled a boner."[57] Weaver laughed, and Faber, because of his winning pitching, was quickly forgiven.

The series turned to New York for Game Three, but rain postponed the action until October 10, leaving the men to mosey around the Hotel Ansonia and nearby entertainment venues. Rowland was happy about the wet weather since it allowed his ace, Cicotte, a full three days' rest between outings. The time off to mend worked, and Cicotte allowed only two runs on eight hits. Unfortunately for Chicago, the extra day's rest cooled their bats, and the Sox offense was completely ineffective against Rube Benton, who pitched a complete game shutout. Jackson went 0-for-4 and the Sox managed only five hits in the 2–0 loss.

The next day, Benny Kauff's two home runs and Ferdie Schupp's complete game shutout helped New York tie the Series at two games apiece. Once again, Chicago was held scoreless and Jackson repeated his 0–4 showing, dropping his Series batting average to .214.[58]

Some believed the tides in the Series had turned and that the Giants had the momentum heading back to Chicago, though the championship was still far from being decided. "We have to win, that's all there is to it," Jackson told a reporter on the train back to Chicago. "I figure either Cicotte or Russell will trim the Giants at home."[59] Jackson was right. Russell started Game Five on October 13, but it took four pitchers to win for the Sox that afternoon. In addition to Russell, Cicotte, Williams, and Faber were finally inserted to conquer New York, 8–5. Chicago scored three runs in the seventh and eighth innings to come from behind and Jackson went 3-for-5 with two runs. Fans at Comiskey Park went ballistic at the finish, and Hugh Fullerton wrote: "It probably will go down in history as the worst, and yet the most exciting game ever played in a World's Series."[60]

Over the subsequent hours, trains packed with players, reporters, and fans departed once again for the "Big Apple" for Game Six at the Polo Grounds.

Thousands of miles away, American soldiers were involved in a global conflict and fighting for their lives. The trenches were being bombarded by mustard gas and the horrors of warfare were taking their toll on a generation of young men. Major League Baseball, to that point, had so far escaped a far-reaching edict calling to service the healthy military-age men within their ranks. But that didn't mean a government order was completely out of the question in the near future. That meant men like Joe Jackson could possibly be drawn into the national army and away from baseball. While the thrilling World Series of 1917 wasn't yet over, the brutal World War being fought overseas was unquestionably on the minds of all Americans, and the future remained uncertain for all.

9

FROM BALLYARDS TO SHIPYARDS

The national pastime enjoyed wide prosperity during the 1917 World Series as the impassioned support of cosmopolitan fans in New York and Chicago did a lot of good for the sport. On the flip side, organized gambling rings took full advantage of the opportunity to cash in, and heavy bettors saturated the scene, looking for gullible suckers. Professional gamblers could spot them a mile away, and the rich businessmen were the real prize. For instance, the upper crust of Chicago's Woodland Bards lived and died with the White Sox. These individuals had plenty of money and a number of them were willing to place thousands down as a demonstration of their faith in their team; it was almost a badge of honor to do so. When the Bards were in New York, local bookies salivated at the potential wagers and many bets were made. After the Sox lost Games Three and Four at the Polo Grounds, an untold amount of money had changed hands.

Nick the Greek, a well-known Chicago gambler, reportedly lost $10,000, while New York big-timer Arnold Rothstein cleaned up $50,000 on the Giants.[1] Gambling reports littered mainstream newspapers and, during the Series, it seemed that everyone was looking for a piece of the action. And why not? Gambling on baseball was a part of the culture and socially acceptable. But there was a dark side to the apparent growing infestation surrounding the game, and baseball's leaders were aware of the problem. American League President Ban Johnson had repeatedly complained about the overt gambling in stadiums and felt certain owners were allowing such behavior to perpetuate, with the two ball grounds in Boston among the worst.[2] Earlier in 1917, a game between the White Sox and Red Sox at Fenway Park was completely halted by riotous gamblers as Chicago players had to literally fight their way to safety.[3]

There were even greater dangers to the integrity of the game if gamblers were able to sink their teeth into the players themselves. The possibility of an athlete finding himself in debt to a gangster and being forced to throw games was far more real than people probably understood at the time. Also, there was an outside chance that the greed of ballplayers would grow to the point where throwing games for gambling money would become a viable option. Of course, to the pure-hearted American baseball fan, such an occurrence was unthinkable. No one wanted to even imagine a situation in which the public's trust would be damaged by the work of conniving players trying to weasel extra cash by losing on purpose. Such a scenario just didn't make sense. But if gambling remained on the periphery of baseball and if gentlemen wanted to partake in such an endeavor, it was seemingly okay by community standards.

The baseball world was transfixed by the World Series between the Sox and Giants, and tensions were high heading into the sixth game at New York on October 15, 1917. One of John McGraw's old friends, a popular oddsmaker named "Broadway" Jack Doyle, predicted the Giants were going to win and placed 5-4 odds that the National Leaguers would tie up the Series.[4] Larry Woltz of the *Chicago Examiner* figured Joe Jackson and the Sox to be fighters until the end, declaring, "There is nothing yellow about the pale hose." Manager Clarence Rowland had his men fired up to play, and with Red Faber on the mound and a team of focused individuals behind him, the Sox were ready to end the Series with yet another dramatic win.

Victory was assured for the Sox that afternoon, and the remarkable action was punctuated by a wild rundown between third base and home plate in the top of the fourth. It all started with Eddie Collins, who hit a quick bouncer at third baseman Heinie Zimmerman. "Zim" threw off the mark to first baseman Walter Holke, allowing Collins to advance to second on the error. Jackson followed with a fly to right field, which was considered an easy play, but Dave Robertson misplayed the ball for the inning's second blunder. Collins went to third, while Jackson was safe at first. Happy Felsch was up next and rapped a grounder into the glove of pitcher Rube Benton who immediately moved toward third, stopping Collins in his tracks. Benton tossed the ball over to Zimmerman and catcher Bill Rariden moved up the baseline, leaving the plate unguarded. Once Collins realized the predicament, he darted for the plate with Zimmerman desperately in tow.

The two runners raced past the out-of-position catcher—the only man Zimmerman could've possibly thrown the ball to—and Collins slid in safely for the score. Zimmerman was hammered by the press for his costly "mistake," but players from both teams later put the blame on Rariden.[5] The Sox continued to benefit in that inning when Chick Gandil followed with a single of his own that scored both Jackson and Felsch. In total, behind a complete game by Faber, Chicago won 4–2, and was declared the world champions of baseball.[6] Jackson's contributions throughout the Series were timely, and he finished with a .304 batting average with four runs, two RBIs, and a stolen base. But once again, it was a total team effort, and the Sox were ready to enjoy themselves. Writer Larry Woltz reported on the celebration, stating: "The scene in the Chicago clubhouse after the game is beyond description. Strong-armed athletes acted as mere children." Felsch, as they began to indulge in alcoholic beverages, shouted, "The strain is over and let's go to it."[7] His teammates fully agreed.

The party continued through the night and the joyous spirits remained during a special exhibition against the Giants at Camp Mills on Long Island the following afternoon. Over 10,000 soldiers watched the two teams perform and Chicago won, 6–3. Jackson, however, was among those absent.[8] (Though he did manage to board the team's train headed back to Chicago and turned up at Comiskey Park on October 18 to receive his World Series check, which amounted to $3,669.32.) The players gave their final goodbyes for the year and Jackson, according to the *Chicago Examiner*, ventured southward with his pal Lefty Williams.[9] When Joe was quoted by the *Chicago Daily News* about his plans, he left out any mention of Lefty's accompaniment. He said: "My wife and I will go to Greenville for a few days and then will beat it for our home in Savannah. I plan to work this off season, and believe me, I'll be in the peak when next season rolls around."[10]

The Jacksons were caught by another reporter in Cincinnati, and Joe cordially offered a few words. He mentioned ex-Reds manager Buck Herzog as having congratulated the Sox after the final Series game and said he had business to take care of, but wanted to relax this winter.[11] In the regular post-Series decompression, the same experts who besieged newspapers with their predictions also had to offer their summations. Grantland Rice centered on aspects he found strange, including the fact that "Joe Jackson got seven hits in three games, and no hits in the other three." Similar, Benny

Kauff, who had two homers, a single, and double in two contests, achieved no hits in the other four games played.[12] He felt there were other oddities, but the randomness of baseball was simply in full effect. On certain days, a superstar lived up to the expectations of audiences, while on others he might prove powerless at the plate. For Jackson and Kauff in the 1917 Series, they epitomized the unpredictability of the national game.

Jackson had no regrets and the money in his pocket was a nice bonus at the end of a long season.[13] But again, his numbers weren't up to his usual standard. Joe was just able to push his average over .300 by the end of the season, and his 162 hits were 15 below Chicago's team leader, Happy Felsch. Felsch also led the club in batting with a .308 average. Jackson was second in the league in triples (17), fourth in runs scored (91), and fifth in RBIs (75). Capitalizing on his name and Chicago's title, companies wanted Joe shilling their products more than ever. "Nuxated Iron certainly makes a man a live wire and gives him the 'never-say-die' strength and endurance," he boasted in one advertisement. "When I see in the papers 'Jackson's batting was responsible for the Chicago victory,' I feel like adding to it—'Nuxated Iron puts the power behind the bat and gives the needed punch to every play.'"[14] Authorizing product endorsements was an easy payday and chances are Joe didn't even have to offer the quote, just give his approval on the deal.

Smart with his money, Jackson paid off his Savannah mortgage with his Series winnings, ridding himself of a significant debt and concern.[15] But there was still another source of incredible anxiety looming for Joe personally, and that had to do with his draft status for the ongoing war overseas. Back in August, the Greenville County, South Carolina, draft board summoned him for a physical examination and Joe went through the motions by undergoing medical testing in Chicago.[16] His mind was made up, though, and he would claim exemption on the grounds of having a wife, a mother, and siblings to support.[17] The local board in Greenville concluded in late September that Jackson was eligible for exemption based on his circumstances, which Joe had expected. But he was also informed that the district board had the final say in the matter and he wasn't yet clear of military obligation.[18]

By late October 1917, various newspapers were freely acknowledging that Jackson had been drafted and ordered to report for duty at Fort Oglethorp in Savannah.[19] Of course, this was staggering news to Sox management, fans, and Joe himself. As far as he knew, the South Carolina District

3778 **REGISTRATION CARD** No. 173

1 Name in full Joe Jackson (Given name) (Family name) Age, in yrs. 29

2 Home address Warner Hotel, 33d & Cottage Grov. Chicago, Ill (No.) (Street) (City) (State)

3 Date of birth July 16, 1887. (Month) (Day) (Year)

4 Are you (1) a natural-born citizen, (2) a naturalized citizen, (3) an alien, (4) or have you declared your intention (specify which)? Natural-born

5 Where were you born? Greeneville S. Car. U.S.A. (Town) (State) (Nation)

6 If not a citizen, of what country are you a citizen or subject? —

7 What is your present trade, occupation, or office? Professional Ball Player. 29

8 By whom employed? Chicago American League B.B. Club
Where employed? Chicago, Ill.

9 Have you a father, mother, wife, child under 12, or a sister or brother under 12, solely dependent on you for support (specify which)? Wife and sister under 12.

10 Married or single (which)? Married. Race (specify which)? Caucasian.

11 What military service have you had? Rank None ; branch ; years ; Nation or State

12 Do you claim exemption from draft (specify grounds)? Sole support wife & sister under 12

I affirm that I have verified above answers and that they are true.

If person is of African descent, tear off this corner.

C

Joe Jackson (Signature or mark)

846

Front page of Jackson's World War I Draft Registration Card. As noted on the document, Jackson claimed exemption because his wife Katie and sister Gertrude, who was under twelve years of age, were dependent on him for financial support. Later it was also revealed that his mother Martha was dependent on him as well.

REGISTRAR'S REPORT

29-2-70

1 Tall, medium, or short (specify which)? Tall. Slender, medium, or stout (which)? Medium

2 Color of eyes? Brown. Color of hair? Black. Bald? No.

3 Has person lost arm, leg, hand, foot, or both eyes, or is he otherwise disabled (specify)? No.

I certify that my answers are true, that the person registered has read his own answers, that I have witnessed his signature, and that all of his answers of which I have knowledge are true, except as follows:

James T. Igoe.
(Signature of registrar)
City Clerk, Chicago, Ill.
By Henry Edler.
Deputy.

Precinct

City or County Greenville,

State S. Car.

(Date of registration)

Back page of Jackson's World War I Draft Registration Card. After Joe's exemption status was denied and he was declared 1A, fit for combat, Jackson sought out a stateside job in the shipbuilding industry. Since his family depended on him so greatly, he felt he deserved exemption from overseas duty.

Board at Greenwood was still deliberating his case. The assertions that he was to report for service were premature, and Jackson continued his winter awaiting the final decision. All across the majors, players, managers, and owners were feeling a greater pinch by the growing scope of the war, and words like "retrenchment" and "reduction" were common in trade periodicals. Salaries were being slashed in certain situations and, in some cases, were drastically cut. For instance, Lee Magee, the versatile infielder-outfielder, was making upwards of $8,300 for the New York Yankees and St. Louis Browns in 1917, but the latter didn't want to pay anywhere near that figure for 1918, offering him in the range of $3,000 to $3,500.[20]

The St. Louis Cardinals rejected the $8,400 demand by twenty-two-year-old infield prodigy Rogers Hornsby, and instead gave him $5,400.[21] Pitcher Grover Cleveland Alexander wanted a $10,000 bonus from the Chicago Cubs on top of his five-figure salary, and journalists scoffed at his bold request. Regardless of how talented the player, owners weren't caving to the extraordinary demands because of an abundance of caution. Joe Vila, a correspondent for *The Sporting News,* was a big proponent of conservatism in 1918 and wrote that owners needed to "curtail expenses if they [expected] to live through the coming season." He condemned the greed of athletes, stating that the players had "become unreasonable and [were] charged with gross indifference to the welfare of the national pastime." Vila warned that such financial hunger in baseball's weakened state risked causing irreparable damage.[22]

Large attendance figures were not predicted for 1918, and even in the most prosperous major league cities, crowds were going to be far lower than the previous year. One notable reason was the fact that a huge contingent of regular stadium-going fans was now serving in the military. The interest in the sport as a nice escape from the painful realities affecting millions of American families would linger, but baseball in general was taking a major backseat to the war effort. In Chicago, Charles Comiskey was one of the most visible of baseball's patriotic owners, and he was proud to see Jim Scott, Fritz Von Kolnitz, and Joe Jenkins serve the military with distinction. In fact, by the spring of 1918, the Sox would have nine stars on its service flag, designating the men who'd committed themselves to the duty of their country.[23] Comiskey planned to donate 10 percent of every home game gate to the Red Cross, and offered his stadium to the military for any use deemed necessary.

In terms of salaries, the White Sox didn't see a dramatic decrease and the team was free of holdouts entering 1918, which was uncommon for a

World Series champion.[24] There were usually at least a handful of players wanting to parlay the title into a raise in their paycheck, but the Sox managed to avoid this issue altogether. Had there been internal grievances against Sox management at this juncture, holding out in an organized fashion would have been the player's best course of action. It wouldn't have been a popular move, all things considered, but fans might have understood if members of the best team in baseball wanted a slight salary increase. Nevertheless, it didn't happen. But, as customary, Joe Jackson was thrust into offseason trade rumors, this time by New York Yankees co-owner Colonel Jacob Ruppert.

"I was thinking perhaps I might take Happy Felsch or Joe Jackson away from Charley Comiskey while I'm here," Ruppert said in a half-serious way upon visiting Chicago in February 1918.[25] But with Comiskey out of town, the New York magnate left empty-handed. Later in the month, Yankees manager Miller Huggins also ventured to Comiskey Park intending to discuss a possible deal for a Sox outfielder with Clarence Rowland. "I'm perfectly willing to talk business with Huggins," Rowland explained prior to their meeting. "They had a story in New York that Joe Jackson might go there, but such talk as that doesn't interest me. We intend to keep Joe, but we might let another one go if we could get a good pitcher. No trade will be made unless I feel sure it will add strength to the Sox, and now I feel that another reliable pitcher on the staff would be acceptable."[26]

Articles in *The Sporting News* indicated that both Comiskey and Rowland were superstitious and wanted to field the same exact team in 1918 that won the championship.[27] If they were able to bolster the pitching rotation, it was believed they'd be even closer to repeating. Louis A. Dougher wrote a column in the *Washington Times* addressing the Jackson gossip and made an observation about Comiskey. "'The Old Roman' is such a sportsman that he would prefer to win the pennant than make another million dollars," also acknowledging that Jackson was likely considered an important cog in the Sox machine. However, Dougher added: "Jackson is no chicken in baseball. He will be thirty-one years old on July 16, and cannot have much of a future."[28]

The Chicago White Sox and its legion of fans were hoping that the opposite was true. Jackson wasn't yet in the twilight of his baseball career. In fact, he still had the potential to once again hit over .350. His 1917 campaign wasn't the best year to judge his on-the-field work, but one had to recognize that he regained his hitting prowess when the team needed it down the stretch and contributed late in the season and into the Series.

But many baseball writers liked to zero in on any shortcomings and paint the game's superstars as being over the hill or having lost "it" when the opportunity was presented. Whatever their motivation, these individuals were drawing hard arguments in claiming Jackson was winding down, and the upcoming season offered an ample occasion for Joe to prove all of his critics wrong.

By the middle of March 1918, Jackson was making final preparations to leave for spring training at Mineral Wells, Texas, and soon boarded a train with Lefty Williams, who also made his winter home in Savannah. The duo arrived in camp on the evening of March 17, ahead of the main body of Sox players from Chicago, and made good use of their time by donning old uniforms and heading out for a brief practice the following morning. Their comrades pulled into the local station later that day, having been held up by train problems, which could have been catastrophic had luck not been with the Sox that day. The situation developed rather suddenly after the train's engine jumped the tracks en route and barely missed tumbling down a hill, taking the rest of the cars with it.[29] Fortunately, the men were safe and healthy, and, in essence, the team was beginning its season with a blessed feeling of having escaped serious injury.

That feeling didn't last long. Sportswriter George S. Robbins noted that spring training for the Sox was quickly becoming known as the "jinx trip," especially after four of its stars were involved in a car accident. Jackson, along with Chick Gandil, Eddie Cicotte, and Ray Schalk were enjoying a simple joy ride when the accident occurred and three of the athletes ended up battered and bruised. Surprisingly, Joe was unharmed.[30] But Jackson's luck ran out a short time later when he was bedridden with malaria. His poor condition was made worse by Katie's own health problems, and the two ailed together in Houston in early April.[31] Figuring he needed time away from the game to recover, Joe asked Clarence Rowland if he could venture ahead of the club to Chicago to mend, but the latter couldn't spare him.[32] The Sox, utilizing two training teams, were grossly understaffed. Jackson fought his way back into the exhibition lineup, but managed to injure his right knee in Kansas and struggled to put any weight on it.

Altogether, the White Sox were performing pitifully on the field in preseason action. They lost games to a number of minor league squads, including Houston, Dallas, Fort Worth, Wichita, and Kansas City, and didn't resemble a major league world championship team in the slightest. The kind of snap, energy, and grit they possessed during the spring of 1917 was completely absent, and the cohesion of teamwork was seemingly a thing of the past. Players were far out of condition and sicknesses and injuries were a constant plague. I. E. Sanborn of the *Chicago Daily Tribune* called the recent work of the Sox the "poorest showing ever made by a big league outfit over a minor league circuit, so far as recalled."[33] But the question being asked was why. How could the Sox have deteriorated that much if they were presenting pretty much the same exact team that won the World Series only months before?

Sanborn, days before his summation of Chicago's exhibition play, wrote that he believed the Sox had a better chance to win the pennant than they did in 1917.[34] Virtually every member of the championship team was back and expected to pull the same share of the club's weight during the campaign. Then what was accounting for their lack of hustle during spring training? What had changed? Speculation was that perhaps the Sox were beginning to experience the same internal problems the New York Giants were accused of suffering from during the World Series. This dilemma was exposed by an unnamed *Washington Herald* writer about a month after the Series ended. The journalist said that the Giants were hindered by being "a team of stars" rather than an equalized group from top to bottom. They were temperamental, striving for "personal glory," and unable to unite for the sake of the club. "The team that has balance is very liable to get the breaks most of the time," the writer explained. "It is balance that counts most."[35]

The journalist stated that Chicago was different from New York in that it only had "several stars," and felt overwhelming self-interests didn't haunt the Sox like it did the Giants. At that juncture it was true. In 1917, Chicago was much more mentally stable and physically robust, and part of the reason was the discipline instilled by an army sergeant beginning early in the spring. The players weren't left up to their own devices, but forcibly pushed into a working schism, and everyone did what was necessary to become a champion. But with the military exercises no longer part of the Sox regimen, the same discipline and balance that worked so well for the team was now lacking. That left Rowland to pick up the pieces, but it seemed as though he was far too overmatched to deal with the various personalities and motivations in the clubhouse. Chicago was a team of stars, much more than the *Herald* writer wanted to admit, and their collective temperamental attitudes probably superseded that of the Giants.

The stress of the war, unquestionably, had a major influence on baseball. In fact, the future of the sport and humanity as a whole were in question.

But the straying minds and fractures in the clubhouse perpetuated anything but team unity. A lack of motivation to get into shape was another factor, and, all told, these elements were central contributors to a losing effort in the major leagues. The Chicago White Sox were not championship material. Actually, despite their abundance of talent, the disjointedness could end up keeping them out of the first division entirely. There was still an opportunity to regain a semblance of control, but the loss of the all-important Kid Gleason—who acted as a buffer between Rowland and the players—to a financial disagreement with management, didn't help matters. Gleason had a gift for handling players regardless of their disposition, and his loss was undeniably significant.

Without Gleason's everyday positivity, joshing, and motivational spirit, the Sox were limping into the season opener a shell of its former self. The initial game reflected the team's lifelessness as four Sox pitchers gave up 19 hits in a 6–1 loss to St. Louis. Jackson, however, was one of the bright spots for Chicago by smashing out two of the club's four hits. Feeling better from his spring injuries, Joe was ready to tackle the season head-on, and set a new goal for himself that had nothing to do with a batting championship. "All my life my ambition was to be in a World's Series and see what I could do," Jackson told a reporter. "Now that my ambition is fulfilled I have another. This is to get into a second World's Series."[36] It was obvious that his enthusiasm was in the right place—and it showed in his on-field play—but some of his teammates didn't seem to share his sentiment. It was as if the atmosphere of the war had deflated their interest in baseball; or maybe it was simply that they had gotten their money the October before and just didn't care.

Jackson's focus on baseball was interrupted by the news that the District Board for the Western District of South Carolina had overruled the decision of his hometown draft board and declared him eligible for the draft.[37] It was ruled that since he had made a considerable sum on the diamond, his wife was not dependent on him, thus, he was an able candidate to enter the army. When Jackson heard his status had been changed to 1A, he was stunned, but seemed to handle the news well. "I'm ready to go whenever they call me," he explained. "And I'll get me a few Boches too, if a good hitting eye proves to be a good shooting eye. Still I don't see how they could move me up to class one when I married long before the war started."[38] In reality, Jackson was unnerved by his status adjustment and held deep concerns for the well-being of his wife, mother, and siblings if he was called overseas.[39]

As the main breadwinner for his family, he took his obligations as serious as anything in his entire life, and no one could have reassured him that things were going to be okay with him off on a distant battlefield. The anxiety would have been too much to even contemplate. Despite his trepidation, reporters almost immediately had him entering the navy and being shipped off within the month.[40] That information couldn't have been any further from the truth, but no one knew what Jackson was thinking. According to Clarence Rowland, Joe was eager to do his part for the American cause. "His absence may mean defeat for us in the pennant race," the Sox manager said, "but if the army needs [him], he will go away smiling."[41] Adding to the overall confusion, an item out of Chicago declared that the "Joe Jackson" named to 1A status wasn't even the famous ballplayer, but another guy entirely.[42] The story, unfortunately for Joe, was incorrect and the government ordered him to appear within days for another physical exam.

The White Sox headed east for a road trip beginning on Friday, May 10, 1918, at Philadelphia. Jackson played in the first two games of the series, including on Saturday at Shibe Park, where he went 0-for-3 in a 1–0 loss. That same day, he appeared before a local draft board for his exam and doctors confirmed that he was 100 percent fit for military service.[43] Joe was informed that his official call to duty wasn't going to be delayed for any reason and that he should be prepared to report between May 25 and June 1. It was a startling turn of events, as he had been granted exemption, only to have it overturned, and now was but a few weeks away from trading his White Sox uniform for that of a soldier's. Joe didn't play a makeup game at Cleveland on May 12, nor did he appear in the lineup back in Philly the next afternoon, and the public was oblivious to a series of major happenings behind the scenes until the morning of May 14, when the news broke nationally. The headline read "Joe Jackson Quits White Sox."[44]

Drastic times called for drastic measures, and Jackson made perhaps the biggest decision of his entire life. He chose to enter an essential occupation instead of playing the odds in combat, and in doing so, felt he would be better able to provide for his family. The choice wasn't made out of fear for his personal well-being, but out of fear for the people he loved. And again, being the sole provider, he was forced to make a judgment call. Of course, his decision was assisted considerably by a persuasive agent of the Harlan and Hollingsworth Shipbuilding Company of Wilmington, Delaware, a subsidiary of Bethlehem Steel, which was his new wartime employer. This unnamed agent reached out to Jackson immediately after his status was changed and offered an easy solution to his problem.[45] The pitch was easy, something most likely along the lines of: "Join the shipbuilding trade, earn a sizable paycheck, and continue to play ball on the weekends." And most important of all: "You'll never set foot on a foreign field of war."

Avoiding the war was not patriotic, but for Jackson his wartime employment for Harlan and Hollingsworth secured him a future. Thus, it also secured his family's future. An article in *The Sporting News* claimed his wife Katie steered him away from the army in the first place, and that he was just abiding by her wishes.[46] There wasn't much more to it, and Joe's choice was made without any prejudice toward military service or the cause of the American people. He set his personal priorities and worked toward solving the impending crisis without hesitation. And at the time, he believed he was still acting within the bounds of patriotism. After all, he was serving the wartime effort by devoting his physical self to the construction of ships—just not with his physical presence overseas. In addition, two of Joe's brothers were actually serving with the American Expeditionary Forces, so the war burden for the Jackson Family, it was believed, was already being met.[47]

In the press, Jackson denied his "jump" to the shipbuilding outfit was specifically tailored to avoid the army, but few journalists were buying it. Joe also said he applied to Harland and Hollingsworth two months earlier and that the decision wasn't reactionary to his 1A status change.[48] Again, it was a difficult sell and individuals very quickly began to call into question his loyalty to America by way of sarcastic remarks or straightforward criticism. Three days after Jackson's announcement, a columnist wrote, "It is hard for everyone to believe that Jackson made this move for any other reason than to escape the draft and save his service to the flag. The affair has a most suspicious look, and the efforts of Jackson to escape service in the army will be closely watched by thousands of fans the country over."[49] Another correspondent added, "Joe Jackson tried to turn a bayonet into a paint brush and was called out by umpire public."[50] A prominent Chicago newspaper editorialized: "We need shipbuilders to win the war, but when a man on the eve of being drafted into the army suddenly finds that he can best serve the nation by painting ships, good Americans will not be very enthusiastic ever seeing him play baseball after the war is over."[51] After a few weeks of constant condemnation, Jackson was fed up and made a few comments of his own.

He had previously made it known that a certain discrimination had forced him into the 1A class when, under normal circumstances, his dependents and lack of savings would have kept him 4A.[52] But now he was defiant about baseball altogether. "It makes no difference when the war ends," Joe said. "I shall not attempt to go back to ball playing to make a living. I intend to make my home here [in Wilmington] and to follow the trade of shipbuilding."[53]

American League President Ban Johnson didn't seem to care whether Jackson ever played another game. "The league doesn't impugn motives of players in this war work," he explained, "but if they took up the job to avoid the trenches, I hope Provost Marshal General Crowder grabs them."[54] Chicago White Sox owner Charles Comiskey was also not happy about Jackson's apparent dodge of war service.[55] He had taken great pride in the selflessness of several of his players to join the military and didn't want the stain of Jackson's self-interests tainting the overall patriotism of his club. Neither Comiskey nor Johnson could see things from Jackson's perspective and they lashed out with hateful authority, dismissing Joe as nothing but a slacker. But there was a logical explanation for his actions, had they attempted to learn his true motivations. The critical press didn't go overboard trying to be accurate either.

George S. Robbins of *The Sporting News* attempted to lessen the assault on Jackson by putting some of the blame on the scheming shipbuilding "scout" who reportedly talked him into joining their operation. "Jackson has made a good target because he's so prominent," Robbins declared, and his words couldn't have been truer.[56] Of the various players to accept essential employment, none were higher profile than Joe Jackson and, in a way, it was easy to use him as an example of weak-kneed athletes running out on military duty. Editorials in various newspapers targeted him without mercy, calling into question his so-called work for Harlan and Hollingsworth. One of them, in *The Sporting News*, demanded, "Come again, Joe, show us the blisters and calluses on your hands." These newspapermen wanted proof that Jackson was really doing something other than earning a nice paycheck for playing ball on the weekends.[57]

A reporter for the *Delmarvia Star* in Wilmington took up the challenge and investigated the claims that players were being pampered on the steel circuit. The stories were found to be false, and the writer noted that the "Harlan ball stars [were] not industrial slackers," adding, "They are answerable to their department heads the same as other employees and are subject to [the] same discipline."[58] The truth of the matter was that Jackson was working hard in support of the American cause. He wasn't a painter for the bulk of his time in the Wilmington shipyards, but a lead man in the bolting-up department.[59] On one fateful day, he was almost injured in a serious accident that killed three of his co-workers, which clearly demonstrated the job's hazards.[60] But despite his hard labor, Jackson continued to be referred to in a derogatory manner and cast aside as a war deserter. These constant insults undoubtedly hurt Joe deep in his heart.

On the weekends, he was able to get back out onto the field and forget about the day-to-day hardships to play the game that came so naturally to him. For his first two weekends in May, as a member of the Harlan and Hollingsworth plant, Jackson was a sideline observer as individuals had to be with the company at least 15 days before taking part.[61] On June 1, 1918, he ventured with the Harlan squad to Sparrow's Point, Maryland, to play the local outfit and contributed two hits in a 5–1 victory.[62] At the time, the Harlan organization was fielding two different teams: one in the more competitive Bethlehem Steel League and the other in the Shipbuilder's League.[63] Jackson's club was among the best in the Steel League and was managed by former Detroit and Chicago catcher Fred Payne, while the secondary team was led by Bill Gallagher. These squads featured many ex-major and minor league veterans, and it wasn't out of the ordinary for an athlete to participate in games for both teams.

To say Jackson was the shining star of the league would not have been an overstatement. He played to the fullest of his abilities and didn't consider giving anything but his best to his employers and fans. That meant he was hitting the ball hard, fielding with great effort, and running the bases with the same kind of energy he displayed early in his career. During a game against Fore River, Massachusetts, on June 15, Joe stole three bases—including home—in a 4–2 victory.[64] He collected three hits against Sparrow's Point on June 29, but Harlan was defeated 7–5. On the mound that day was Jackson's former Sox teammate and close friend Lefty Williams, who also recently defected to Harlan by accepting a day job as a boilermaker.[65] Williams was joined in his jump to Harlan by catcher Byrd Lynn, another of Jackson's White Sox pals.

Whereas Harlan's Steel League club was ushered out of the pennant chase, the company still had a chance to win the Shipbuilder's title and executives shifted Jackson from the former to the latter in August. On September 14, 1918, at Phillies Park in Philadelphia, Joe led his team to a victory over Standard Shipbuilding of Staten Island, New York, in the final game of the Shipbuilder's World Series to capture the William G. Coxe Trophy. Harlan won, 4-0, and Jackson had three of his team's four hits. A writer for the *Delmarvia Star* explained, "It was plainly noticed that Joe was in his real fighting spirit on account of being out of the game in the last two contests, for when he stepped to the rubber as first hitter in the second, he bounced on the first over and it was only stopped by the scoreboard [for a double]." He also added home runs in the sixth and eighth innings, guaranteeing Harlan's Atlantic seaboard shipyard championship.[66]

On September 21, 1918, Jackson played alongside young National League sensation Rogers Hornsby in an exhibition between the two Harlan clubs. The duo, under the watchful eye of Fred Payne, beat out Bill Gallagher's squad in a quiet 1–0 victory.[67] Jackson finished his Steel League season with a .393 average, to go along with 24 hits, seven runs, and eight stolen bases in 17 games.[68] His statistics in the Shipbuilding League are unknown, but his work in bringing home a title was lauded by his superiors at Harlan and Hollingsworth. As 1918 went on, the overall tenor toward the shipbuilding renegades seemed to lessen as journalists found other topics to focus on. It still wasn't known whether the public would ever welcome the likes of Joe Jackson back onto a major league diamond, but, even beyond that, it wasn't known whether Joe would ever consent to appear on a big-league field again. One thing was clear: bad feelings were being harbored on all sides of the debate, and Joe wasn't going to easily forget what had transpired.

10

CHICAGO'S HOUSE OF CARDS

There was little question that the Chicago White Sox were doomed to fail in 1918. The team slumped all through spring training and was only loosely holding it together through the first month of the season before Joe Jackson departed for Wilmington, Delaware. His demoralizing exit, followed in turn by Lefty Williams and Byrd Lynn, as well as Happy Felsch to an essential occupation in Wisconsin, were the final nails in the coffin for Clarence Rowland and Charles Comiskey. There was nothing salvageable from their championship season and every facet of the team's makeup suffered in some form or fashion. When it was all said and done, the Sox had 43 less victories than in 1917 (57–67) and placed sixth in the American League.[1] For a team with so much potential to repeat, and with the support of baseball experts predicting that it would indeed happen, Chicago's free-fall into oblivion was embarrassing to everyone attached to the club. As a result, big changes by Comiskey were anticipated.

Comiskey was having a tough year both mentally and physically, and several times vented his frustration to the press. He was adamant in his beliefs about Jackson, Williams, Lynn, and Felsch, and perceived their actions to not only be a flat-out desertion of his club, but a coordinated ploy to evade their patriotic duty as Americans.[2] "I don't consider them fit to play on my ball club," he told a reporter.[3] "There is no room [for any players] who wish to escape the army draft by entering the employ of shipbuilding concerns and steel mills. Players like [Jim] Scott and [Red] Faber, who have enlisted in the army and navy, respectively, have my best wishes, and I'm pulling for them. The Government ought to get after baseball slackers like Williams, Lynn, and Joe Jackson. They should be put into the army, where they rightfully belong."[4]

A former major leaguer himself, Comiskey was always known as a ballplayer's ballplayer. Early in his career as an owner, he was the kind of magnate who mingled with his men, knew their strengths and weaknesses, and had so much day-to-day knowledge that he could seemingly step onto the field at any moment to manage his club. He was relentless in his hunt for new players and always chasing another pennant. But as he got older, Comiskey began to lose some of his famous and popular personality. He was slowed by recurring illnesses and bogged down by the health concerns of his wife and son, leaving him cynical and tired. Comiskey also distanced himself from his players; it wasn't a sudden shift either, but occurred over a matter of years. It got to the point that many of his men rarely ever saw him in person.

This change wasn't personal, but rather reflective of Comiskey's overall condition. On top of that, it was apparent that instead of forming relationships with his players, as he'd previously done, he was increasingly viewing them as regular business commodities. In the cases of several of his stars, he paid tens of thousands of dollars to obtain their services, and therefore expected first-class results. That included Joe Jackson and Eddie Collins. These five-figure acquisitions, Comiskey felt, were the gateway to league pennant honors, and if they lived up to their reputations then championships were a lock for Chicago. In fact, on paper, the White Sox had a near all-star team and anything but a first-place finish was a major disappointment. Comiskey was big at internalizing his fury, and every game the Sox lost ebbed a little more at his insides. Based on that fact, it wasn't exactly surprising that he often suffered from stomach disorders. Sometimes he had to retire to his private office at Comiskey Park because the stress of watching a close game was too much for him to bear.

Without closer contact to Comiskey, players formed their own impressions of "The Old Roman." To them, he was not dissimilar from any other owner in the way he sat back and collected a predominant share of the profits. In their eyes, he was up on a pedestal—barking orders at Harry Grabiner, the team's business manager, as well as manager Clarence Rowland—and never getting his own hands dirty. Comiskey, from the reports they'd read, was made of money, probably with cash to burn, and lived a lifestyle they could only dream about. Some players on the team, like many others elsewhere in the majors, felt uneasy about the way owners perpetuated unfairness by not meeting their demands for greater raises. It didn't make sense to them. After all, they were the reason fans paid to attend games and were the real celebrities, not the owners. These same players, regardless of the club they were on, doubtlessly complained whenever they got the chance, criticizing management as being tightfisted and obsessively greedy.

Neither the absence of Comiskey's presence nor the players who were grumbling with any frequency did much to help the atmosphere in the Sox clubhouse. But Comiskey wasn't coldhearted toward his men. Not in the least. He ensured they were taken care of on long road trips to spring training by booking special trains with extraordinary luxuries. Following the 1917 pennant victory, he paid for a large banquet dinner for his team in celebration at the Boston Tavern.[5] His Woodland Bards staged another congratulatory party a few nights later at Chicago's Edgewater Beach Hotel.[6] These were first-rate events and although Comiskey did not attend the Boston party, he was on hand to see his players treated like royalty by their faithful fans back in Chicago. Once the World Series was won in 1917, Comiskey had only great things to say about his players. "They fought only as champions can fight," he told a reporter, "and I want to thank them for their splendid work. Every member of our team deserves the greatest praise."[7]

The banquet and nice words were thoughtful, but the memorable deed from Comiskey following his team's last World Series championship in 1906, in which he awarded his men a handsome bonus (four times what was given to the losing Chicago Cubs), was not repeated in 1917. And if Sox players were anticipating the same kind of reward in 1917, the heartache, disappointment, and resulting animosity was probably just human nature. The reason for Comiskey's failure to duplicate his liberal act of 1906 was not acknowledged. In fact, the entire discussion of a World Series bonus was disregarded by Chicago journalists. On top of that, once the Sox returned to the "Windy City" after defeating the Giants, Comiskey didn't sponsor any parties, parades, or other gatherings to commemorate their achievement. It was as if the pennant-winning galas were enough to satisfy his interest and, again, Chicago reporters didn't seem to think it was worth mentioning.

The First World War came to a conclusion on November 11, 1918, and there was a general sigh of relief across the globe. But, despite reasons to the contrary, major league owners weren't optimistic that business was going to be any better in 1919 than it had been during wartime. In their

In 1907, before he entered Organized Baseball, Jackson (second from left, standing) played with the Victor Mills team in Greer, South Carolina, and earned quite a reputation as a slugger.

Playing with the Savannah Indians in 1909, Joe Jackson led the South Atlantic League with a .358 batting average.

Joe gained his first taste of widespread fame in 1908 as a member of the Greenville Spinners in the Carolina Association. He batted .346 in 87 games before making his Major League–debut later that year for the Philadelphia Athletics.

With the New Orleans Pelicans in 1910, Joe (seated, third from right) won his third straight minor league batting championship, achieving a .354 average in 136 games. The twenty-three-year-old was ready to return to the majors and did so in September 1910, this time for the Cleveland Naps.

On July 19, 1908, Joe married Katie Wynn in a small ceremony in Greenville, South Carolina, and the two remained together for the next forty-three years, ending only with his death in 1951. Without question, Katie was the love of his life and his best friend.

As Jackson pummeled Southern Association pitchers to another minor league batting title in 1910, an artist for the *New Orleans Times-Picayune* newspaper fashioned this cartoon depicting the inevitable—Jackson's expected transition to the big leagues.

Photo from the public domain, originally run in 1910 by the Times-Picayune *("What Every Fan Knows")*

JACKSON LEADS ALL LEAGUE BATTERS

The great batting stars, such as Cobb, Lajoie, Crandall, Wagner and others, are playing second fiddle to Joe Jackson, Cleveland's right field. A batting average of .411 in 62 games makes the Lake City fans joyful.

Wherever baseball is known Joe Jackson is famous; wherever men smoke there you'll find FATIMA Cigarettes starring.

Joe Jackson Fatima Cigarette Premium, circa 1913.

Photo by The Pictorial New Co., New York, for the Fatima Cigarette Company, from the public domain.

Undeniably, Jackson was a remarkable hitter and his lifetime .356 batting average ranks third all-time behind Ty Cobb (.366) and Rogers Hornsby (.358).

Photo by Charles M. Conlon, from the public domain.

Almost from day one of his major league career, Joe Jackson (right) was a determined challenger for Ty Cobb's American League batting title. Although he came close several times, Joe was never able to best his foe, and the two remained good friends away from the diamond for years.

Possessing excellent eyesight, Joe was dangerous with both a baseball bat and a rifle. One of his passions was trapshooting, and his aim was nearly perfect.

Of all his teammates on the Chicago White Sox, pitcher Lefty Williams was Jackson's closest friend, and the two were often inseparable. As shown in this 1917 photo, Jackson (right) and Williams enjoyed the outdoors and hunted whenever they got the chance.

Jackson was acknowledged by his contemporaries as being one of the greatest natural ballplayers they'd ever seen, and despite the efforts of some managers and coaches to change his on-field style, Joe relied on his instincts throughout his career to great success.

A photographer at Comiskey Park in Chicago obtained a rare frontal view of Joe's powerful swing during batting practice. Always good natured, Jackson probably got a good laugh about it afterwards.

Humongous compared to most regular sized bats, Jackson's "Black Betsy" was remarkably large, measuring 35 to 36 inches in length and weighing nearly 50 ounces.

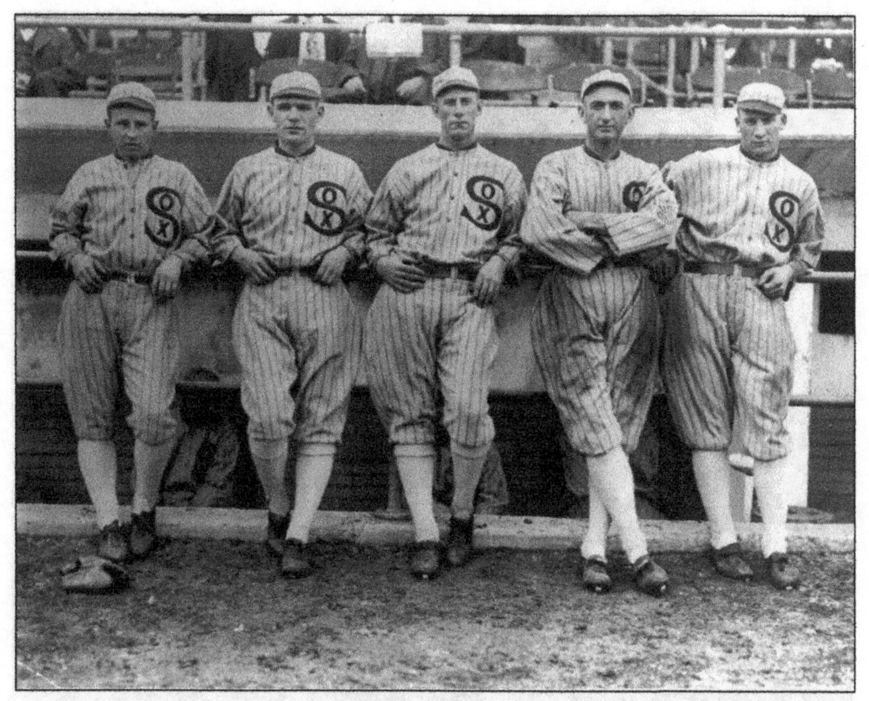

During the latter part of the 1910s, the Chicago White Sox had five men capable of outfield slots on any given day. Nemo Leibold, Eddie Murphy, Shano Collins, Joe Jackson, and Happy Felsch (from left to right) each offered the team a different combination of skills, and helped Chicago win the 1917 World Series.

Desperate to rid his team of the "Hitless Wonders" moniker, Chicago White Sox owner Charles Comiskey stocked his club with star-caliber players. By 1917, he had a quintet of talented outfielders including Joe Jackson, Shano Collins, Happy Felsch, Eddie Murphy, and Nemo Leibold (from left to right).

As the call went out for individuals to enroll for the US Army draft in World War I, Joe Jackson was more than happy to do his patriotic duty and registered. However, he later determined that he would best serve his country, and his family, by joining a shipbuilding outfit in Wilmington, Delaware.

Criticized for jumping to the shipbuilding league during World War I, Joe maintained that he was just as patriotic as those who entered the military, and worked dutifully for the Harlan and Hollingsworth Shipbuilding Company. On the weekends, Jackson (ninth from left) played ball for the company and was the biggest superstar in the so-called "Paint and Putty League."

The 1919 Chicago White Sox, considered by many experts to be the greatest ballclub in major league history. Unfortunately, due to the efforts of the corrupt "Black Sox," the team failed to live up to its potential and lost the 1919 World Series to the Cincinnati Reds. Joe Jackson is in the top row, second from right.

In tune with his amiable nature, Joe was a mentor to innumerable up-and-comers, and willing to offer advice to anyone who asked. Jackson (right) often spoke with future home-run king Babe Ruth, and the latter even mimicked Joe's batting style, helping him achieve great fame as a power hitter.

The infamous "Black Sox" in a Chicago courtroom for their 1921 trial. Joe Jackson is seated second from right, and next to him are Buck Weaver, Eddie Cicotte, Swede Risberg, Lefty Williams, and Chick Gandil (right to left).

On the stand in his 1924 trial against the Chicago White Sox over back pay, Joe Jackson spoke impressively and won over both the jury and many of those in attendance. Ever personable and witty in his own way, Joe was one of the most memorable figures in baseball history.

Despite a jury awarding him a victory in the trial, the judge overturned the decision and jailed Jackson for perjury. The judge felt there were too many discrepancies between Joe's 1924 testimony and his 1920 Grand Jury statement to let the jury's decision stand.

Following his banishment from Organized Baseball, Joe retained his pride and fun-loving personality. He continued to play on the outlaw circuit and, regardless of the size of the town, enjoyed it as much as ever. In this 1924 image, Joe and Katie shared a moment in front of a dugout in Waycross, Georgia.

As a member of the Waycross (GA) Coast Liners in 1924, Jackson batted .475 and helped his club win a regional championship.

Jackson (third from right), shown with his 1925 Waycross Coast Liners team, remained a baseball attraction all over the South. Stories about his old major-league feats never diminished while, at the same time, he continued to hammer the baseball with extraordinary slugging power. He might have slowed down on the basepaths, but he never lost his sharp batting eye.

Although he was without a formal education, Joe was a spirited entrepreneur throughout his life. For many years, Joe (center) and Katie (left) operated a successful dry-cleaning business in Savannah.

After relocating back to Greenville in the 1930s, Jackson opened a liquor store in the western part of the city and operated the business until his death in 1951.

Jackson was always proud of his baseball achievements. In his later years, he posed with a trophy he was given in 1917 for winning a distance throwing contest at a benefit game in Boston. His remarkable toss went 396 feet and 8 ½ inches.

Joe (third from left) was never forgotten by the baseball fans of Greenville and, in 1948, was honored at a special "Joe Jackson Night" gala at the Brandon Mills Park. Over 2,000 people were on hand to pay tribute to their hometown hero.

Neighborhood kids in Greenville witnessed Jackson's generosity and kindness firsthand, and many of them were recipients of free ice cream, compliments of "Shoeless Joe."

In 1949, Jackson (right) agreed to be interviewed by journalist Furman Bisher and spoke openly about the 1919 "Black Sox" scandal for the first time more than a quarter century. The interview appeared in the October 1949 issue of *Sport* magazine and, in the article, Jackson maintained his innocence of any wrongdoing in the fix.

Martha Jackson (center), the family matriarch, loved her children and took pride in their success. While the baseball public knew her eldest as "Shoeless," he was just "Her Joe," and that's what she called him. Joe (left) was not the only ball player in the family. His brother Jerry (right) was also a minor leaguer of note in the Carolina region.

Still his pride and joy, Joe displayed his famous "Black Betsy" bat to a photographer in 1949, decades after his final major league ballgame. In 2001, "Betsy" was auctioned off for $577,610, a record amount for a bat, and to this day retains a mythical legend all its own.

When the opportunity presented itself, Joe and Katie enjoyed getting back out to the park and watching the national pastime. During the summer of 1947, the couple had one such occasion, and saw the Brandon Braves play ball in Greenville.

Fun to be around, Joe was always smiling at the ballpark and his genuine likability made him one of the most popular players of the Deadball Era.

Although he was more outgoing as he got older, Joe was surprisingly bashful around photographers and reporters early in his baseball career. At one point, he was even superstitious about having his photograph taken and avoided them whenever possible.

paranoia, they were ready to accept further retrenchment and salary reductions, plus a cut in the number of regular-season games from 154 to 140. These devices were nearly all implemented with the business end of the game in mind and to protect the financial status of magnates. Comiskey saw his home attendance in 1918 drop an astonishing 28.5 percent (almost 500,000) over the previous season; Chicago had always been considered one of the best baseball towns in the country.[8] A boom period was certainly possible with thousands of fans returning from overseas and with people more open-minded to amusements, but owners remained cautious.

As was the case in years prior, the introduction of salary cuts—or the threat of such a maneuver—was inviting players to rebel. Comiskey was acutely aware of that happening when contracts were sent to players early in 1919. Any number of his men could be rendered discontent by the monetary numbers offered and reject the sum outright. They could mutiny as an entire club if his reductions were too steep and create quite a ruckus. It would leave Comiskey with little option but to pay his men better, especially if he wanted his stadium filled anywhere close to capacity. But this was all theoretical because Comiskey didn't plan to decrease his salary list. His team was approaching 1919 as it had two years prior, with one of the largest payrolls in the history of baseball. Comiskey, however, was keenly aware of his team's lack of synergy in the recent season and was looking to quickly rebuild morale.

The only answer to that problem rested in an old-school baseball veteran who spent the previous season away from the big leagues at his home in Pennsylvania: William "Kid" Gleason. As one newspaper noted in the midst of Chicago's 1918 team strife, "It is apparent Kid Gleason is missed. He was the peacemaker on the club last year and managed to keep the players in line so well that there were positively no disgruntled ones on the club, and they gave the team their best efforts at all times."[9] Gleason, who sat out because of a grievance over his salary, was not being asked to support Clarence Rowland this time around. Instead, Rowland was returning to the minors to manage the Milwaukee Brewers in the American Association, and Comiskey was handing the reins of the ship to the good-natured ex-ballplayer, giving him a nice paycheck to go along with it. Gleason agreed, and with him instilled as the new manager, the Sox had a chance to regain some of its lost fighting spirit.[10]

Gleason, throughout his tenure in Chicago, was an immense resource and friend for the players. He provided quick wit, a profound sense of

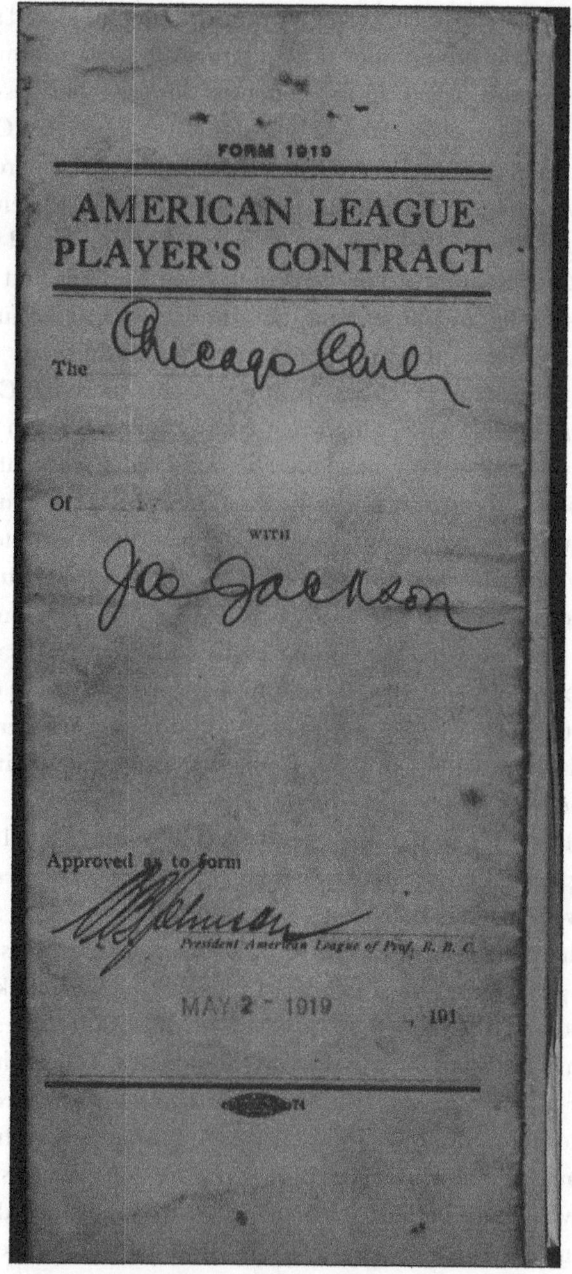

FORM 1919

AMERICAN LEAGUE
PLAYER'S CONTRACT

The Chicago Club

Of

WITH

Joe Jackson

Approved as to form

President American League of Prof. B. B. C.

MAY 2 - 1919 , 191

Following a contentious period with a shipbuilding corporation during the war, Jackson made his return to the Chicago White Sox in 1919, ready to reestablish himself among baseball's best. This photograph shows the front page of his 1919 contract.

11. All the terms and conditions herein have been fully considered by each of the parties hereto, and this agreement embraces the entire contract between the parties and any agreements not contained herein shall be void.

12. The club owner may at its option, at any time prior to January 1 next succeeding the termination of this contract, notify the player of its election to renew this contract for a term of one year; and upon the club owner's giving such notice—which may be by mailing notice to the player at his last known place of address—of its election to renew the contract, the parties hereto shall enter into a written contract for such renewal term, which contract shall be in all respects, except as to compensation, identical with this contract. The compensation shall be as agreed upon by the parties.

It is further agreed that if the party of the second part is a member of the Chgo Club in good standing he shall be paid the amount of $750.00 at the close of the 1919 season making the total compensation for the season (not to exceed $6000.00)

In Testimony Whereof, The parties hereunto have executed this contract in duplicate, each of which shall be considered an original, one copy being retained by the club owner and one copy by the player, this 29 day of ...., A. D. 1919

Chas A Comiskey

(SEAL) By Joe Jackson

Witnesses:

The second page of Joe Jackson's 1919 baseball contract with the Chicago White Sox, signed by team owner Charles Comiskey and by Joe himself. Jackson earned approximately $6,000 for the season.

humor, and was always relatable. At times he more resembled a jolly and wise uncle than a coach, and his toughness was often underestimated. Standing 5-foot-7, he was easily dwarfed by many athletes, but was strong as an ox and willing to fight at the drop of a hat. During his baseball career, he wasn't one to walk away from a confrontation and, if fisticuffs were the only answer to a problem, he was unafraid to stand up to a man twice his size. His energy on the field was contagious and players knew that if they were struggling with a mechanical flaw, Gleason's advice was usually enough to break their spell. He also preached discipline and was not the type of manager who'd let his players run roughshod over the establishment. He was an excellent man to depend on, and Chicago was in the midst of a new day with him at the helm.

Meanwhile, Joe Jackson continued to make his presence known in Delaware and Pennsylvania that winter. According to a press account, he turned up in Reading, Pennsylvania, to inquire about a job with the Reading Steel Casting Company in November 1918.[11] A few weeks later, the same newspaper indicated that Joe was not only still with Harlan and Hollingsworth, but going out for the company's basketball team.[12] His future in Major League Baseball was unsettled, and journalists speculated at length about the status of all the sport's essential workers. Even though he was no longer in the spotlight, much of the scorn still remained. A writer for the *Washington Times* noted that baseball didn't need a blacklist because the fans would see to it that the jumpers were punished enough. "As Jackson's courage is not considered of the highest," the writer explained, "he would never be able to endure the storm of criticism the stockyards workers would hand him the first day he appeared out against the fence in left field. Well, it won't be gentle stuff."[13]

Nevertheless, in one of his first official acts as manager of the White Sox, Gleason convinced Comiskey that the shipbuilding jumpers were needed if Chicago had any chance of success in 1919. He wanted Jackson in left field, and if the stockyard workers wanted to roast Joe for a while to get their animosity out of their system, Gleason believed Joe could handle it. But it was also pretty much guaranteed as soon as Jackson started belting out doubles and triples that he'd once again have the favor of the bleacher section at Comiskey Park. In addition to Gleason's prodding to reinstate Jackson and his fellow shipbuilders to good favor, a pocket of influential fans did likewise, and the combination eased Comiskey's mind to the idea.[14] In the end, Comiskey rejected options to trade Joe to Cleveland and New York, which would have strengthened his rivals, and gave Gleason the go-ahead to welcome the famed left fielder back to Chicago.[15]

With this decision in place, contempt sparked again. "Another soldier boy came back to us the other day," a reporter for the *Washington Herald* sarcastically noted. "Joe Jackson, who used to be on duty in the cleaning department, is the hero this time. Joe, we congratulate you upon your safe return."[16] However, W. J. Macbeth of the *New York Tribune* believed the widespread backlash was fading and felt people were ready to "forgive and forget."[17] But was Jackson ready? For the previous eight months he'd been the target of ridicule, condemned for his lack of patriotism and nerve, and was criticized in innumerable personal ways. Now that Comiskey and various sportswriters were willing to accept him back into the baseball fold, people were forgetting that Joe himself had to pardon the vicious critics without receiving any form of apology. He was being asked to overlook the vitriolic commentary and resume his career as if nothing had happened. With no one taking the blame for the unwarranted attacks.

There was still plenty of resentment. Only friends had taken his side in the matter and, despite the scant defense offered by writers here and there, the overwhelming context of reports about Jackson were negative. Kid Gleason wanted to move forward and put everything that had occurred behind them. He was asked about Joe and the new Sox manager replied, "He'll be out there playing left field and 'Happy' Felsch too. They're my boys, and they'll work their heads off for me."[18] Gleason tried to catch up with Jackson in the Wilmington area in January 1919, but Joe had returned to Savannah to spend time with family. Gleason was able to locate Lefty Williams, who was hard at work in the boiler-room, and "Kid" persuaded him to rejoin the Sox once a $180 payment, which was owed to the pitcher, was made.[19] Before the end of January, contracts were sent out to Jackson, Williams, Felsch, and backup catcher Byrd Lynn.[20]

Regarding his salary, Jackson was offered $1,000 per month, amounting to $6,000 for the year.[21] It was essentially the same figure as his last contract, and for anyone who'd read Comiskey's venomous comments about Joe the year before and understood that the Sox magnate did not want him playing ball for his club again, it was a sure sign that the owner was extending an olive branch. But on the other hand, people had wondered and, based on certain statistics, presumed that Joe was mightily underpaid compared to other major league stars at the time. While Jackson was considered a heavy-duty offensive weapon, the general perspective about his playing ability was not all glowing. Even when Comiskey purchased him in 1915, he acknowledged that Joe had been in decline for two years and that it was a "gamble" to a certain extent.[22] Jackson wasn't a perfect player and still had faults that needed to be addressed.[23]

Prior to the 1916 season, many pundits agreed that in a straight trade with Jackson going to New York for Fritz Maisel, the Yankees were getting the bum part of the deal. Maisel, it should be quickly noted, would end his career with a lifetime .242 batting average in six seasons of professional ball. But then and there, George S. Robbins, a pro-Chicago correspondent for *The Sporting News,* wanted the third baseman for the Sox and couldn't see the benefits to keeping Joe around, writing that Chicago "could afford to part with Jackson for Maisel."[24]

A reporter for the *New York Herald* wrote that "Jackson once was a great player," whereas Maisel was considered a young star with unlimited potential.[25] Bill Donovan, then Yankees manager, added: "It is a gamble how long [Jackson] will be of major league value."[26]

Well-known Chicago expert James Crusinberry said a few months earlier that Chicago Cubs outfielder Frank Schulte (.270 lifetime hitter) was Jackson's "equal," and that the National Leaguer broke up "many a game of ball in the pinch, while Jackson seldom [did]."[27] Another Chicago journalist, I. E. Sanborn, picked Red Sox left fielder Duffy Lewis (.284 lifetime hitter) over Jackson in a head-to-head comparison. "Joe Jackson has thousands of admirers," Sanborn wrote in 1916, "but I doubt if there is a manager in the game who would not select Duffy Lewis if he had the choice."[28] Louis A. Dougher of the *Washington Times* explained, just prior to the 1917 World Series, that New York Giants outfielder George Burns was a "far better fielder and base runner [than Jackson]."[29] Jackson's worth was arguable to these writers, but there was little doubt that the Yankees would have taken Joe in a split second had Chicago wanted anything less than Maisel in a trade. Other teams would've been happy taking him as well.

An article appeared in the March 1916 issue of *Baseball Magazine* entitled "The Man Who Might Have Been the Greatest Player in the Game," and it was all about Joe. The author wrote, "It remains for the future to tell whether or not he will bring to Comiskey's club that wonderful ability which is his by divine right." And at the end of the lengthy piece, the writer left it open by saying that Jackson "might perhaps even yet" live up to that amazing proclamation. Three years had passed, and with 1918 discounted for obvious reasons, Joe was still trying to reach his optimal potential for the

Sox without distractions, extraordinary slumps, or other distressing occurrences. But it was clear that Jackson was not considered the best player in the American League, nor was he a leader on the field or in the clubhouse. Kid Gleason understood his importance, though, and that was why he pushed for Joe's return before doing anything else as Chicago's manager. To Gleason, Jackson was imperative to his team's success.

Altogether, the White Sox were a unique bunch and had been for a number of years. They exemplified diversity with college educated, illiterate, business-savvy, and ruffians intermixed, joining together on the field to wage war on the diamond. The climate of the clubhouse was often jovial, as one thing most players had in common was a stark sense of humor. The players could find humor in most anything, and whether they were ragging on each other or telling a wild story from a night out on the town, they were frequently doubled over in laughter. And they were an entertaining group in any kind of public setting. In April 1916, while in the town of Shawnee, Oklahoma, the Sox participated in a practice session using only their imaginations. There was no actual ball in play, and their actions were all for the amusement of the crowd on hand.[30] Another time, in Mineral Wells, Texas, they had people in stitches as they acted out football maneuvers with nothing but a medicine ball.[31]

Happy Felsch definitely lived up to his name. During a session of batting practice at Detroit in 1917, he was accidentally knocked out after a bat slipped from Jackson's hands following a swing. When he awoke a few minutes later, Felsch was not angry in the slightest, but instead laughing. He thought it was hysterical, and played that afternoon with a huge knot on his forehead.[32] One year during spring training, Columbia University grad Eddie Collins figured out the exact mathematical location for second base, insisting that it was the "square root of the sum of the squares of the two sides of the triangle," according to the *Chicago Daily Tribune.* Felsch of course had a snappy retort, and his reply had everyone dying. "That's nothing; you ought to watch me extract the cube root of a triangle of pumpkin pie."[33]

The Sox were easy with their smiles and it wasn't all about performing before a crowd, as they freely joked and joshed each other in the clubhouse. They were a likeable and relatable group, and it was no surprise as to their popularity in recent years.

But there were other sides to the White Sox, one of which stood out a little more than the rest. And, as might be expected, it had to do with money. In 1916, reporter James Crusinberry described Comiskey's men as "money players" for the first time and he was talking about the way the Sox came together to beat out the Cubs in the City Series every year.[34] It was as if the players smelled the greenbacks and rose to the occasion to ensure they'd take home the winner's share of the pot. Crusinberry's words were not malicious in tone and no one was offended.

A year later, in the buildup for the World Series, Charles Dryden wrote, "Being fond of money and having the incentive to go and get it is going to be a powerful factor on the side of the Sox."[35] It was the same overall premise as Crusinberry's comments and, once again, referenced their collective yearning for bigger cash payouts. There was nothing wrong with being interested in monetary rewards for winning games, and the Series was the dream of all major leaguers; both for the thrill of playing for a championship and making several thousand dollars for a few days' work. Of course, it had to be assumed that there was a tremendous amount of honor in winning a baseball championship and, to professionals, it was a nice tribute to a hard-fought season. But when money was the sole purpose of playing hard in a series and there was absolutely no personal pride at stake, baseball was deprived of the sportsmanship the ticket-buying audience came to expect.

For some members of the White Sox, money was their only driving force. Baseball was nothing but a business to them; a gateway to suits, nice cars, and property. In that way, it was all about garnering better deals for themselves mostly by obtaining improved contracts. These were the real "money players." Additionally, there were politics in the Sox clubhouse; a pecking order devised by management, and certain players—without question—were seen to be held in special favor by Comiskey. Eddie Collins was at the top of that select list. Gleason also acknowledged the second baseman's extraordinary importance. "Collins is the most valuable man I have ever seen in a ball club. . . . Collins combines everything that makes up greatness; brains, courage, hitting ability, speed, and baseball instinct."[36] But the perceived special treatment of Collins caused unrest and jealousy within the Sox ranks.

This unrest started first and foremost with his salary. Collins was signed at a guaranteed $15,000 per year for five years in December 1914. The contract, inked during the heated war with the Federal League, was an egregious anomaly when compared to the rest of the Sox. No other player even came close to that amount of money; it was even more than double of Jackson's pay. But there were other factors to his salary than just a bidding war with the Federal League. Collins was a leader both in the clubhouse and on the field. In fact, he was Chicago's on-field captain and disseminated information from management when necessary. His intellect was a constant aid during ballgames and he performed his all-around abilities with consistency. In terms of the White Sox roster, no one performed similar duties. Now, that didn't mean Collins should have been making double of what Jackson did, and the disparity caused much friction for the legitimate "money players" on the team. As far as Jackson was concerned, he had no real problems with Collins.[37]

But Buck Weaver, Chick Gandil, and Happy Felsch *did* have personal reasons to dislike their on-field captain. Beginning with Weaver, who was the team's captain prior to Collins being named to the post, there was a hostility that had been slowly growing over the years.[38] The two worked together as a skilled double play combination, and Eddie went to great lengths to coach Weaver in ways to improve his defense on the left side of the infield.[39] Weaver, however, was immensely competitive—even with his own teammates—and put more focus on his yearly statistical comparison with Collins than turning the perfect double play. In 1917, he was only five points behind his rival at season's end, with a .284 to Collins's .289. The following season he led the Sox captain by 24 points, finishing 1918 with a .300 average compared to Collins's .276. Weaver also achieved a team-leading 126 hits, which was 35 more than Collins. These factors illuminated his value to the club, and he felt he was just as important as Collins (and should so be compensated).[40]

That was why, in early 1919, he sought a $2,000 raise from Comiskey. George S. Robbins of *The Sporting News* indicated that Weaver was making in the neighborhood of $4,000 a year, an astounding $11,000 less than Collins. Additionally, Robbins declared Buck the "greatest drawing card on Comiskey's team," which would have seemingly entitled him to a better paycheck than he was receiving.[41] Comiskey finally agreed, and Weaver's salary was raised to $7,250 in 1919.[42] Needless to say, it was still less than half of what Collins earned.

Chick Gandil, the brawny Sox first baseman, had an even longer history with Collins than Weaver, and his relationship was built on much more hostility. Seven years earlier, when Gandil was with Washington and Collins Philadelphia, the two butted heads several times on the basepaths, resulting in a broken nose for Chick, a near spiking to Eddie, and a lot of ill feelings.[43]

Gandil was not the kind of guy to forget a broken nose, particularly when it was caused by Collins's irresponsible behavior at second base. On top of that, Gandil was a polar opposite of Collins in the way they grew up, were educated, and entered baseball. As a kid, Chick never had the opportunities of a middle- or upper-class lifestyle. He broke out on his own as a teenager and traveled throughout the western part of the United States, using his size and strength to do manual labor. Before he was twenty, he landed in Cananea, Sonora, Mexico, forty-odd miles south of the US border, and worked in the copper mines. Using the name "Chick Arnold," he joined the camp's independent baseball team and did well for himself. He also fought on occasion. On September 16, 1907, before four hundred people at the National Theater in Cananea, Gandil knocked out a local boxing celebrity, John Bernal of Tucson, in three rounds. The *Bisbee Daily Review* reported that Bernal successfully hit him "but once during the fight."[44]

Even at a young age, Gandil displayed his internal grit and fortitude, and it was evident he possessed an innate fearlessness that few others could claim. His toughness was worn on his sleeve as he rose up through the minors and entered the big leagues in 1910, and an observer could tell he was rough-around-the-edges just by looking at him. He put his entire body on the line in every game he played, often risking injury, and was a valuable asset to his club. Away from the diamond, he was socially adept among sportsmen at downtown pool halls and bowling allies all over the league circuit. When he played in Washington, he even took a job working for Frank Sherman at the latter's famous Royal Billiard Parlors.[45] Gandil was a popular man in those circles and made friends with all walks of life, from reputable businessmen to degenerate gamblers.

Notably, Gandil shared one trait with Eddie Collins: both were leaders. People simply gravitated to them for their charisma and experience, and Gandil had loads of infectious self-confidence. Chick was a nonconformist in some ways, and routinely got into hot water with the managers of the clubs he played for. At Washington, for instance, he smoked cigarettes and his habit drove manager Clark Griffith up the wall. But Gandil was unflinchingly stubborn when he wanted to be, and it was said that his dismissal from the Senators was due to this issue over cigarettes.[46] In Chicago, a few of the younger athletes looked up to him, and it was relatively easy for Gandil to form a clique of like-minded pals to hang out and swap stories. In fact, the grouping of various cliques was a common theme throughout the Sox clubhouse, and players were more inclined to join their buddies rather than talk with others with whom they had little in common.[47]

This has always been a common occurrence but, in terms of building team camaraderie, managers hated dealing with factions. It was a detriment to the success of any club and usually stirred up lots of infighting. In 1917, the cliques of the White Sox were diminished by the military component of their discipline, and players reached a sustainable level of teamwork to become champions. The following year, within the chaos and uncertainty of war, factions blossomed within the Sox and uncooperative personalities began to develop. Bad blood also expanded with a growing hostility toward management, those in favor with management and anyone outside their select faction. Even though these emotions were running high, the internal dissension hadn't yet caused Chicago to collapse entirely and become an altogether unproductive ballclub. But the problems were ingrained within the factions, the rogue players, and brewing in those who were discontented with how things had progressed.

Happy Felsch's problems with Eddie Collins were generally limited to a quarrel they had during the 1918 season, but their fight was no small affair. Comiskey speculated that their clash had something to do with Happy quitting the team in early July, but he had several different things on his mind at the time, including an awareness of the "work or fight" decree by the US Government.[48] Collins wanted to start anew in 1919 and told a reporter that Felsch was the "best young player in baseball."[49] During the winter, Felsch kept himself busy selling Christmas trees in Milwaukee and didn't hastily rush into making a decision about returning to baseball. On February 10, 1919, he turned up in Chicago and met with Comiskey. They talked for hours, hammering out their differences and, in the end, Happy signed to play another year with the Sox.[50]

Without question, Felsch, Weaver, and Jackson were more likely to hang out socially with Chick Gandil than the faction led by Collins and Ray Schalk. Jackson's pal Lefty Williams was also included in the pool-playing sect, as were Gandil's pals Swede Risberg and Fred McMullin. The seven players were much more brawn than brains, embracing street smarts rather than formal education. And many of them were fighters, too, just like Chick. Weaver and McMullin displayed their physical prowess in fighting their way off the diamond at Fenway Park back in June 1917 after angry rioters rushed the field.[51] During a trip to New York in May 1918, Risberg delivered a swift punch to a man who talked "roughly" to a woman working for the Red Cross, and later said he used his left hand "because he did not want to kill the fellow," according to the *Chicago Daily Tribune*.[52] A few months later, Swede punched out an umpire in California after landing on the wrong end of a close play.[53]

As for Jackson, he was not known for any fistic aggression, although the story behind the alleged fight with a sheriff in 1915 wasn't completely known. Joe did, however, understand the complexities of factional strife on a baseball club. He'd lived through it while in Cleveland, and personally had been part of a Southern group of players who always comingled with each other. In 1914, there was a painstaking internal battle among the Naps, and Louis A. Dougher of the *Washington Times* described it as a feud "between 'town and gown,' collegians and non-collegians, with [Joe] Birmingham leading the 'high brows' and Nap Lajoie the 'roughnecks.'" A player confided in the writer at the time, admitting that "There [was] no chance for such a team to win the pennant, not while they're fighting among themselves."[54]

Similar to the situation in Chicago, Jackson leaned toward the non-collegian-roughneck group because he felt more comfortable around people he could relate to. He liked the hard-nosed style of baseball and agreed with Lajoie when the latter told a reporter, "The trouble with Cleveland is that there is too much of that rah-rah college stuff and not enough real baseball."[55] To them, it was more about instinctual game play, fighting for runs, and never giving an inch to an opponent than applying textbook formulas. Jackson relied on his natural abilities more so than anything else. After all, he didn't have the background for anything else, and listened to his manager and fellow players for guidance. In the outfield, Joe had a good system with Felsch in center field, and the two were highly successful in handling things defensively. But there were known weaknesses in the Sox scheme and Jackson, as one of the non-collegians, certainly saw some of the more advanced baseball techniques go right over his head.

The White Sox were not known to be a cerebral club. The unscholarly far outnumbered the scholarly, and Chicago was prone to mental mistakes on the field. Hugh Fullerton, a Chicago-based writer, pulled no punches in a column about the Sox in September 1917. He wrote, "[Clarence] Rowland has a hard team to manage, in that few of them do much thinking on the ball field." Additionally, he claimed the Sox were vulnerable to "fits of self-satisfaction and carelessness," while examining the areas of play in which the team was deficient. Seeing that 1918 was a wasted year, many of the weaknesses of 1917 were going to be prevalent in 1919 if Gleason didn't tackle the issues during spring training. That meant he needed to stress improved baserunning, better small ball, and strengthening their pitching rotation.

The need for smarter play was essential, and everyone had to step up their game to meet the demands of the upcoming season. In fact, it was crucial that the Sox regained its lost synergy and crushed whatever internal dissensions that were brewing. But within the non-collegian clique, there was potential danger on the horizon. This trouble was far-fetched, but possible if the street smart "money players" realized just how far they could take advantage of the naïve and unschooled members of the club, and pushed their luck in a for-profit scheme. In the realm of professional baseball and considering the type of honor and respect shared among players, plus the high level of sportsmanship they lived and breathed, any kind of cockeyed scheme was considered absurd.

But as ego-driven baseball ran more and more rampant, and as the greed of players grew, the probability of a wacky ploy to siphon money from owners or audiences rose, whether it was coordinated holdouts or some other strategy. For the Sox, the only hope was that Kid Gleason and Eddie Collins nipped any kind of uprising in the bud. And all it usually took was for one man to speak up and reveal the plan, cutting off the illogical conversation once and for all. Chicago's house of cards was flimsy, built on a combination of great baseball strength and disruptive personalities. Needless to say, 1919 was going to provide many thrilling moments for enthusiasts and create a memorable new chapter for the sport; not only in Chicago, but in the annals of major league history.

THE BIRTH OF THE "BLACK SOX"

The factional groups were well established in the Chicago White Sox locker room headed into the 1919 season. Unfortunately, for manager Kid Gleason, there was very little he was able to do in terms of any attempt to divide and conquer. In response, he hoped to create an overall umbrella of peace and harmony that superseded any increasing acrimony and allow the team's natural baseball talents to pave the way for success. With regard to salaries, players had to deal with management on their own, and the various cliques played no part in negotiations. All Charles Comiskey wanted from his roster was an honest exhibition of their God-given talents on the field. (Of course, he wanted them at their absolute best all season long.) On the other hand, players expected to be paid twice a month, while also receiving the many perks of being a big-leaguer on the American League circuit. They also desired a fair salary amount, and it wasn't uncommon for players to temporarily hold out during the preseason while discussing better terms.

Holding out for improved salaries was an absolute right for major leaguers. Ty Cobb, Nap Lajoie, Honus Wagner, and many of the game's top superstars used this technique to get more money from owners and, while it was frowned upon by traditionalists, baseball writers and fans accepted the practice as normal. Unlike most teams, the Sox players were in a unique bargaining position going into the 1918 season. Being the 1917 World Series champions, they probably had more say in terms of receiving improved contracts. However, no members of the team took advantage of the opportunity.

A year had since passed and, as mentioned earlier, Buck Weaver was anxious to rebuff the so-called conservative front by owners and requested a raise. Comiskey, in recognizing Weaver's importance, acquiesced.[1] *The Sporting*

News mentioned that Swede Risberg and Lefty Williams were in the same boat, and terms were supposedly adjusted well enough for both men to sign prior to the team's departure for spring training.[2]

Jackson bided his time after receiving his 1919 contract as experts continued to speculate about a potential trade. He weighed his options, and undoubtedly realized that he was not in the best politically smart position to become a holdout himself. But it was still within his right to do so if he felt it was completely necessary. Bitterness still endured and, in February 1919, James Crusinberry of the *Chicago Daily Tribune* took it upon himself to ask the "common man" whether Jackson would be welcomed back to baseball with open arms. The respondent, a waiter at a Loop restaurant, replied: "I'll holler my head off at him as soon as he comes upon the field. He don't belong there. He don't belong in the game. He quit 'em last summer, didn't he? He was afraid to stick and take his medicine, wasn't he? He was afraid of the trenches, wasn't he?"

The restaurant's manager, however, differed in his opinion. "Why shouldn't he play for 'em?" he asked. "No one can hit 'em any harder."[3]

Ex-major leaguer Fritz Von Kolnitz, who played 24 games with the Sox in 1916, was a longtime friend of Jackson's from South Carolina. He understood Joe's plight and felt a strong need to defend his actions of the year before. "It has always been a puzzle to me why Joe was picked out of the hundreds of shipyard workers and persecuted," Von Kolnitz wrote in a widely circulated letter. "You know and I know the main reason. He was a star in his profession and the small-mindedness of some people makes them delight in blaming anyone high up whom they can criticize. As a 100 per cent American, Joe has always stood for square in my opinion and my only motive in writing this is to give the impression of a man in the service who knows Joe Jackson probably better than any other man."[4] Von Kolnitz was not just a military serviceman, but had achieved the highest grade (Major) of any former player during the war, and his words were consequential. Jackson no doubt appreciated his efforts.

With support from Comiskey, Joe was given approval to return to baseball from the National Commission, lifting the final official barrier that kept him from rejoining the Sox. All that remained was for Jackson to sign his contract, and any hesitation on his part was reasonable under the circumstances. It was believed he did want to return, though, and there was some speculation whether Kid Gleason would venture to Savannah to deliver a persuasive speech.[5] But that action wasn't necessary, as Jackson's signature arrived at the club's Comiskey Park offices on February 21, 1919. Of all those with the club, "Kid" couldn't have been happier.[6] "I knew the big fellow would come around all right," the manager exclaimed.[7] And with his signature, the "old 1917 gang" was reunited for another dash at the pennant.[8] It must be acknowledged that the Sox roster, one-by-one, personally accepted their salary terms, and the team was ultimately free of holdouts.

Spring training was again held in Mineral Wells, Texas, west of Dallas, and Joe journeyed into the "Lone Star State" with Katie by his side. They were running a bit late, however, and missed linking up with the Sox special train as it passed through the Fort Worth area. After running into an acquaintance with a car, the Jacksons enjoyed a ride over to camp and arrived on March 23.[9] Gleason arranged for two-a-day practice sessions and divided the team into halves for exhibition games. Cold weather and rain put a literal damper on their conditioning plans as Joe nursed sore extremities during the early going. He also wore a rubber shirt under his uniform to aid in weight loss, but was in prime shape by early April. An observant Chicago correspondent noted that Jackson, along with Happy Felsch, had "caught the Gleason spirit" and looked more motivated than ever.[10]

Jackson was reinvigorated on the field, but the controversies surrounding his shipyard employment remained a hot topic for sportswriters. In a syndicated column in April, Hugh Fullerton predicted that Jackson was "in for a hard summer." He believed the "constant abuse of the crowd [would] affect his work," and explained that fans "[would either] forget the incident entirely or drive him out of baseball."[11] For that reason, Jackson was at the public's mercy. He had no idea what the reactions of audiences were going to be, and all he could personally control was how well he performed. So far that spring, he was utterly determined to play his best type of ball—which he was doing. He delivered multi-hit games in Little Rock and Memphis (including two triples in the latter contest) while driving one out of the park in Louisville.[12] He almost homered again at Cincinnati on April 20, but was robbed by the Reds' star outfielder, Edd Roush.[13]

Kid Gleason was fortunate as the Sox were able to present the same exact opening day lineup as they'd featured two years before. The outfield consisted of Nemo Leibold in right field, Happy Felsch in center and Jackson in left, while the infield was made up of Chick Gandil (first base), Eddie Collins (second base), Swede Risberg (shortstop), and Buck Weaver (third base). Ray Schalk was behind the plate and Lefty Williams, who went 17–8 in '17, was again on the mound. Interestingly, Chicago faced the same opponent in the St. Louis Browns at Sportsman's Park. But this time, instead of Williams being knocked out of the game after one inning, he pitched a complete game for the Sox on April 23, 1919. Lefty received staggering support from his teammates, and the motivated contingent powered out 21 hits in a 13–4 victory.[14] Jackson was fired up and delivered three of his team's hits, including a double and an RBI.

To add on to that great Opening Day start, Jackson went 10-for-18 with three doubles and a home run in the four-game series with the Browns. Subsequently, at Detroit, he garnered another six hits in 12 at-bats, and was batting .533 after seven games.

While he was performing masterfully at the plate, he shined in the field as well. Against the Browns on April 26, he raced to the fence to catch a difficult drive by outfielder Baby Doll Jacobson, and prevented two runs after grabbing a lightning shot by Tigers catcher Oscar Stanage on April 30.[15]

Already setting an incredible pace, Jackson was soon to face his biggest test as the club headed home for its opener on May 2. Everyone wondered how local fans were going to react to his first appearance back in uniform. It was hard to imagine a segment of the baseball public not holding a grudge and perhaps voicing their disapproval. But at the same time, his on-field play was extraordinary and, for die-hard enthusiasts, if having Joe back in the lineup was the catalyst to victory, they would be all too willing to let bygones be bygones.

And that's exactly what occurred. A special group of "Joe Jackson Rooters" from the stockyards—complete with a full band—was on hand at Comiskey Park to demonstrate their full support for the slugger.[16] In fact, the rooters stopped the game when Joe went up to bat for the first time and furnished him with a gold watch. Additionally, the loyal left-field bleacher section cheered him each and every time he went to the plate, and other fans reacted positively when Joe smashed his fifth double of the year.[17] Although the Sox were defeated by the Browns, 11–4, the affair was auspicious because the remaining tension surrounding the shipyard jumpers was lifted by the South Side fans. Jackson was welcomed back with open arms and, as far as some Sox followers were concerned, it was as if he never left.

The reigning World Series champion Boston Red Sox entered Chicago for an important early-season clash in mid-May, and Jackson was right in the thick of things. He doubled home the only run in a 1–0 pitcher's duel between Eddie Cicotte and Carl Mays on May 14, allowing his team to take the win. The next day, in what one Chicago reporter called the "best battle in years," the Red Sox edged out Gleason's warriors, 6–5, in 12 innings. Joe went 1-for-3, but his finest contributions came in the outfield where he stole hits from Stuffy McInnis and Babe Ruth. However, in the fifth inning, he proved to all fans that his heart, body, and spirit were still deeply committed to Chicago. It was in this inning that he rushed to the outfield wall to catch a blast by Del Gainer, only to lose his balance and smash his head on a metal fence. A lesser player might have taken the rest of the day off, but Joe took a few minutes to regain his senses and returned to the game.[18]

But like the Jackson of old, Joe refrained from heeding the laws of smart baseball at times, and did what he felt was right regardless if it hurt the team. Against Philadelphia on May 17, he had an opportunity to sacrifice Eddie Collins to second after the latter walked. The Sox were down by one run and advancing the baserunner was critical, but Joe decided to swing away. He hit the ball "harder than he ever hit in his life," according to the *Chicago Daily Tribune*, but it went right to second baseman Red Shannon and triggered a double play.[19] The Sox lost that contest, 1–0, but Joe had a way of making up for his foibles. The very next afternoon, it was his hit that allowed Chicago to win a 1–0 battle against Philadelphia, and a Sunday crowd of over 20,000 at Comiskey Park roared in elation.[20]

Jackson's enthusiasm was at a fever pitch. His batting average remained around .390 for the first month of the season, and for several weeks Joe was hitting above .400. On May 30, 1919, he snagged a drive off the bat of Cleveland's Bill Wambsganss in left-center, and sportswriter James Crusinberry wrote that it "probably was the best [catch] of his career."[21] With Eddie Collins and Happy Felsch underperforming on offense, Jackson was picking up their slack. But Chicago's success, though, was a team effort, and the entire roster was contributing day to day. For that reason, the Sox had held first place since the season began and rarely displayed signs of slowing up. However, Jackson couldn't maintain his breakneck pace at the plate and his average dropped 102 points from .411 to .309 between May 16 and June 16. The Sox also fell to third place on June 23, giving up ground to the Yankees and Indians in what was quickly becoming a tight pennant race.[22]

The combined effects of a hitting slump and a short-staffed pitching staff were responsible for Chicago's dramatic demise. Pitching was a problem all year, as Kid Gleason was relying mainly on two individuals, Eddie Cicotte and Lefty Williams, to win games. Red Faber, who usually would've been dependable, was completely out of sorts, allowing twenty-five-year-old Dickey Kerr, a 5-foot-7 rookie, to step into the void. Kerr was originally being used out of the bullpen but was soon pushed into a starting role and would ultimately go 13–7 with a 2.88 ERA. In total, Gleason would use seventeen different pitchers over the course of the season—a handful for just a singular appearance—and centrally leaned on the sturdy arms of his top stars. But Kerr and Faber, and to a lesser degree Dan Danforth and Grover Lowdermilk, ate up innings while giving Chicago a little variety on the mound.

Gleason knew the importance of having four strong starters in a pennant fight.[23] He had optimal faith in Cicotte and Williams, but was worried about the rest of the team's consistency down the stretch. And if the Sox managed to make the World Series, how could his club win without at least one other steady hand? Essentially, if obtaining another pitcher was not possible, Gleason needed Faber and Kerr to shore up the weaknesses. Players upping their game to make up for deficiencies was a great strength for Chicago. The Sox were a crew of veterans and it was a rare day when the entire roster was taken by a dry spell. If a couple of players were having a bad day, the others usually made up for their handicap.

On July 6, 1919, Jackson was responsible for driving in two runs in a 4–1 victory, and Chicago's triumph kick-started a crucial six-game winning streak over Detroit and Philadelphia. During the midst of that run, the Sox regained first place and quickly began to expand its lead. Not before long, the American League's primary battle shifted to a fight for second place, as four teams were engaged in combat: New York, Cleveland, Detroit, and St. Louis. As for Jackson, the *Chicago Daily Tribune* remarked that he was back "on his ancient trail for a batting championship," and with a .352 average regained the league lead.[24] He was having his best season in years, but nothing he had done so far in 1919 evoked the kind of fan reaction that occurred at Comiskey Park when he hit a 10th-inning home run to win a game against the Yankees on July 20. Over 30,000 spectators witnessed the heroic feat live and responded with reckless abandon.

Jackson's teammates paced him from third to home and then mobbed him in a celebratory embrace at the plate. He was lifted onto their shoulders for a rousing exit from the field as fans cheered themselves hoarse. "The demonstration given Joe Jackson after the game was the greatest seen at the Sox park in ten years," a Chicago writer observed.[25] Joe's popularity in the "Windy City" was never greater, and he was living up to his previous reputation as one of baseball's heaviest hitters.

The team survived the slumps and normal bumps in the road while working through injuries to preserve its first-place status into August. Following an

Eastern road trip, Kid Gleason announced: "The White Sox are stronger right now than they've been at any time this year."[26] The news was music to the ears of baseball fans in Chicago. While no one wanted to jinx the team with similar praise, the quiet mumblings about a probable spot in the World Series were getting louder and louder as each day passed.

Notably, the legitimate "money players" of the Sox were way ahead of the public and press when it came to dissecting the potential of the World Series. Matt Foley of the *Chicago Herald and Examiner* revealed that these unnamed athletes already had "divided their World's Series money," meaning that they had calculated what they were to personally receive if they made it to the big event.[27] This wasn't something the players were figuring in October just prior to the games, but rather two months prior in early August; well before the pennant was even settled. So as far as the "money players" were concerned, they were already caught up in the hype brought on by the approaching. As Gleason later admitted, "My boys like something to play for," and sometimes players relaxed a little too much when there was "no incentive to win."[28]

These were haunting realities about the state of Major League Baseball. The "money players" permeated the sport across all sixteen big-league clubs, and their philosophies were arguably the predominant mind-set of the Deadball Era. In fact, baseball was a business to these men, and it was treated that way from the beginning to end of each season. For many of the "heroes" of baseball, idolized for decades, they didn't play for the love of the game like most modern day depictions claim, but were on a pathway to financial independence while working only six months a year. William A. Rafter of the *Brooklyn-Standard Union* wrote about this situation following the 1916 Series. He explained: "Much of the romance heretofore attached to players was taken off at the last World's Series melee, when it became known how the players figured the profits before the Series started, but failed to figure anything else."[29]

Now here were the Chicago White Sox, two months before the 1919 Series, calculating their profits and demonstrating their callousness about baseball's purity. But Matt Foley's column was far from just a one-time leak of sensitive information. The Sox players didn't seem to have any problem openly discussing their thoughts about money as it related to the Series. On August 29, 1919, still several weeks before the pennant was decided, Harry Neily of the *Chicago American* attained more insight into the mind-set of Sox players. His column featured the headline "Split of World Series Money

Worries Sox," and discussed a proposal by the National Baseball Commission to divide part of the Series income with the second- and third-place teams. The actual breakdown of such a concept was unknown, and players were up in arms.

Surprisingly, Buck Weaver was the first Sox athlete to publicly demonstrate the qualities of a "money player." He was quoted by Neily as saying, "What I would like to know is what are we going to get out of this series? The players don't know. It doesn't look as if anybody else does." Another player, who remained anonymous but was described as "one of the hardest working members of the Sox [and] a fellow who never quits on the field," also spoke out. He said: "I would not play for a flat sum of $2,100, and I guess that half the other fellows on the Sox wouldn't. The club owners ought to tell us now how the money is to be split. There isn't any doubt about how much the commission gets or how much each club officer will haul down, but if we got to split with the second and third clubs in each major league, we certainly ought to know about it before we go into the series."[30]

The comments by the unidentified player were striking, especially when he declared that "half the other fellows on the Sox wouldn't" agree to play for $2,100, which amounted to a third of some salaries and about half of others on Chicago's payroll. But for these dissenters, they expected more from their Series work. It wasn't about the pride of winning a World Series or the honor they'd bring to South Side fans in Chicago, but rather the cash they themselves would pocket. There were selfish reasons to worry about the capital to be earned, and players weren't hiding their emotions. At the center of this bastion of angst was Chick Gandil, who Louis A. Dougher of the *Washington Times* called a "great money player" in 1917.[31] Of all the Sox, Gandil was perhaps looking out for his own interests more than anyone else, but it wasn't completely spiteful. He had genuine personal reasons to do so.

Gandil's central concern was for his family. His wife Laurel loved their hometown California and disliked the East.[32] Her desire to stay West was an important factor in his decision-making and, prior to the 1919 season, it appeared that Chick was ready to slow things down and remain close to home. In fact, he actually reached out to the San Francisco Seals of the Pacific Coast League about a job with the club, and was prepared to completely sever ties with the Sox.[33] One report in *The Sporting News* claimed that Gandil had received approval from Charles Comiskey to take the minor league opportunity, but the claim was erroneous.[34] Comiskey wanted Gandil back at first base for Chicago, and so Chick had no other option but to either return to the Sox or retire from Organized Baseball. It wasn't a blackmail-type situation but rather followed the regular rules of OB, particularly the reserve clause which gave Comiskey the right to hold on to Gandil regardless of what the latter wanted.

In April 1919, incidentally, a faction of White Sox players expressed joy when a court in Washington, DC, gave a verdict to the Baltimore franchise of the defunct Federal League. In essence, the decision formally attached the stigma of "monopoly" to Organized Baseball, and if the verdict was upheld on appeal, the entire structure of the game was going to be transformed.[35] Journalist I. E. Sanborn heard players discuss the topic and found that a "minority" supported the court's decision and wanted a swift elimination of the reserve clause. "This, they believe, will enable them to command higher salaries than heretofore, because it will permit them to sell their skill to the highest bidder," Sanborn wrote. Other players, however, felt salaries would ultimately decrease if such changes were enacted.[36] Sanborn purposely withheld the names of those in the minority but, considering Gandil's recent situation, it wouldn't have been surprising to learn if he was one of the most vocal.

There is also a good probability that Gandil was dismayed by the news about the National Commission's efforts to shrink the Series pot for players. If 1919 was going to be his final season, he wanted to maximize his financial payday, and the Series was the best way to do so. But Gandil had a longer history of discontent with Comiskey, stretching back to his rookie year in the majors. It was 1910 when he began his big-league career with the Sox and played over 70 games at first base. He was well suited on defense but struggled at the plate, hitting a mere .193. Sox management figured he needed more refinement and sent him to Montreal of the Eastern League, a demotion Gandil never forgot.[37]

To that point, though, Gandil had given the Sox all he had on the field. He played through pain and injury, including knee problems, a stomach illness, and a near appendicitis, which caused him to lose 14 pounds.[38] In early June, he fought Cleveland outfielder Tris Speaker and ended up a bit bruised, but to him it was all part of a day's work.[39] Nonetheless, Gandil was widely known to be temperamental, and since other players looked up to him his downcast attitude had a way of becoming contagious in the clubhouse. Simply put, his words had a significant effect on others and contributed to the segregation of personalities. By August 1919, his clique was focused on the Series. They were tabulating percentages, griping about potential losses forced upon them by new Commission rules, and were certainly more concerned about profits than baseball glory.

There were a lot of number crunchers in the White Sox ranks, and manager Kid Gleason was no exception. "We figured if we went on the next eastern trip Sunday night with 77 wins, no club has a chance of beating us," he told a reporter in Detroit. "We doped it out that way a week ago. Last night we won our 77th game and we have four more before starting the final swing through the east. What about the World's Series? Can you think of any ball club that can beat a team like the Sox?"[40] Exuding confidence, Chicago ventured to Washington on the evening of September 7, and players hoped to finish off the pennant race with a victory in the quickest possible manner. Gleason was particularly eager, as he wanted to begin resting some of his overworked stars. At the top of that list were Eddie Cicotte, Lefty Williams, and Ray Schalk. Cicotte necessitated rest anyway after taking ill on the train en route to Washington.[41]

Jackson had the good fortune of bringing Katie on the final road trip east, which provided some comfort during a crucial time. The *Chicago American* noted that she also went with the Sox in 1917 when the club won the pennant, and declared her an "omen of good luck."[42] This time around, Chicago did just about everything right, and although the team didn't clinch the league championship on the road, they won eight of 12 games, including a run of six straight. For Jackson, he began the trip with an average hovering around .350 and ended it the same way. He contributed a few multi-hit games at Philadelphia, New York, and Boston, collecting several doubles, triples, and a home run—his seventh of the year. However, it was while in Boston that Jackson was confronted by an off-the-field proposition that was both unexpected and startling. The provocateur was none other than Chick Gandil, whose mind continued to work the angles and whose attention remained squarely on the World Series.[43]

After all the contemplation about money and figuring the upsides and downsides of Series participation, Gandil came to a peculiar conclusion. He deduced that it would be financially smarter to actively fix the Series than to play it honest. In this case, the players' share for throwing games could result in a total amount more than 400 percent greater than what they would normally gain, of course, dependent on specific circumstances falling into place. It was life-changing money for Gandil's family, and since he wanted to stay in California after the 1919 season anyway, the potential profit from such a scheme made sense. Additionally, Gandil saw the possibilities of double and triple dealing to maximize his own profit. The entirety of the plot was going to be sizable with scores of moving parts, but Chick was more than comfortable to begin the maneuvering. In fact, he had already broached the subject with Eddie Cicotte and Lefty Williams in New York just days before.[44]

Cicotte was receptive to hearing more about the plan, and met with Gandil and Bill Burns—a former major leaguer turned oil-lease peddler who entered the conspiracy as a middleman between the players and a gambling operation. The trio discussed a $100,000 deal involving five crooked White Sox players, and at $20,000 apiece it was far and away a greater reward than the estimated $3,500 winner's share that was normally awarded.[45] On the surface, talk of throwing baseball's most esteemed event was an abomination, and men who'd devoted most—if not all—of their adult lives to honest game play would cringe at such a disgraceful conversation. But in New York on September 18, 1919, Cicotte and Gandil inched a little closer toward making it a reality. And when the secretive meeting ended, Burns went off to manipulate the gambling end of the scheme while Cicotte did some personal reflecting. Like Gandil, he saw the money as a way to help his family, and so needed more time to think.[46]

As for Gandil, he was a busy man and immediately began recruiting players. He didn't waste time and quickly involved his trusted comrades Swede Risberg and Fred "Mac" McMullin. The latter was an often overlooked member of the Sox franchise, but was valuable to Kid Gleason and known for his smarts.[47] But with the addition of twenty-four-year-old infielder Hervey McClellan to the Sox roster, the need for McMullin as a utility player was becoming less and less. His name was dangled by sportswriters in trade rumors and there was additional speculation that he was unhappy with his salary after a holdout earlier in 1919.[48]

Around the same time, *The Sporting News* reported that McMullin and Risberg both yearned to stay in California, similar to the thinking of Gandil, and were considering leaving Major League Baseball behind.[49] If that was again the case, joining an operation that could strengthen their financial situation on the way out was logically sound. With Risberg and McMullin on board, Gandil targeted Lefty Williams before the Sox left New York for Boston, and the pitcher was not overwhelmingly enthusiastic about the idea. He wanted to ponder things over and agreed to discuss it again at a later date.[50]

Next on the list was Joe Jackson, and Gandil waited for a private moment between the two in Boston. According to Jackson's 1920 Cook County (IL) Grand Jury testimony, Chick initially asked him if he would "consider

$10,000 to frame up something," without specifically identifying the objective. Likely confused by the question, Joe asked what he was talking about, and Gandil explained that the World Series was the intended target. "I said no," Jackson later admitted, and the conversation rapidly came to a conclusion. But Gandil wasn't done going after him, not by a long shot. He cornered Jackson again back in Chicago as the season was coming to a close, and offered to double the amount to $20,000, which was the originally planned sum Gandil talked about with Cicotte and Burns in New York, going to each of five players.[51] The $10,000 offer, presumably, was Chick's way of stiffing Joe right off the bat, but Gandil was the only one who knew about it at the time.

Jackson, again following his Grand Jury testimony, turned Gandil's second proposal down. Of course, nobody knows what the exact conversation was or the amount of pressure and influence the latter put forth, but Jackson did acknowledge that Chick told him that he "could either take it or let it alone," but the fix was "going through."[52] This line of persuasion was also used on Williams, and was exceedingly effective.[53] Both Jackson and Williams accepted the word of Gandil that the plot was happening with or without their involvement, and decided to at least make a few bucks in the process. As a result, Jackson agreed to participate in the throwing of the 1919 World Series.[54]

There was no hiding the fact that Jackson was uneducated. He was street smart to a certain extent, not generally "stupid," but a bit naïve. He often looked to others around him for their intellect and leadership on the field, such as Joe Birmingham in Cleveland and Eddie Collins in Chicago, and that was immensely helpful throughout his career. Off the field, however, Joe was "one of the oddest characters in the game's history," as sportswriter W. R. Hoefer explained in 1917.[55] He was utterly unique in so many ways and there was no question that he was one-of-a-kind. But his decision-making was sometimes faulty. The *Greenville News*, his hometown newspaper, described it best in 1915 when it declared: "Joe is a spasmodic sort of a fellow and like in all other of his dealings, he acts quickly and unexpectedly." The article added that Jackson had signed a contract to perform a theatrical act "before he realized what he had done."[56]

Chicago writer George S. Robbins called Jackson a "somewhat erratic person," and viewing a handful of instances over the course of Joe's life, a case could be made to support that statement.[57] His controversial action in 1915 when he refused to join Cleveland because he was performing on vaudeville is a perfect first example. It was believed that Joe was influenced by a clever manipulator who preyed on his lack of sophistication. George B. Greenwood was the smooth talker in this case, promising big money as an actor and businessman, and Joe ate it up. He honestly figured he had a future on the stage, and was threatening to walk away from Organized Baseball because of it. But everyone who knew him recognized it as complete nonsense, and even Katie was imploring him at the time to give up the delusion and return to the diamond.

Some months later, veteran player-manager Joe Tinker of the Chicago Whales Federal League club convinced Jackson that the Indians had violated his contract, thus creating a windstorm of controversy.[58] But the situation was generally baseless and unnecessary. It was another instance of Joe being influenced by a brainy conniver. In 1918, Joe was again pinpointed for manipulation by cunning agents representing Harlan and Hollingsworth, and while he was doing what he felt was right for his family, the way he was ushered into the shipbuilding field was not altogether on the level. From the point of view of the White Sox, Joe was behaving in an underhanded manner and running away from his pending military obligations.

Perceptively, a reporter in January 1919 noted that "Joe was more susceptible to the power of suggestion than most players." Continuing, the journalist wrote, "A fellow player or a friend could persuade him . . . he was a much-abused person or could make him feel tickled with conditions on the team."[59] The combination of making rash decisions and being easily influenced and manipulated were detrimental to Jackson throughout his life, but never more so than when Chick Gandil began working on him in September 1919. It was in Joe's makeup to be in preservation mode, but he hated looking like a fool and definitely didn't want to show his weaknesses to Gandil or his teammates. He undoubtedly didn't ask the right questions to cover himself during the early stages of the plot, particularly the aspect of getting the cash before Game One, and was left wide open for exploitation. Jackson was far out of his league on this one.

So were Happy Felsch, Lefty Williams, Eddie Cicotte, and Buck Weaver, who was also pulled into the scandal. These men were either complicit, persuaded through coercion, or agreed outright to participate in the fix for personal reasons, yet none of them realized just how damaging the scheme would ultimately be. Although these players were baseball-smart, they were far from intellectuals. Felsch possessed a sixth-grade education and, in 1920, called Gandil the "wisest one of the lot," illustrating the latter's mental superiority over his co-conspirators.[60] Regarding Jackson, Shano Collins—a hard-nosed veteran of the Sox since 1910—later said he pitied Joe because of how easily influenced he was.[61]

Probably Joe's biggest mistake was not consulting his most important advisor: his wife Katie. In fact, she was left in the dark until the scheme was already well into motion. Had she been informed, Katie would've more than likely interfered to some extent to protect him as she had always done. She was his voice of reason, his conscience, and acted as a motherly figure in the way she guarded his interests. Hugh Fullerton once wrote that Jackson was "something of a boy himself," clearly referring to his purity in mind and vulnerability.[62] Left to his own devices, Joe was at risk. He needed the wise voice of someone who truly cared about him. Gandil, his teammate, was not such a person. He could not be depended on to look after Joe's best interests, and Jackson was no longer on a playing field he could dominate by way of natural ability. The sharks were navigating around him, and the legendary "Shoeless Joe" was about to fall from grace.

12

THE CONSPIRACY UNFOLDS

Understandably, as America's national pastime, baseball was long embraced by the public as the image of sportsmanship and wholesome competitiveness. The game was played hard but true, and the players themselves were admired for giving everything they had in order to win for the sake of their club, the fans, and their own personal honor. The high-octane energy of games was palpable throughout the stands, and it was nearly impossible not to be drawn into the action. But during its history, baseball had experienced a number of ups and downs and survived several damaging periods of scandal. One of the most explosive situations occurred in 1877, when four members of the Louisville Grays were permanently banned from the sport after revelations of dishonesty were exposed.[1] The leaders of Organized Baseball worked to ensure those on the wrong side of honorable gameplay were severely punished, establishing a precedent and warning to anyone else considering a corrupt practice on the field.

For the most part, baseball avoided any backbreaking exposures of crooked work, but the suspicions of fixed games flared up from time to time. Even during the 1918 World Series, speculation about the genuineness of certain plays inspired conversation, but little else came of it. In the end, there was no firm proof. But the line between honest ballplayers and professional gamblers looking for an edge was not all that profound. In fact, big money bettors were closely situated on the periphery of baseball. In addition, shadowy figures routinely mixed with players in public situations, including in hotel lobbies and pool halls. In terms of the Chicago White Sox, gambling was prevalent among those in the Woodland Bards, the club's official rooter organization. Notably, ex-World Featherweight champion Abe Attell joined the Bards on their special train between New

York and Chicago during the 1917 Series, and the former fighter was well known for his gambling proclivities.[2]

Always looking for insider information, the diminutive 5-foot-4 Attell was in the right place at the right time two years later when Bill Burns was shopping around the gambling plot he discussed with Chick Gandil and Eddie Cicotte in New York. It should be mentioned that Attell was not Burns's first choice as a co-conspirator, as he originally tried to establish a connection with multimillion-dollar gambling maestro Arnold Rothstein to no avail. Burns quickly found Attell to be far more accessible than the notorious bookmaker, who prided himself on secrecy and protected his interests by dealing with only select associates. To Rothstein, Burns might have been pitching a solid idea, but he wasn't trusted enough to form a partnership. He was just not a syndicate man. But Attell didn't care. He saw an opportunity to make big money and hitched himself to the Burns scheme almost immediately.

Attell sold himself to Burns as a middleman between the Sox and Rothstein, which was a complete fabrication, but smartly used to shore up a key role for himself in the scam. He even brought in his friend David Zelcer who under the name "Bennett" was said to be Rothstein's envoy for the deal, and Burns bought the fable hook, line, and sinker. Further explaining that he'd arrange the $100,000 payment for the players, Attell was designated the primary source of funds for the fix, according to what Burns knew at the time. And for his efforts in delivering the money to the tainted athletes, Burns would also garner a percentage.[3] It was a solidly laid plan, at least as far as Burns could see, and he waited to talk with Gandil and Cicotte in person to explain the specifics in detail.

However, Attell wasn't the lone moneyman involved in the fix, thanks to Gandil's shrewd manipulations. While the Sox were in Boston on September 19–20, 1919, he broached the subject of a Series swindle with longtime friend, forty-eight-year-old Joseph J. "Sport" Sullivan. For the greater part of two decades, the solidly built Sullivan was a prominent member of the New England athletic community. Socially adept and smooth in his operations, he confidently mingled with all types of people—from the pool hall hustlers to the wealthy in downtown hotels. Sullivan's greatest asset was his knowledge, and he excelled in all-things baseball. His easygoing relations with ballplayers opened the door to exclusive information that aided his gambling investments and solidified his place among Boston's leading bookmakers. Gandil figured that having "Sport" recruited would bolster the financial output of the fix, and their interests quickly merged into a separate cash agreement for upwards of $80,000.[4]

Most of what is currently understood about the 1919 scandal nearly a hundred years after the fact is still open to debate and interpretation. There are many different versions of what happened and it is nearly impossible to say with absolute certainty that "this or that account is exactly what occurred" between the members of the White Sox and their gambling counterparts. For instance, a number of newspaper outlets would later claim that Hal Chase, the infamous first baseman, was the linchpin for the entire conspiracy. The allegations surfaced that Chase was responsible for bringing both Abe Attell and Bill Burns onboard, and that it was Attell, not Gandil, who initially reached out to Sullivan with an assist from Chase.[5] Yet another depiction claimed that Sullivan was the point of origin for the fix, and that he went to Gandil with the idea.[6] But there are clear and obvious discrepancies, and enough doubt is cast to offer the necessary reminder that the story of the 1919 scandal is anything but cut and dry.

With regard to Joe Jackson, there is an important question: Did he have any other legitimate reasons to consider endangering his baseball future in such a shaky proposition other than being coerced by the statement that the fix was on whether he was involved or not? The simple answer is yes, he did. With the goal of attaining $20,000 for his participation, Jackson anticipated raking in more than three years' salary in one series. Joe had previously admitted that he was fully content with leaving baseball behind after obtaining enough money, and that he was eager to settle into a quieter farm life.[7] But that was in 1912, and Jackson was a much different man in 1919 than he was at that time. He was still interested in making money, but his baseball success had made him one of the most popular stars in the game. Leaving the sport on short notice made little sense, especially since his career was progressing so well and he was likely headed toward immortal glory with his peers in any future hall of fame.

But Jackson was much more sensitive. For a period of seven to eight months between May 1918 and January 1919, he was relentlessly abused and shamed by the press corps. Baseball writers, editorials, and other commentaries slammed his decision to work in the shipyards, condemning him in nearly every way possible. The constant remarks were humiliating, drawing into question his manhood, his ethical sensibilities, his devotion to his country, and every word took its toll. He even told a reporter during the midst of all the chaos, "I shall not attempt to go back to ball playing to make a living."[8] Jackson was undoubtedly saddened by the overwhelming backlash and knew that some of the reporter's resentment had trickled down to the public as well. It was completely unwarranted, he felt, and he managed to live with the criticism each day. Only nine months had passed since the bulk of the condemnation ceased, and not all had been forgotten.

In fact, some fans wouldn't let him forget. During a trip to Detroit in early September 1919, rowdy spectators yelled "shipyards!" at Jackson, hoping to interfere with his game-time concentration.[9] He was usually able to ignore the drunken outbursts of instigators, but the symbolism behind such remarks did nothing but remind everyone of the cruelty he'd received. Within the White Sox camp itself, there were issues that remained unresolved, and much of it related to owner Charles Comiskey. In February, sportswriter George S. Robbins boldly declared: "Jackson has been manhandled and lambasted in a rough manner here, and President Comiskey himself is responsible for the feeling to a great degree, for Commy never has retracted in print what he said about Joe."[10] In another column, Robbins wrote: "We would like to see Commy come out in the open and give Jackson the glad hand. If Comiskey is lukewarm about Jackson, he can't expect the fans to be any other way, especially those who panned him last summer."[11]

While it is not known what, if anything, was said between Comiskey and Jackson in private, it is not believed "The Old Roman" made a public statement withdrawing his previous criticisms. That in itself was enough to leave Joe with a bad taste in his mouth about the Sox, and taking all things into consideration leaves the question: How much real passion did he still have for baseball? He played solid ball in 1919, and his natural abilities were evident as much at the plate as they were in the field. But what was his mind-set? Is it possible that he had anything but animosity toward Comiskey and the press for what he'd been put through? Did he want revenge? Or did he see the $20,000 he was to receive in the fix as a way to finally break free from the Sox and baseball forever?

His agreement to be a part of the conspiracy, and the peace he made with his own conscience as to what was about to happen, might have been predicated, in part, on that fact. But Jackson wasn't a natural schemer, nor was he a gambler. The details of the scam were far outside his realm of understanding. He didn't comprehend the bigger picture: where the growing nature of the fix involved dozens and dozens of components. Jackson didn't understand that such a revelation jeopardized his good name inside and outside of baseball and made him susceptible to any number of potential dangers, including criminal prosecution. Everything he'd worked for throughout his life—his upstanding reputation, his idol status among kids, his astronomical lifetime batting average—would forever be tainted in such an instance, and Joe was either too unaware to understand or just felt the reward outweighed the risk.

A number of secret meetings about the soon-to-be-rigged Series were staged before the White Sox officially captured the American League pennant on September 24, 1919. Jackson contributed two hits in the 6–5 triumph over the St. Louis Browns, and the home crowd at Comiskey Park was thoroughly enthused by the victory.[12] However, many of those same fans were equally disappointed by the performance of the Sox in their subsequent four games, which were the final contests of the regular season. Instead of finishing the campaign with a commanding display of their abilities, Chicago lost all four (one to St. Louis and three against Detroit). "I was extremely sorry to see the Sox play the manner of ball they revealed yesterday," explained longtime fan Dad Kentmor. "It pained me deeply to see our boys play that way. It has been said they are the greatest money team ever assembled, and I guess that is the right dope. There was nothing at stake for them yesterday and they played like a bunch of amateurs."[13]

It was another "money team" reference, but this time made by a fan. Kentmor went on to say, "In the World's Series they will play wonderful ball because they have the incentive of the winning end of the melon before them." Harvey T. Woodruff of the *Chicago Daily Tribune* seemed to agree, pegging the Sox to win over their National League opponents, the Cincinnati Reds. He actually referred to Kid Gleason's club as the "greatest aggregation of money players in baseball."[14] The same went for George S. Robbins, who made a striking comment in the August 28, 1919, edition of *The Sporting News* in sizing up Comiskey's players going into the series: "The Sox are great money players. Show that gang a bunch of coin and they'll do almost anything except commit murder."[15] No one outside the secretive cabal grinding away on the Series fix knew just how accurate the words "money team" were, as the corrupt members of the Sox plotted a record monetary output for players in the event's history. They were forging ahead without the consent of owners to their financial score, and weren't exactly getting executive approval from the National Baseball Commission.

Chick Gandil, Swede Risberg, and Fred McMullin were motivated to go ahead with the idea from its inception. With Gandil leading the way, the trio planned a special confab for the Warner Hotel in Chicago—not overly far from Comiskey Park on the South Side—on September 29, 1919. According to the later recollections of Lefty Williams, who attended the meeting, the roster of participants included Gandil, Eddie Cicotte, Happy Felsch, Buck Weaver, plus the Boston gambler "Sport" Sullivan and his ally "Brown," who was later identified as Rachael Brown.[16] Joe Jackson wasn't present but, by the end of the meeting, a total of eight Sox players were officially tied to the fix whether they wanted to be or not. There was no way to disavow knowledge of what was going to be attempted, and if anyone wanted to back out, the only way was to spill the beans to an outsider and throw his teammates at the mercy of the law.

For the conspirators, having Jackson involved was a major coup. His hard hitting was certainly a key to Chicago's success, and his participation inspired confidence in their ability to follow through. But Eddie Cicotte was even more important. The right-handed pitching ace was going to start two, possibly three games during the Series, and if he was lobbing them over the plate, how could the scheme fail? Cicotte, known for his intelligence, took his time in deciding whether or not to play ball with Gandil, and thoroughly weighed his options. Money, he decided, was the answer to his problems, particularly when it came to paying off his farm's sizable mortgage, and so agreed.[17]

The winner of 29 games during the regular season, Cicotte was acknowledged as one of the sport's finest pitchers, and he told a reporter earlier in 1919 that he could easily pitch for another ten years.[18] But with just half that time as a pro, his status as a future Hall of Famer was pretty much guaranteed. So, like Jackson, he had plenty to lose. Unlike Jackson, Cicotte smartly demanded $10,000 in cash up front and refused to commit his services unless the money was in his possession prior to the start of Game One. "I didn't want any promises," he later admitted.[19] But promises were precisely what Jackson was banking on, taking Gandil at his word that increments of cash would be delivered promptly after each game.[20]

With the World Series fast approaching, sportswriters offered detailed analysis of the two clubs, comparing and contrasting their various styles.

The Cincinnati Reds were a balanced group led by manager Pat Moran, and finished their pennant race with a nine-game advantage over the second-place New York Giants. Center fielder Edd Roush, who began his career with the Sox as a twenty-year-old in 1913, was not only leading the Reds in hitting but the entire National League with a .321 average. Third baseman Heinie Groh was fourth in the league with a .310 average, while three other starters were in the .270 range. As a club, Cincinnati was hitting .263, tied for second in the league with the Brooklyn Robins, and six points behind the Giants. Pitching was the Reds' strength, and Moran had five reliable starters: two lefties and three right-handers. Southpaw Slim Sallee was on the losing end of the 1917 Series as a member of the Giants and was looking for a bit of revenge. His 21 regular season wins were second in the league.[21]

Conversely, the Sox still lacked depth on the mound, but Kid Gleason wasn't worried. He believed in his top two pitchers, knowing that Eddie Cicotte and Lefty Williams had enough talent, conditioning, and resiliency to overcome whatever challenges they faced against the Reds. He also gave them time to recover from the strain of the regular season. "Cicotte says his arm hasn't a trace of lameness," Gleason told a reporter on September 30, "and that means Eddie is ready for the World's Series of 1919. About the only worry I had was Eddie and now I have none."[22] Harry Neily of the *Chicago American* once wrote that Gleason knew "more about the White Sox than anybody in the world," and if he was confident in the shape of his men headed into the Series, who was to doubt him?[23] But Gleason had no clue that Cicotte and Williams were now on the take, and with his star hurlers intentionally trying to lose, the Sox were doomed before the first Series pitch was thrown.

On the political side of things, a majority of owners voted in favor of extending the Series from seven to nine games. The move was sponsored by National Commission chairman Garry Herrmann, and Sox supporters figured it was a sly way for Herrmann to assist Cincinnati because of Chicago's limited pitching staff. After all, Hermann was also a part owner of the Reds. Charles Comiskey was the only man in both leagues to vote against the change, even though the maneuver guaranteed more money for him in the long run. However, he denied his vote had anything to do with his club's limitations.[24] Comiskey wasn't stupid, though, and was keenly aware of how things stood. At that same time, he was holding a personal grudge against his former friend, American League President Ban Johnson, as to the way the latter and the National Commission handled the rights to veteran right-hander Jack Quinn, who was sent to the New York Yankees after Quinn had pitched for the Sox in 1918. Quinn would've potentially filled Chicago's need as a third or fourth starter, and Comiskey was still sore.

The tainted members of the White Sox received their marching orders, the gamblers placed their bets, and the home plate umpire called for "play ball" on Wednesday, October 1, 1919. Over 30,000 people watched from the stands at Redland Field for Game One in Cincinnati, as Cicotte took the mound in the bottom of the first inning. Facing second baseman Morrie Rath—another former Sox castoff—Cicotte threw the first pitch for a called strike. The next sailed high and hit Rath directly in his shoulder, giving him first base.[25] Only later was it revealed that Cicotte's errant pitch wasn't an accident, but purposeful. By hitting Rath, he silently conveyed the message that the fix was on.

Due to the nature of his state of mind in 1919, his afternoon on the mound was no better against the Reds. He pitched for 3 2/3 innings, giving up six runs on seven hits with two walks before Gleason had enough and pulled him. Jackson made his first plate appearance in the second inning, leading off against Dutch Ruether, and slashed one at shortstop Larry Kopf. The latter bobbled the ball and then proceeded to throw it over the first baseman's head, allowing Jackson to reach second on the error. Happy Felsch sacrificed him to third and Chick Gandil singled him home for the first Chicago run . . . their only score of the contest.[26]

The rest of the game was relatively uneventful for the White Sox, with Jackson going 0-for-4 at the plate. The Reds, on the other hand, pummeled Sox pitching for nine runs and 14 hits, winning 9–1. Shano Collins, who started in right field for the Sox, later admitted that by the first game, rumors of a fix had circulated throughout the clubhouse. "I had heard some talk but we all laughed at it," he explained. "Cicotte of course had been badly beaten in the opening game. But we were willing to make allowances for that. You see 'Knuckles' had been complaining of a sore arm during the last month of the regular season. [Additionally], we were willing to accept the explanation that he gave . . . that McMullin had scouted the Reds for two weeks and that he, Cicotte, had pitched according to McMullin's dope, all of which he said was wrong. So we figured it was only an off day for him."[27]

But Collins was in the dark to the genuine truth that his teammates were indeed crooked. In fact, behind the closed doors of the club's hotel, Jackson inquired to Gandil about the first installment of his owed money.[28] Gandil didn't have a good answer. He reportedly was given the shaft by Bill Burns and Abe Attell, leaving the players high and dry.[29] More promises were made and players were again ordered to lose in Game Two the following day. Lefty Williams went to the mound and held the Reds to only four hits, but gave up four costly earned runs. "Our second defeat . . . when Lefty Williams was on the rubber, was unexpected," Collins told a reporter. "In this game we outhit the Reds better than two to one and yet we were hopelessly beaten. Of course, Williams' wildness was mainly responsible. But long afterwards in comparing the respective scores and figuring our ten hits against the Reds four we made note of the fact that none of our ten hits came at the right time."[30]

Jackson achieved his first hit of the Series in the second inning when he smashed a double to left-center, but was stranded at third when the inning closed. In the fourth, he followed Buck Weaver's single with one of his own, but subsequent batters failed to move them along. Joe had an opportunity in the sixth to drive home a run with Weaver on second, but struck out on three straight pitches. He achieved his third hit of the afternoon in the eighth with two outs, but it had no influence on the game's final totals.[31] And with that the Reds were victorious in Game Two, 4–2. With the Series heading to Chicago for Game Three, players checked out of their hotel and boarded a train westward. While en route, they discussed the two previous games at length, trying to get a beat on what was happening, but were incredibly stumped by the turn of events.[32]

Once again, Jackson asked Gandil about his money, and again Chick didn't have a response other than to blame Burns and Attell for not fulfilling their part of the deal.[33] The crooked players had done their part, purposefully striving to lose the first two games of the Series.

Looking at Jackson's performance, the question to be asked was: What had he contributed to the fix? He'd gone 3-for-8 at the plate for a .375 batting average, garnered a double and a run, and played flawlessly in the field. Twice he went to bat with men in scoring position—in the sixth inning of both the first and second games—but failed to produce. In the past, when Jackson was having a bad day or acting indifferently on the field, everyone knew it. For instance, a writer for the *Cleveland Leader* in 1912 noted seeing Joe "loaf" going after a ball "many times."[34] In June 1913, a reporter felt his "sulking" actually cost the Naps a game.[35] His downcast attitude was obvious.

So far, for Jackson, there was no sulking, no apparent miscues, and nothing he had personally done to raise suspicion. His role in the active fix was minimal, but Joe still wanted the money he was promised. When Gandil failed to produce the cash, he was left with very few options. It wasn't like he could complain to a reporter, and he certainly was in no position to go over Chick's head and converse with the higher-ups. Jackson was out on a vine with his compatriots and at the mercy of those unscrupulous characters he agreed to join. But facing Gandil and Swede Risberg with any type of aggressiveness was also looking for trouble, as both were imposing tough guys. And that was a situation Jackson was going to avoid. Needless to say, the intimidation shown by Gandil and Risberg was going to prevent anyone from running off and ratting on the deal. For the time being, each of the players involved were supposed to lay low and wait it out.

But Jackson didn't know that Gandil had collected $10,000 from Burns and Attell after the second game, just before leaving Cincinnati.[36] And he wouldn't see a dime of it. Additionally, Burns passed along Attell's orders, indicating he wanted the Sox to win the third game to improve the overall odds for the Series. According to the testimony of Burns in 1921, Gandil and those privy to the inside information agreed, but once back in Chicago, Chick notified Burns that the third game was going to have the same result as the first two. That, in turn, motivated Burns, his pal Billy Maharg (who had been with him on the scam from the start), and Attell to bet heavy on Cincinnati, assured that the Sox were going to throw the game. However, Burns later realized Chick had no intention of losing the third game. In a double-cross fashion, as a way to punish the gamblers for not paying up, the Sox went forward and beat the Reds, 3–0.[37]

That version was told by Burns himself, who felt personally deceived because of Gandil's suspected lie. Yet in 1920, Jackson claimed the crooked members of the club really tried to lose the third game, and Chicago won only because the honest Sox stepped up.[38] If this was true, then Gandil never lied to Burns and didn't double-cross the gamblers purposefully. It was just the result of the chance involved in such a scheme. With a number of nonparticipants actively trying to win, the result was never guaranteed. Going back to the third game itself, the honest Sox were more enthusiastic than ever to win, and Kid Gleason was determined to have his men in the right frame of mind before the contest began.

Shano Collins later remembered: "When we reported at the grounds, Gleason called us into the clubhouse, chased out the trainer and clubhouse boy, and then read the riot act. He told us that the word was going around that some of the Chicago White Sox had sold out the Series and that it was up to us to throttle the rumor. This talk put us on edge, and we went in against the Reds to give them a real battle. Little Dick Kerr pitched this game, and it was the first of the Series we won. We never knew, Kerr never dreamed that he and four loyal players were downing Cincinnati and half of his own team. The alleged testimony of Jackson and others has stated how little Dick won in spite of treachery by his mates. And even at that it took a couple of lucky breaks to get us the decision."

Rookie Dickey Kerr was the star of the day. He held the Reds scoreless with his pinpoint control and the Sox offense came up with three runs to push Chicago to its first victory of the Series. Strikingly, the team was in a fighting mood; utterly refusing to relent on its path to victory. Eddie Collins nearly came to blows with Reds utilityman Jimmy Smith, and only Gleason prevented a fistfight. "Then Jackson and [pitcher Ray] Fisher had a row because Fisher shot one at Joe's bean and Joe bunted one toward first base, daring Fisher to go over and cover the bag," Gleason explained. "Joe was mad enough to have spiked him, too, but nothing came of that."[39] Altogether, Jackson went 2-for-3 with a run in the game, including base hits to start the second and sixth innings. He eventually scored in the second, but was caught trying to steal second in the sixth. Joe had another opportunity in the third inning with two men on, but errantly popped up his bunt attempt to first baseman Jake Daubert.[40]

If Gandil and his allies in the fix consciously decided to win behind "busher" Kerr in the third game, either Jackson was left out of the plan or refused to admit it based on his later revelations.[41] But looking at the box score, it was obvious those players tied to the conspiracy were more motivated to win than they previously demonstrated. They contributed five of the seven Sox hits, two of the three RBIs, and all three runs. Gandil himself was responsible for both of those RBIs, and Risberg added a triple.[42] Burns and Attell learned very quickly that the players had a measure of recourse if they didn't honor their end of the deal. As for Kid Gleason, he was thrilled by what appeared to be a full renewal of his team's unity and drive to win. Fans and local sportswriters were also revitalized by the victory, and with the usually competent Cicotte returning to the slab for Game Four, hopes were high in Chicago.

But Game Four was a lifeless effort by the Sox players. They compiled just three hits off Cincinnati pitcher Jimmy Ring and were unable to score, while the Reds garnered five hits and two runs. Cicotte, instead of building upon what Kerr had started, shamelessly disappointed, and his fifth-inning performance was the turning point of the contest. The madness started with one out and Pat Duncan at the plate. Duncan hit a grounder up the middle and Cicotte made a nice stop. He rushed his throw to Gandil at first, but the peg was way off target, allowing Duncan to reach second. Larry Kopf followed with a single to left field. Jackson made a great stop and unflinchingly threw toward home plate to prevent Duncan from scoring. Surprisingly, Cicotte stepped in front of the ball to cut it off, and it ricocheted off his glove for his second error of the inning. Duncan scored on the play and Kopf continued on to second. Greasy Neale proceeded to add to Chicago's misery by smashing a double over the head of Jackson in left, scoring Kopf, and giving the Reds a 2–0 lead.[43]

"The . . . game was another upset," Shano Collins explained. "I think it was here that our players really began to be convinced that there was something really wrong. We were feeling rather downcast that night. I don't mind saying right now that some of us began to pay a little more attention to the stories that were circulating more widely every hour."[44] Jackson went 1-for-4, and his double to start the second inning initiated a potential rally, but Cicotte drew the third out with the bases loaded. After the contest, Lefty Williams visited his [Jackson's] room at the Lexington Hotel in Chicago's South Loop and delivered $5,000 in cash, compiled of "mostly fifties."[45] This would be the only crooked money of the entire conspiracy that Jackson would see, and was but one-fourth of his promised amount. Williams was actually given $10,000, but kept half, as it was the only cash he'd seen to that point as well.[46]

Jackson was bought and partially paid for by gamblers at that juncture, and nothing in history could change that ugly truth. Prior to being paid, he was definitely complicit and possibly committed to doing his part in the throwing of games. But, after cash changed hands, the famous "Shoeless Joe" was unequivocally stained by the corruptness of the 1919 baseball scandal. According to Jackson's Grand Jury testimony, Katie first learned about the fix that same night following the fourth game, and she "thought it was an awful thing to do."[47] Nobody knows what was said between them in their hotel room that night, but it is likely Joe gained a better perspective of what he'd involved himself in from his wife than at any previous time.

No one on the team was going to be the straight-shooter that Katie was, and none of his co-conspirators were looking out for his best interests like she had always done. It is within good probability that Katie informed Joe just how much trouble he could be in for his faulty thinking.

Incidentally, touching upon Jackson's mind-set a little more, it must be noted that Cincinnati applied a heavy dose of psychological warfare during the Series. "The Reds were primed to abuse and insult certain Sox players with the idea of getting them angry," Hugh Fullerton later wrote. Twenty-four-year-old utility player Jimmy Smith, "a hot head and fighter at heart," was a base coach for the Reds and the lead instigator. He worked on Eddie Collins relentlessly, nearly drawing the Sox captain into a physical altercation. Fullerton noted that Jackson was targeted for abuse as well.[48] Of course, Jackson was thin-skinned about his wartime duty with Harlan and Hollingsworth, and the Reds took advantage of that unique sensitivity. As the *Indianapolis Star* reported, "The Reds . . . annoyed Joe Jackson intensely by constantly referring to the shipyards league."[49] It seemed that part of his life was something he'd never live down.

With the Reds ahead three games to one, the Series appeared nearly out of reach for the Sox, but Chicago fans yearned for a turnaround. They wanted to see the real club of 1919; a team many people considered to be the best ever constructed. Things didn't improve in the fifth game at Comiskey Park on October 6, the day after a Sunday rainout. The Sox were ineffectual behind the pitching of Lefty Williams, achieving three hits and no runs against the mastery of Reds pitcher Hod Eller, who struck out nine in a 5–0 victory. The loss left the Sox players (at least those who were trying) nearly comatose in a Series they were supposed to win.[50] Jackson was completely shut down by the right-handed Eller, and went 0-for-4. Twice he went to the plate with men in scoring position, and twice he failed to bring them home.

The Series returned to Cincinnati for Game Six on October 7, and it was do or die for the Sox. Kid Gleason called upon Kerr again, and Dickey pitched 10 innings of hard-nosed baseball. In the end, the Sox won 5–4, and Chicago was able to live another day. Jackson went 2-for-4 on the day with a run and an RBI, and contributed to big rallies in the sixth and tenth innings. Twice, though, he was doubled up on the baselines after the defense made difficult catches—once by Edd Roush in the eighth and the other by Larry Kopf in the tenth. In the fourth inning, Joe made a spectacular defensive play of his own by snaring a fly by Jake Daubert and launched a perfect throw to catcher Ray Schalk to nail Morrie Rath at the plate.[51] Jackson garnered another two hits the following day in Game Seven, helping the Sox beat the Reds, 4–1. This time, Joe's clutch hitting drove in runs in both the first and third innings, and Cicotte went the distance to halt Cincinnati's charge for a fifth and final Series victory.[52]

There has been ample speculation that dissatisfied Sox conspirators decided to forge ahead after the fifth game (Cincinnati was leading 4–1) and make a serious comeback attempt to win the Series outright. The wins in Games Six and Seven were indicative of a team effort, and Cicotte's performance in the latter contest was more in tune with his regular season showing. Gamblers who'd bet on Cincinnati going all the way were dismayed by the sudden burst of energy displayed by Chicago, and it was alleged that Lefty Williams was menaced by a mysterious man prior to Game Eight to ensure the Sox would lose. If it did indeed happen, the threat to Williams and perhaps to his wife as well was cause enough for Lefty to pitch about as poor a performance as a major leaguer could. On October 9, 1919, at Comiskey Park, Williams lasted but part of the first inning and gave up four runs on four hits.

Jackson provided some excitement in the third inning by hitting the first home run of the Series into the right-field bleachers. He also added a double in the eighth which scored two runs. In the bottom of the ninth, with two outs and two men on, and the Sox trailing by five runs, Jackson grounded to second baseman Morrie Rath to end the game and the Series.[53] The Cincinnati Reds won, 10–5, and captured the 1919 World Series title. Following the game, Kid Gleason told a reporter: "The Reds beat the greatest ball team that ever went into a World's Series. But it wasn't the real White Sox. They played baseball for me only a couple or three of the eight days. Something was wrong. I didn't like the betting odds. I wish no one had ever bet a dollar on the team."[54]

As could be expected, there was a certain amount of "resentment [by members of the Sox] toward some of the players who did not perform up to expectations," as observed by a writer for the *Chicago Daily Tribune*.[55] The failure of these men to execute their ordinary level of play made them possible suspects in the growing rumors of a Series fix. Of those involved, Chick Gandil batted .233, Happy Felsch .192, Swede Risberg .080, and the Sox defense committed an uncharacteristic 12 errors in eight games. So uncharacteristic, as they had made 176 errors as a team in 1919, which was the second lowest in the American League that season.

For Joe Jackson, he played well, carrying the highest batting average of the Sox regulars (.375, 12-for-32), and the most hits (12—a World Series record), runs (5), RBIs (6), and highest slugging percentage (.563). He also made no errors. Captain Eddie Collins, who was one of the Series disappointments, acknowledged Joe's work in the *Chicago Daily News*, stating that Jackson "maintained his reputation with the stick." Ray Schalk agreed, noting, "Joe Jackson hit as hard as he did during the season, or even a little better."[56]

Writer Oscar C. Reichow added, "Jackson certainly demonstrated that a World's Series makes little difference to him. He played up to his standard."[57] However, not everyone felt a high average was representative of a player truly performing on the level. "Some of the men accused of crookedness have pointed to the fact that they hit well up in the averages for this Series, and that their fielding was well-nigh faultless," said Shano Collins. "I won't argue with them along this line. I will only state that very few of these hits were made at the proper time and that errors were made just when they cost the most."[58] Jackson failed to produce a total of eight times when men were on base, seven of them with runners in scoring position. These facts are not definitive proof of Jackson's contributions to the fix, but it does highlight other mitigating factors of his Series play. In truth, no one to this day can say for sure whether Jackson played honest and true baseball during the 1919 World Series. All we have are the stats, and they only tell part of the story.

13

EXPOSED AND SHAMED

The whispering and unsubstantiated reports circulating the World Series did not halt with the climax of Game Eight. Not by a long shot. The rumors continued at a fevered pitch, and excitable journalists were chomping at the bit for any type of insight into what was potentially the biggest story in baseball history. Many of these same journalists diligently compiled a list of suspected White Sox, the athletes most likely involved based on their missteps during the battle with Cincinnati. But fearing libel lawsuits, they were hesitant to make open accusations in their regular newspaper columns because there simply was no firm evidence one way or the other. No one could say with confidence that any particular member of the Chicago club was, in fact, crooked.

White Sox owner Charles Comiskey, American League President Ban Johnson, and the National Commission were obstructed by the same legalities. All things considered, Comiskey, a lifelong baseball man, was facing an immense embarrassment, and, with the most to lose by a destructive scandal, initiated a private investigation to sort through the mess. He offered $10,000 for proof, and his emissaries scrambled to find anyone claiming knowledge of a fix.[1] However, some sportswriters weren't yet convinced of any transgressions. Joe Vila, a well-known New York baseball expert, was one of them. "The Reds captured the big title fairly, squarely, and honestly," he declared in *The Sporting News*. "Fools there were, not baseball men, who tried to create the impression that there was something screwy about the Series, but you'll always run across such skeptics no matter where you go."[2] Non-believers insisted the Sox were overrated, its pitchers run down from the strain of the regular season, and were plainly beaten by a superior ballclub.

Collyer's Eye, an alternative newspaper in Chicago devoted to the stock market, gambling, and various professional sports, was heavily active in reporting on the fix in the weeks and months following the Series. Frank O. Klein, the paper's "special investigator," boldly declared that seven of Comiskey's players were "under suspicion," and made a brief comment touching upon an extraordinary motivation for Sox conspirators overlooked for the most part heretofore. Klein wrote, "The plunging Texans, for whom a trap nicely baited was set and sprung."[3] The Texans he was referring to were a group of millionaire oilmen from Wichita Falls, who ventured from their southern hamlet with gobs of money, fully prepared to back the Sox to the hilt.[4] Led by Chicago native Jack Art, a heavy Texas oil investor, the estimated twenty-five businessmen were prime fodder for gamblers. It is also very likely that they were seen as vulnerable targets for the tainted Sox themselves, as the players knew the faction was attending the Series for gambling purposes.

Back during spring training, the Sox were the vulnerable ones. A correspondent for *The Sporting News* called the players "easy marks for salesmen," citing their unabashed eagerness in purchasing oil leases after being promised fortunes beyond comprehension by fast-talking Texas agents.[5] Even as late as September, just before the Series began, Joe Jackson was considering the idea.[6] With regard to the susceptibility of the pro-Sox Texas contingent in a fixed Series, Chick Gandil might have had personal reasons for wanting to see the oilmen duped. Early in his career he played ball for Amarillo, and the latter was engaged in a heated feud with the Wichita Falls club. There was apparently bad blood on both sides of the diamond, and the memories still resonated with Gandil more than a dozen years later.

While Klein, Hugh Fullerton, and other journalistic sleuths worked the angles and lifted the veil on the guilty conspirators a little at a time, the honest Sox players went to their winter residences stunned by the turn of events. "Before we left Chicago, rumor had already hinted that eight of the White Sox were involved in the scandal," Shano Collins explained. "We started to figure out who these could be by a process of elimination. And one by one we were able to decide, although there was nothing tangible upon which to base our suspicions. We were just like you and a good many others—we couldn't prove anything. Some of us got into communication with each other during the winter, and by the time spring arrived we had practically decided upon who the traitors really were."[7]

The usually reserved Ray Schalk couldn't contain his rancor, and without specifically declaring the men guilty told *Collyer's Eye* in late 1919 that Jackson, Gandil, Eddie Cicotte, Lefty Williams, Fred McMullin, Swede Risberg, and Happy Felsch "would be missing from the lineup in 1920."[8] Notably, Buck Weaver was previously acknowledged by Klein as being "clean as a hound's tooth."[9] But Eddie Collins believed something was up with Weaver's play, and cited an example in the first inning of the opening game against the Reds. "The first man up for us was Leibold (sic)," Collins remembered. "Nemo singled and when I attempted to sacrifice him I forced the lad at second. The next man up was Weaver. On the second ball pitched Weaver gave me the 'hit and run' signal and I was caught off second the proverbial mile. When I returned to the bench I immediately accused Weaver of not even attempting to hit the ball."[10] Weaver would be the eighth member of the Sox to be associated with the plot.

Eddie Murphy, who participated in three Series contests for the Sox as a pinch-hitter, disagreed with Schalk and thought Joe Jackson put up a heroic performance. "Jackson's hitting was wonderful," he declared. "He was robbed of a number of hits by sensational fielding, but even so he came through with many a timely clout."[11] Cleveland sportswriter Henry P. Edwards, who covered Jackson throughout his tenure with the Naps, felt Joe's weaknesses during the Series were much more evident on defense, stating, "Joe Jackson and Happy Felsch messed up more fly balls to their gardens in the eight games than they would do ordinarily in two entire seasons." Edwards didn't believe the Series was fixed, though.[12] Observers definitely had a variance of opinions on the play of Jackson, which later caused many arguments as to whether he was an active (or even willing) participant in any scam.

Nevertheless, Jackson was affiliated with the other seven suspects, and the $3,254.36 he made as part of the loser's share of the Series pot was withheld by team officials, pending the outcome of an investigation.[13] Before the end of October, he sent a letter to Sox headquarters—specifically to Comiskey—and inquired about the money he was due. Comiskey responded on November 11, 1919, and addressed the "adverse talk . . . reflecting on [his] integrity in the recent World's Series," and invited him to return to Chicago to discuss the situation (even offering to pay his expenses to and from Chicago). Comiskey denied he had anything to do with holding up his share of the Series funds, and recommended Joe contact Kid Gleason instead. A few days later, Jackson responded, denoting his surprise at being tied to the controversy, and insisted "my playing proved that I did all I could to win." He told Comiskey he sent a letter to Gleason, further inquiring about his Series share, and would agree to appear and clear his name once he heard back regarding his money.[14]

Comiskey didn't put any additional pressure on Jackson to make a formal statement about the Series and, on December 14, after a two-month investigation, revealed that no evidence proving the guilt of his players had been found. "I am now very happy to state that we have discovered nothing to indicate any member of my team double-crossed me or the public last fall," he announced.[15] The inquest wasn't yet over, Comiskey confirmed, and he declared: "If I land the goods on any of my players I will see to it that there is no place in Organized Baseball for them. There will be no white-washing or compromising with crooks, but as yet not one bit of reliable evidence has turned up."[16] Soon thereafter, the withheld Series shares were released to the suspected Sox players, and the regular offseason baseball talk took the attention of fans. As far as they were concerned, with no new information being dispensed, the 1919 Series was a thing of the past.

For the "money players" of the White Sox, the cash-grab of the corrupt Series didn't dissuade them from seeking greater salaries from management headed into 1920. Realistically, it took a bold kind of man to hijack the biggest event in baseball for money, then to hold up his club—the same club he purposely injured by throwing games—demanding to be rewarded for his prowess. But that is exactly what Cicotte, Weaver, and Jackson did. Less than a month after the Series ended, it was claimed that Cicotte wanted $15,000 to play ball for Chicago in 1919, while Jackson wanted $10,000. Cicotte, a 29-game winner in his 1919 campaign, was even quoted as saying, "The Sox can afford to pay me $15,000 a year and I think my record of 1919 satisfies the fans I am entitled to it."[17] Their collective brassiness reflected men of apparently clear conscience, and there were no signs of simply wanting to make good for the sake of the Sox, its owner, or the fans in light of what they had done.

If you only considered his regular season performance (.351 batting average, which was fourth in the American League, 181 hits, 31 doubles, 14 triples, and 96 RBIs) and his Series statistics (.375 batting average, 12 hits, 6 RBIs), Jackson was a logical choice for a salary bump. After all, his $6,000 was paltry compared to some of the league's other top stars and based on his numbers alone, he deserved an increase. But there were always extenuating factors when it came to Joe's career. Prior to the 1919 season, he was breaking back into baseball after quitting the team during the war. Comiskey didn't see any reason to give him any kind of a raise at that contentious juncture. Now, a year later, Joe's name was connected to perhaps the greatest scandal in the sport's history. His traitorous actions were unpardonable if true, and once again Comiskey was more than a little hesitant to reward him for a job well done.

But the sixty-year-old Comiskey was being held over a barrel. Nothing was in the record establishing the guilt of his men, and they were essentially untouchable in the eyes of the law. The players remained on his active roster and he literally had three options. One was to initiate a fast and painless trade, pawning the allegedly tainted players off to another owner. Another was to undercut their salaries with the understanding that they would never play for that lesser sum and force them into retirement. And finally that he could re-sign them and let 1920 develop naturally. Since Comiskey had no idea if real evidence would ultimately be presented, he was rolling the dice and allowing fate to dictate the course. In a way, both Comiskey and Jackson were both in the same boat in that regard, and until something concrete was presented, both sides were going to continue as normal.[18]

According to insider gossip, Comiskey did work the trade angle for most of the supposedly crooked players during the winter months, and Jackson was indeed involved in those talks. Joe LeBlanc of *Collyer's Eye* reported that Jackson was going to the New York Yankees in a straight trade for Home Run Baker. However, Jackson's final destination was Boston, LeBlanc noted, "as one of the terms of the sale of Babe Ruth to the Yankees was that [owner Colonel T. L.] Huston replace the 'Home Run King' with a hard-hitting outfielder."[19] Ruth, incidentally, hit 29 home runs for Boston in 1919, and was sold to the Yankees for a record $100,000 on December 26. *Collyer's Eye* also claimed Buck Weaver and Swede Risberg were headed to the Yankees as well, while Chick Gandil and Fred McMullin were going to be traded to Los Angeles of the Pacific Coast League for ex-Chicagoan Jack Fournier and a pitcher to be named.[20] Finally, Happy Felsch was to be sent to Philadelphia for pitcher Scott Perry.[21] None of these rumors, however, panned out.

From the letter he received from Comiskey, Jackson was well aware that his name was circulating among the purported Series fixers. However, he obviously felt his ground was sturdy enough to press for a raise. He set his mind on a three-year contract for $10,000 annually, with the 10-day clause eliminated, and rejected the initial offer of $7,000 offered by Comiskey in a letter to Jackson on January 29, 1920. The latter amount was $1,000 more than he received in 1919, and Comiskey felt it was a "very liberal increase." Jackson disagreed. He made it known that he had an opportunity to expand his "Billiard Business" and make more money than was being proposed. The best the Sox could do, under the circumstances, was give him a two-year agreement worth $7,000, but again Joe turned it down.[22] By February 13, 1920, Jackson's holdout was national news, and it was clear he was prepared to quit baseball if his terms weren't met.

Harvey T. Woodruff of the *Chicago Daily Tribune* understood Jackson was using his poolroom enterprise as leverage to get a bigger salary, but simply declared, "His business probably won't interfere with his playing ball with the White Sox this coming season."[23] There was no reason why he couldn't maintain his company back home and still aid the Sox in a pennant race. Fed up with the lack of progress, Comiskey sent Sox business manager Harry Grabiner to Savannah to discuss contract specifics with Jackson in person. Grabiner had already spent part of February in the South, overseeing the layout of the diamond for spring training at Waco, Texas, and was more than willing to venture eastward to help the Sox cause.[24] At the time, though, Jackson was facing some personal issues, as his sister Gertrude was battling an illness. The timing of Grabiner's arrival was inopportune but, to fulfill the obligations of the club, the latter went ahead with his mission.

And with Grabiner's arrival, Joe signed his contract. He agreed to a three-year deal worth $8,000.[25] The specific details of the signing and exact contents of the contract would later come up in court proceedings, but as far as Jackson was concerned, he was returning to the Sox for the 1920 baseball season with a $2,000 raise. It should be noted that Grabiner was not coy with Jackson about the alleged fix and openly talked about the subject. But Joe didn't admit a thing, withholding the evidence Organized Baseball needed to crack the story open. Jackson was all too ready to move on. Upon arriving in Waco for spring training on March 16, Jackson displayed his upbeat attitude. "I'm going to do my best to lead the American League in batting this year," Jackson told a reporter. "I won't say that I'll beat Cobb's record, but I'm going to hustle for the lead at the start and try to hold it."[26] His motivation was reminiscent of earlier in his career when he was starved to beat Cobb for the batting title. But that enthusiasm had waned recently. Whether Jackson was feeling inspired by his new contract or compelled to prove himself in light of the Series allegations, he was nonetheless ready to have his best season in more than half a decade.

Right from the start of spring training, Kid Gleason was battling an uphill fight. He was without any of his starting infielders for a good part of the first week, and Chick Gandil sent word he was leaving Chicago to manage an independent club in Idaho. Gandil's pals Swede Risberg and Fred McMullin were also threatening to leave the Sox, and writer Hugh Fullerton felt the trio's exit presented a major problem. "Perhaps nothing could be worse for baseball than this," he declared. "If three or more players quit after all that has been charged against some of the players, the fans will at once jump at the conclusion that the charges are true and that the men 'got theirs' and are willing to quit."[27] Gandil and his cronies did "get theirs," and Chick was more than willing to demonstrate his freshly acquired wealth by purchasing a new home in California. Whereas Risberg, McMullin, Buck Weaver, Eddie Cicotte, Lefty Williams, and Happy Felsch eventually joined Jackson in camp, Gandil went into a self-imposed retirement.

As a result of all the chaos, Gleason wore the hallmarks of "mental distress," *Chicago Daily Tribune* reporter James Crusinberry noted, and the Sox manager experienced "bales of trouble with eccentric and mercenary players."[28] Once the holdouts were reeled into camp and everyone went to work, Gleason attempted to restore Chicago's championship form. But there were other complications bubbling underneath the surface which couldn't be righted by Gleason's immense baseball knowledge and leadership. "Suspicion pervaded the White Sox atmosphere," Shano Collins explained. "We were two different outfits in the same club. Eddie Murphy, [Red] Faber, [Dickey] Kerr, Eddie Collins, [Roy] Wilkinson, [Nemo] Leibold, and one or two others of us hung closely together. The others made up a group by themselves. The old days of card playing and knocking about together had passed away. It's tough when you can't trust the man beside you. That's the way we felt.

"You might have noticed a difference in the way the players acted. In batting practice before the game, at Comiskey Park, as well as along the circuit, the loyal players stood at one side of the plate and the others were by themselves. We seldom spoke, excepting to discuss a play or something connected with the game. There was no more friendship among us."[29] Camaraderie was always a crucial element in Chicago's success and the absence of cohesion, the lack of trust, and failing confidence stripped the Sox of many of its most important characteristics. The house was divided to its core and Kid Gleason was the one man in the middle trying to sort it all out. It's no wonder the strain was showing . . . and the season had yet to start.

Jackson engaged in a little roughhousing with catcher Byrd Lynn, one of his closest friends on the team, toward the end of the exhibition schedule, and "dislocated his Adam's apple," according to what Gleason told a journalist. Lynn apparently inflicted the injury with a powerful headlock, but Jackson dismissed the seriousness of it, claiming he only had a cold. He missed a game in Memphis on April 8, but was back in harness when the season kicked off on April 14 against Detroit at Comiskey Park. The Sox won the initial contest in 11 innings, 3–2, yet Jackson was ineffective at the plate. But his offensive firepower came to life in subsequent games and aided Chicago to a 10–2 record. Joe's batting average remained above .400 for the first three weeks of the season and he had a 12-game hitting streak going before being stopped by right-hander Stan Coveleski of Cleveland on May 5. During that difficult series with the Indians, wherein the Sox lost four of five, Jackson's average dropped 48 points to .386.

While in St. Louis, also in early May 1920, Jackson and Lefty Williams were mistakenly nabbed as "suspicious characters" by plain-clothes police officers as they were walking back to their hotel after a show. The officers were apparently so sure of the players' dubious identities that they pointed their pistols at them before the situation was cleared up.[30] The month of May was a difficult stretch for the White Sox, as the club went 13–16, falling to fourth place, and Jackson's average dropped to .355 on May 31—the lowest it would be all season. Additionally, he missed four games because of ptomaine poisoning.[31] He tried to skip the doubleheader against St. Louis on May 31, but Kid Gleason convinced him to play despite his continued illness.[32] The American League pennant was up for grabs after all, and each of the top six clubs—Cleveland, Boston, New York, Chicago, Washington, and St. Louis—played solid championship ball at times. But by the end of June, the race tightened into a three-way fight between the Indians, Sox, and Yankees.

At Washington on July 14, 1920, Jackson made two embarrassingly poor decisions in the field to cost the Sox a win. The first instance occurred in the fifth inning with two men out. Sam Rice was at bat with two runners on when he lined one toward right field. Joe, who was playing in right instead of his normal left-field position (because left in Washington was considered a "sun field"), tried to make a daring grab on the fly, but failed. The ball bounced past him and rolled all the way to the wall, allowing Rice and the two runners ahead of him to score. Three innings later, Braggo Roth, a player involved in the 1915 trade that sent Jackson to Chicago, lifted a fly near the right-field foul line. Jackson overran the ball, which dropped for a triple, and another run scored. Washington ended up winning the contest, 6–4. A reporter for the *Chicago Daily Tribune* believed that had Nemo Leibold been in right for the Sox that day instead of Jackson, the result might have been different.[33]

Two days later, Jackson avenged his mistakes before the Griffith Stadium audience in Washington by going 3-for-4 with three runs, four RBIs, and a grand slam. His round tripper came in the ninth inning and gave the Sox the win, 8–5.[34]

In August, Chicago achieved first place during an important East Coast road trip, and Joe's slugging was the driving force for the club. At Shibe Park in Philadelphia on August 20, he drove in five runs with homers in both the first and second games of a doubleheader. Altogether, he went 5-for-9 with four runs and seven RBIs on the day, and the Sox proved their dominance over the Athletics, 7–4 and 5–2 (forfeit).[35] Chicago remained in first heading into Boston on August 30, but the team was hanging on by a thread. And not only was the clubhouse environment still unstable, but there was a growing belief that the 1919 Series suspects were continuing to fix games.

"You may remember our last visit this year to Boston," Shano Collins later explained. "Just before we came there the Red Sox had started a spurt and were beating all comers. This allowed us to creep up to the top, or very near it, for we had been fattening at Cleveland's and New York's expense. And we reached the Hub with a splendid chance to go away out in front. Well, we lost all three games. Cicotte was batted out of the box. Our men were hopeless at the bat. The big stickers fell down miserably. I have heard a lot about certain players watching the scoreboard while playing in the Hub and not trying as hard as they might. Well, I am not going to discuss that. I only know that we lost three straight to the Red Sox, that our defeat put the Indians in first place and that we left Boston with every hope blasted."[36]

The three losses at Boston were part of a string of seven straight defeats overall, sending the Sox in a spiral toward third place. A few days later, Chicago regained second from the Yankees, but the pressure to regain the lead proved too much for Gleason's men. Aside from a brief stint tied for first on September 10, the Sox were unable to retake the top position. They finished the 1920 season with a 96–58 record, in second place behind Cleveland. The Indians, following the accidental beanball death of the popular shortstop Ray Chapman on August 17, were the sentimental favorites to win both the league pennant and World Series.[37] They knocked off the Sox and Yankees to capture the American League flag and then toppled the Brooklyn Robins in seven games for the World Series title. For fans country-wide, it was a befitting end to what had become a tragic season.

Backtracking a little bit, baseball as a whole was faced with another heart-breaking situation the last week of September 1920, and this one tied directly to the conspiracy of 1919. Chief Justice Charles A. McDonald of the Cook County (Chicago, IL) Criminal Court organized a special grand jury to investigate gambling in the national pastime, and planned to call innumerable witnesses from players to owners to sportswriters. There was literally no telling which direction the investigation was going to go, but the size and scope of the inquiry was sure to unsheathe many of the game's hidden skeletons. Jackson, for one, saw the writing on the wall. He told Happy Felsch before practice one day that he'd soon be facing the inquisitors, "the way things looked."[38] He was concerned, and rightfully so, because there was a wide range of possible implications which could include potential criminal charges.

The grand jury began its inquest during the final days of the 1920 season, and cast a pretty large shadow over the White Sox. In fact, the mainstream media, which had avoided printing the names of those suspected to be involved in the scandal, decided to publicly name the eight Sox players involved in the alleged "scandal" on September 25.[39] Jackson and his mates were on the front pages of newspapers from coast to coast, and although there still wasn't evidentiary proof, the insinuation of their guilt was loud and clear. That same day, the Sox were finishing up a three-game series at Cleveland, and the fans at Dunn Field, who never were all that polite to Jackson to begin with, leveled the Sox with a torrent of insults. "I wish you could realize how downcast we felt, how ashamed we were when we had to face that big crowd of fans at Cleveland," Shano Collins remembered. "I can hear those yells of 'crook,' 'traitor,' 'look out for the grand jury' yet ringing in my ears. It's a wonder that the fans didn't mob some of the team."[40]

Jackson played through the outbursts, hammering two doubles and a home run in four at-bats. The next day, the club was back in Chicago for a Sunday afternoon contest against Detroit. A throng estimated to be between

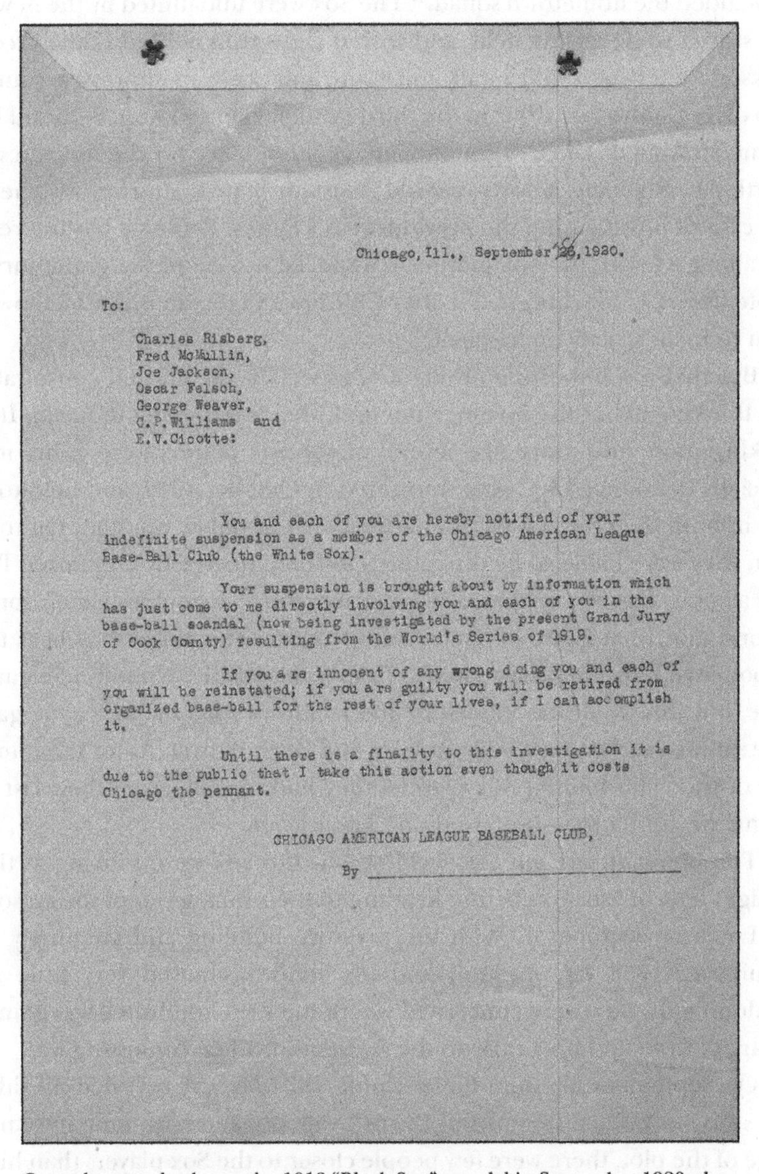

Chicago, Ill., September 28, 1920.

To:

Charles Risberg,
Fred McMullin,
Joe Jackson,
Oscar Felsch,
George Weaver,
C.P. Williams and
E.V. Cicotte:

You and each of you are hereby notified of your indefinite suspension as a member of the Chicago American League Base-Ball Club (the White Sox).

Your suspension is brought about by information which has just come to me directly involving you and each of you in the base-ball scandal (now being investigated by the present Grand Jury of Cook County) resulting from the World's Series of 1919.

If you are innocent of any wrong doing you and each of you will be reinstated; if you are guilty you will be retired from organized base-ball for the rest of your lives, if I can accomplish it.

Until there is a finality to this investigation it is due to the public that I take this action even though it costs Chicago the pennant.

CHICAGO AMERICAN LEAGUE BASEBALL CLUB,

By ______________________

Once the news broke on the 1919 "Black Sox" scandal in September 1920, the Chicago White Sox immediately issued an indefinite suspension to those implicated in the World Series fix. In the letter given to the players, it clearly stated that they would be reinstated if found innocent of wrongdoing. But none of the men were ever exonerated in the eyes of Organized Baseball and remain banned from Major League Baseball to this day.

25,000 and 28,000 spectators took in the game and, despite the abundance of reports casting aspersions on members of the team, fans warmly applauded the hometown squad.[41] The Sox were undaunted by the newspaper stories while on the field, and scored eight runs behind Eddie Cicotte. Jackson went 0-for-4 with a walk and a run, and made an impressive running nab of Ty Cobb's line drive in the third inning. Chicago won, 8–1, and kept within striking distance of the Indians. In attendance for the festivities was Hartley L. Replogle, a forty-year-old Assistant State's Attorney assigned to the case of investigating the previous year's Series. Replogle was interested in calling a few of the Sox players to a special session of the grand jury on September 27, but cancelled it after Chicago's victory in order to allow the men to focus strictly on baseball.[42]

But that was impossible. Everyone, especially the alleged conspirators, was thinking about the investigation and what it was going to mean. It was looking more and more like several of the Sox players were going to be officially denounced for what transpired in October 1919, and held to the fire in both the criminal court and the court of public opinion. On top of that, they were liable to be disciplined to some degree by Organized Baseball as well. The Sox returned to Comiskey Park on September 27, for the second and final game of their Detroit series. This time, they beat their opponents, 2–0, and Jackson went 1-for-3 with an RBI.[43] Nobody knew at the time, but this would be "Shoeless" Joe Jackson's final major league game. The same would go for Swede Risberg and Buck Weaver. As for the remainder of the eight tainted Sox players, they had already given their last big-league performance—but just didn't know it yet.

The pennant was not yet decided, but the Sox were looking at three straight days of vacation before heading to their final series of the season at St. Louis on October 1. With the pressure building and seemingly new admissions each day, Jackson and his cohorts enjoyed very little rest. Undoubtedly, they were concerned where the next bombshell was going to emanate from and how close to the fix the individual confessing was.

On September 27, from Philadelphia, Billy Maharg revealed his side of the story and, since he was Bill Burns's top ally and had immense knowledge of the plot, there were few people closer to the Sox players than him.[44] Finally, it got to be too much. The following morning, the heaviness upon the shoulders of Eddie Cicotte forced a breakdown and he confessed to the grand jury that the 1919 World Series was indeed fixed. It was the first direct evidence from a player actually involved in the plot. Cicotte was emotional, and the *Chicago Daily Tribune* noted that he explained his side of the story "in tears and in shame."[45]

Cicotte admitted to receiving $10,000 in cash and declared: "From that night until this morning I have lived a thousand years. I have suffered agony day and night. It has been terrible. I wish to God I had not taken the money. If it had not been for Chick Gandil I would have been a winner again this year. He is to blame for my downfall. I never pitched a crooked game before. He told me how easy it was to make ten thousand that no one would ever know about. Before Gandil became a ball player he was mixed in with gamblers and low characters in Arizona. That is where he got the 'hunch' to fix the series. Abe Attell and three Pittsburgh gamblers agreed to back him. Gandil first fixed Williams and McMullin. Then he got me in on the deal and we fixed the rest."[46]

The confession from Cicotte sent a bolt of lightning through the world of professional sports and rocked baseball to its foundations. Joe Jackson heard the news that morning and was conflicted. On one hand, he feared the continued intimidation of Swede Risberg, particularly after the latter threatened to "bump [him] off" if he confessed. On the other, he wanted to get out in front of the growing scandal and get his version on the record before he was steamrolled by the confessions of whoever else was talking. After initially talking with White Sox lawyer Alfred Austrian and Charles Comiskey, Jackson decided to own up to what he'd done and accept his share of the responsibility.[47]

"I heard I'd been indicted," Jackson later explained. "I decided that these men couldn't put anything over on me. I called up Judge McDonald and told him I was an honest man, and that he ought to watch this thing. He said to me, 'I know you are not.' He hung up the receiver on me. I thought it over. I figured somebody had squawked. I got the idea that the place for me was the ground floor. I said, 'I'll tell him what I know.' He said, 'Come on over and tell it to me.' I went over. I got in there and I said: 'I got $5,000 and they promised me $20,000. All I got was $5,000 that Lefty Williams handed me in a dirty envelope. I never got the other $15,000. He said he didn't care what I got. That if I got what he thought I'd ought to get for crabbing the game of kids, I wouldn't be telling him my story. I don't think the judge likes me."

As could be expected, Joe was completely vulnerable and had been carrying the lies and burden long enough. He ventured to the criminal court building under the watch of Austrian and entered the jury room, prepared to answer each and every question in earnest. With his memorable Southern drawl, he did his best to recount the Series fix as he remembered, delivering facts, figures, and other information as he was asked, often responding with a polite "yes" or "no, sir." Similar to Cicotte, Jackson pinpointed Gandil as the broker for the entire deal. "He was the whole works of it," Joe admitted. "The instigator of it."[48] The timeline of certain events was also a priority for State's Attorney Hartley Replogle, his interrogator, and Joe was asked when he received the cash from Lefty Williams, when certain games were supposed to have been fixed, and when he spoke with his fellow conspirators.

Replogle asked Jackson specifically about the fourth game which Cicotte pitched in Chicago, and Joe remembered it well. He cited the "wildness of Cicotte" as the standout feature and, after being asked if he "fielded the balls [in] the outfield to win," Joe responded in the affirmative.[49]

However, Cicotte felt Jackson's poor fielding, combined with his own, helped the Reds win. "The second game I pitched I went a little better," Cicotte explained. "But in the fifth inning [Pat] Duncan knocked an easy grounder and I let off an easy peg to Gandil, which was wide and high—just high enough to pull Chick off the bag. Duncan came home with the run when I fed [Larry] Kopf an easy one, which he hit to Joe Jackson. Jackson helped the run on its way. When he made a poor return of the ball he threw over Schalk's head. [Greasy] Neale followed with a double into Jackson's territory. Both Jackson and myself presented these two runs to the Reds. The game was won by the Reds, 4–2."[50] Others believed Jackson's throw was on target to get Duncan at the plate.

Jackson always asserted that he never played to lose. He accepted the dirty $5,000, but his work at the plate and in the field was honest all around. Interestingly, part of the confession attributed to Jackson printed in the press differed from the official transcript of his grand jury testimony. For instance, in the *Sun and New York Herald*, Joe reportedly said that he had received the $5,000 under his pillow "after the first game."[51] But in his actual testimony, he admitted receiving the cash after the fourth game, and it was delivered by Lefty Williams, not found under his pillow.[52]

It is arguable whether Jackson exhibited the same kind of remorse and emotion that Cicotte did in his confession. The latter made it abundantly clear that he had suffered with regret for a year and if he could take back the things he did, he would. In Jackson's testimony, there was only a single instance in which Joe appeared to display his utter disgrace. It occurred when Replogle asked: "Weren't you very much peeved that you only got

$5,000 and you expected to get twenty?" Jackson answered: "No, I was ashamed of myself."[53] On the surface, it seemed that Jackson was admitting certain humility for taking part in the crooked affair, but there is another interpretation of his answer. He might have simply been stating how ashamed he was for allowing himself to be swindled out of the full amount. This interpretation ties to the statement Jackson made later on that night when he reminded reporters, "I never got that $15,000 that was coming to me," seemingly still bothered by Gandil's broken promise.[54]

Jackson also said, "I wasn't wise enough like Chick to beat them to it."[55] Altogether, these comments could be read several different ways and it is tough to interpret the true intentions of his words. But the one thing that remained consistent was how Joe felt about the criticism he received for his wartime work. "They ruined me when I went to the shipyards," he bellowed the evening of his grand jury appearance. It was obvious he wasn't yet over the abuse he suffered. The wounds inflicted on him were as raw as they were in early 1919, as he slowly integrated back into the good graces of Organized Baseball. Always prideful, Joe wasn't the kind of man to purposefully disgrace his family's good name and, during the war, he worked as hard as the individual next to him, serving the American cause. The 1919 Series scandal, though, was damaging his name about as bad as could be imagined.

After delivering his lengthy grand jury testimony, Jackson was surrounded by a group of young kids, the base of his popularity for years and years. Saddened by the reports, the children looked up at him, and one inquired, "It isn't true, is it, Joe?" Jackson grimaced and answered, "Yes, boys, I'm afraid it is."[56] If he wasn't fully engulfed by shame before, the realization of disappointing countless young fans who idolized him probably did the trick. Later that night, he told a reporter, "I don't care what happens now. I guess I'm through with baseball."[57]

14

BANISHMENT

The commotion surrounding the "Black Sox" scandal grew to epic proportions, and within the span of a day, Joe Jackson had become one of the most infamous people in the country. Showered with attention, he remained fearful for his life, as the threat issued by teammate Swede Risberg echoed in his head. The criminal gambling elements involved in the 1919 Series fix were probably not too thrilled by his confession either, even though he didn't know enough about them to properly disclose their identities or any incriminating information. Everything had cascaded downhill so quickly, all stemming from the initial admission by Eddie Cicotte on the morning of September 28, 1920. Within hours, White Sox owner Charles Comiskey issued an indefinite suspension order for the seven active players tied to the controversy. Then at noon, the Cook County Grand Jury issued a true bill (indictment) for each of the same seven men—plus Chick Gandil—for conspiracy to commit an illegal act.[1]

With an expected trial months away, Jackson wanted out of Chicago at the first opportunity. But before he made his getaway, his closest friend on the team, Lefty Williams, followed his lead by also confessing to the grand jury. But in Joe's anxiousness on the grand jury stand, he drew into question whether Williams was telling the truth when he told him he too only received $5,000. He believed his pal, along with Gandil, Risberg, and McMullin "cut [the crooked money] up to suit themselves."[2] It wasn't exactly a glowing testament to their trust and friendship. Nevertheless, Jackson and Williams departed Chicago together a few days after their confessions and landed in Greenville, South Carolina, where they, along with their wives, planned to stay with Joe's relatives.[3]

The two suspended Sox players had big plans for their winter. Back in August, they made preliminary arrangements with Dr. J. L. Moorefield of St. Petersburg, Florida, to join a winter league based in the "Sunshine State." In fact, Moorefield received a letter from the pair on September 10, inquiring about a possible residence in the area.[4] Less than a week before Joe admitted to being part of the fix, the *St. Petersburg Daily Times* reported that he was going to manage the local winter league franchise, while Williams was going to lead the pitching staff.[5] The escape to beautiful Florida after the grueling season was something to look forward to but, needless to say, the exposure of the 1919 Series scam changed their plans. The league went on as planned, using replacements for both Jackson and Williams.

There was immense disappointment for what Jackson had done in both of his acknowledged hometowns, Greenville and Savannah. Baseball officials in Greenville displayed their collective discontent by blocking the lease of its field for an exhibition game starring Jackson, which normally would've been a big selling attraction. Two cotton mills did likewise the following day, halting any attempt for Joe to appear on a local diamond.[6] The *Savannah Morning News* mentioned that area fans didn't want to initially believe the stories from Chicago, but came around after word of Jackson's confession. A certain amount of "astonishment" circulated in the aftermath of the news.[7] On October 17, the two couples arrived in Savannah from Greenville and checked into the Hicks Hotel. They requested privacy, shunning interview requests, and hotel employees respected their wishes.[8]

Nationally syndicated columns and newspaper editorials freely judged Jackson for his role in the Series scandal. Hugh Fullerton, who wrote that Jackson "never [was] a great ball player, excepting in hitting power" in March 1920, was one of the most prominent.[9] He wrote a long column in the *New York Evening World* on September 30, rehashing his stark rise from "mill boy" to superstar, declaring that Jackson "had become the hero of millions." Fullerton continued: "There came a day when a crook spread money before this ignorant idol, and he fell. For a few dollars, which perhaps seemed a fortune to him, he sold his honor. And when the inevitable came, when the truth stood revealed, Joe Jackson went before a body of men and told the story of his own infamy."[10] Another writer stated, simply: "We speak of the passing of Joe Jackson, hero, and the coming of Joe Jackson, the scorned."[11]

Sportswriter Charles Dryden made light of the baseball scandal by naming his "Benedict Arnold All-Star Team," of course including the corrupt Sox, Hal Chase, Lee Magee, and Heinie Zimmerman. "The Benedict Arnold All Stars contemplate a series of winter games on an indoor circuit which includes Leavenworth, Joliet, and Atlanta," he added, and proclaimed Abe Attell and Bill Burns bookers for the tour.[12] Harvey T. Woodruff in his "In the Wake of the News" column in the *Chicago Daily Tribune* came up with a "White Sox Musicale" for the suspended players, and designated song titles for each man. For instance, Williams was the vocalist of "I May Be Gone for a Long, Long Time," and Gandil: "I Got Mine, Boys." Jackson's rendition of "I Know I Got More Than My Share" was pegged to be an instant classic, but unfortunately the concert was a figment of Woodruff's comedic mind.[13]

Badly in need of legal counsel, Jackson and Williams hired James H. Price, a friend of Joe's from Greenville, and received important advice. A few weeks later, Joe surprised a lot of people when he boldly denied ever participating in a crooked game. "I have never confessed to throwing a ball game in my life," he proclaimed, "and I never will."[14] He was essentially walking back the previously established ties connecting him to the fix and launching a campaign to clear his name. It was the first stage of a multilevel legal strategy, but many journalists weren't impressed. "Some people like to impress upon the world how really foolish they are," a *Collyer's Eye* editorial began. "Joe Jackson made [a] considerable fool of himself when he started out to throw games in the 1919 World Series, but he's adding to the magnitude of his folly by now, down at Greenville, denying that he made any confession to that effect before the grand jury. Joe better forget the denial and stick by the confession or he'll fool himself right into jail."[15]

Jackson wasn't the only member of the dishonest Sox to become noticeably braver after receiving legal guidance; Buck Weaver was similarly confident. Ironically, the former third baseman was willing to bet $500 that he was going to be back with the Sox in 1921.[16] Jackson and Williams added to their self-assuredness after slipping back into Chicago around the middle of January 1921, and quietly hired an aggressive middle-aged attorney named Benedict J. Short.[17] Under Short's direction, the men refuted any assumption that they had confessed to a "conspiracy" the previous September, which again drew much criticism. "These men may jump from the frying pan to the fire," responded Judge Charles A. McDonald, who presided over the grand jury and heard their confessions. "They face a possible maximum penalty of five years in the penitentiary at present, if they are found guilty, but a perjury charge might make it much harder."[18]

The risks of perjury, plus the ominous threat of prison time, were major concerns, but Short was quickly lining up a scattershot defense. Part of his scheme was to discredit the honest White Sox players by drudging up a story from late in the 1919 season, wherein Chicago was said to have given Detroit a series to allow the Tigers to clinch third place. Not only that, but the clean Sox athletes were alleged to have bet on the games as well. American League President Ban Johnson heard the convoluted tale and felt the tainted players were trying to specifically injure the reputation of Eddie Collins, "one of the cleanest and finest men" in baseball. The *Chicago Daily Tribune* reported that Jackson and Williams were responsible for initiating the spread of this "yarn" while at a South Side hangout.[19] Another aspect of Short's battle plan was to attack owner Charles Comiskey on several different fronts, trying to turn public opinion against "The Old Roman" and toward the indicted players.

A report out of Philadelphia in early 1921 seemingly offered the ex-Sox an opportunity to get back on the field much sooner than expected. George H. Lawson invited the group to join his newly fashioned Continental League, stating: "I fully believe that the fans will be ready to forgive the erring men and grant them another chance."[20] Whether that opinion was true remained to be seen, but the players didn't buy into Lawson's plan and his league only had a brief existence. Jackson remained in Chicago through the early part of the year and attended several preliminary hearings before Judge William E. Dever. His attorney, Short, was joined by lawyers representing his former teammates, forming an intimidating combination of legal minds.

On the other side of the coin, Assistant State's Attorney George E. Gorman was the head of a solid prosecutorial team. Considering all the elements and the overall subject matter, the public was anticipating a grueling yet revealing court battle.

The prosecution requested a six-month postponement for the trial in March, yearning for the extra time to strengthen its case. Jackson and Buck Weaver were up in arms about the delay, as both wanted the case over and done with so they could return to play in the 1921 season. At that point, Judge Kenesaw Mountain Landis, the recently named high commissioner of Organized Baseball, stepped in to erase any possibility of that occurring until a court case could be staged.[21] "All of these players have been placed on the ineligible list and must vindicate themselves before they can be readmitted to baseball," he declared.[22] Shortly thereafter, on March 16, 1921, the White Sox unconditionally released Jackson, Weaver, Lefty Williams, Swede Risberg, Fred McMullin, Happy Felsch, and Eddie Cicotte, formally severing all ties between the Series fixers and the Chicago club.[23]

However, the next day, the State's Attorney's office dismissed its case against the seven players, but promised to charge them again within days.[24] It was apparent that the prosecution was struggling to formulate a sound enough case against both the players and gamblers. One of the most troubling issues they faced was the confirmation that Jackson, Williams, and Cicotte had changed their minds and rejected turning state's evidence, a fact in which the original case was built around. Without their firsthand testimony, they were lacking the overwhelming evidence they needed to prove a conspiracy. And there were additional circumstances not yet revealed to the public that would also prove detrimental. With the entire world watching, Gorman and his associates had to appear confident they could produce a guilty verdict and bring the allegedly corrupt players to justice.

An important question that cannot be overlooked is: Why did Jackson, Williams, and Cicotte renounce their confessions and refuse to testify on behalf of the state? There are several probable answers to this question. The most logical is the fact that once these three men were informed by legal counsel that the prosecution had little chance of achieving a guilty verdict on conspiracy charges without their testimony, they realized that they were essentially incriminating themselves if they went forward as planned. On top of that, the trio was compelled to sign immunity waivers before giving their confessions, relinquishing their right to refuse that same self-incriminating testimony. They were locked in, but the prosecution—and maybe even the defense by that juncture in March 1921—had realized that the original immunity waivers were stolen from the State Attorney's office sometime during the transition from one state's attorney administration to another.[25]

The loss of the immunity waivers was a huge blow to the prosecution and a major coup for Jackson and his ex-teammates. For Joe, though, he later claimed that he was "half drunk" when he signed the document and was given promises of protection, easing his mind to the point in which he would've "signed [his] death warrant if they had asked [him] to."[26] Nevertheless, once the waivers were gone and Jackson declined to cooperate, he was a step closer to being free from any prosecution. That didn't necessarily mean he was going to be exonerated in the eyes of Judge Landis, Organized Baseball, and the public, but rather off the hook for criminal charges. The Cook County Grand Jury indicted the seven ballplayers again before the end of March 1921, along with Chick Gandil and ten other individuals, all part of the gambling clique.[27] A bond of $48,000 each was set for Jackson and his cronies, although it was knocked down to $7,500 per man.[28]

The prosecution still needed time to prepare, leaving everyone a bit antsy. Not wanting to be completely sidelined without an income stream, Jackson and his mates considered setting up an independent (outlaw) club to play semiprofessional squads outside the bounds of Landis and Organized Baseball. Backed by a financial investor, George K. Miller, Joe was going to be joined by Williams, Risberg, McMullin, and Felsch in the endeavor, while Weaver and Gandil were considering it.[29] To be known as the "Major Stars" or the "South Side Stars," the club started booking dates against semipro and professional outfits, the initial against the Aristo Giants at Murley Park on April 17. But there was almost immediate backlash from various baseball organizations, including the Chicago Baseball League, the National Baseball Federation, the Central Industrial Baseball League, and the Umpires' Protective Association, each warning managers not to play against the ineligible ex-Sox crew.[30]

Field owners were also weary and disapproved applications by the "Black Sox." As a result, the April 17 contest against the Aristo Giants was postponed. Jackson was a big believer in what they were doing. "I think it will go over big when we get the chance to break in and show what we can do on the diamond," he explained. "Personally, I could play all the baseball I wanted down south, but I'd prefer to play up here. If our bunch gets together for this team like it's lining up, we certainly can play the ball, and that's what the crowds want to see. I don't think there would be any trouble."[31] According to press accounts, an estimated 6,000 people were eager to see the former hometown stars perform in their first battle as an outlaw combo on May 9. And so, Lefty Williams pitched Jackson, Weaver, and Felsch to a 7–2 victory over Aristo, and the United News service shared the news nationally.[32] With that, the ex-Sox were back in business.

Sportswriter Hugh Fullerton, however, was unimpressed. In fact, he figured the attendance to be much lower. He wrote: "The shamelessness of baseball in some quarters is shown by the fact that the Chicago "Black Sox," defying public opinion, played a game of ball in Chicago and escaped uninjured. Hardly enough persons went to the game to mob them, but they played."[33] Soon, reports emerged claiming the outsiders were drawing as many as the real White Sox for their weekend extravaganzas, and one journalist noted that "contrary to expectations, [they were] not 'razzed,'" by the ticketholders, but rather encouraged.[34] Their media hype had crowds at upwards of 15,000 by June, but attendance was likely far less. Another baseball correspondent observed that Jackson was as "big as a house," weighing 40 pounds heavier than normal, and was eating Cracker Jacks and drinking soda throughout an active game. It was also mentioned that the morale of the former major leaguers was "low."[35]

They were undoubtedly perked up by the start of their criminal trial in late June 1921, hoping that it would lead to a painless not guilty verdict. Of the eight members of the "Black Sox," all were present in court except Fred McMullin, who was still in Los Angeles. The presiding judge was Hugo Friend and between the seven players, there were at least eight affiliated defense attorneys, which included Jackson's main lawyer, Benedict J. Short, and Thomas D. Nash, the representative of Buck Weaver and Swede Risberg.[36] Assistant State's Attorney George E. Gorman was joined by three others, including John R. Tyrrell, Edward Prindiville, and George F. Barrett. The two sides wrangled over potential jurors for over two weeks, haggling and occasionally arguing passionately to get their point across. It was during this period that the gist of the defense team's strategy was revealed; not only to those in the courtroom, but to the public as well.

First and foremost, the defense questioned the legitimate possibility of a thrown major league game, especially with the eyes of players, managers, and umpires closely scrutinizing every play. They played up the fact that the athletes themselves were underpaid, forced to pay 50 cents to have their uniforms laundered, and treated "more like the beauties in the sultan's harem than free men."[37] Notably, owner Charles Comiskey was vilified in the proceedings, while the defense tried to garner sympathy for their clients. At the same time, it became apparent that the prosecution was going to rely heavily upon the testimony of Bill Burns, the middleman between Abe Attell and the crooked Sox. Burns was dug up by American League President Ban Johnson near the Mexican border and promised immunity to turn state's evidence. His insight, which was replacing that of Jackson, Williams, and Cicotte, was expected to be highly damaging to the defense's chances for victory.

And it was. Burns detailed his knowledge of the fix from the initial meetings prior to Game One through the eventual double-cross perpetrated by both sides. He had particulars, dates, and firsthand awareness of the fix that could not be refuted. The *Chicago Daily Tribune* called his testimony "the most dramatic yet" of the trial. He named names throughout, but quickly acknowledged afterwards that he never once implicated Jackson. The prosecution didn't make anything of it, and promised that other witnesses would connect him to the plot.[38] Three days later, they made good on their pledge, and Jackson was officially drawn into the fray. As expected, the disappearance of the immunity waivers, confessions, and other "confidential records" pertaining to the case was a hot topic. Ban Johnson boldly blamed New York gambling chief Arnold Rothstein as being behind the theft, claiming he paid $10,000 for the documents because he was concerned he was incriminated by the confessions.[39]

Rothstein wasn't implicated in any way, nor was he indicted by the Cook County Grand Jury. The fact that he was essentially being allowed to walk away scot-free was not lost on the defense, and attorneys openly wondered why the big shots of the Series fix weren't being targeted. No one had a good answer. During the fight over admitting the confessions into the record, Jackson appeared on the stand for a bench hearing without the jury present on July 25, 1921. His "quaint dialect and humorous answers made it an entertaining morning for the spectators," the *Chicago Daily Tribune* reported. He was startlingly honest about his alcoholic intake, claiming he was "half drunk" when he spoke before the grand jury, then "got drunk" that night. The attorney asked him if he left town after he was done at the State's Attorney's office, and Joe replied, "No, I got tee'd up again."[40]

Jackson never spoke before the actual jury, but his confession, along with those of Williams and Cicotte, were admitted. In the end, the 12 jurors were asked to determine whether the eight players "conspired, confederated, and agreed together . . . to procure divers large sums of money by means of and by use of the confidence game."[41] In the final argument presented by the prosecution, Edward Prindiville highlighted the confessions of Jackson, Williams, and Cicotte, and asked: "What more convincing proof do you want than the statements made by the players? When the scandal broke, they sought out the state's attorney's office and made their confessions voluntarily. The public, the club owners, and even the small boy playing on the sandlots have been swindled."[42] Before he finished his statement, Prindiville asked the jury for a "verdict of five years in the penitentiary and a fine of $2,000 for each defendant."[43]

Benedict Short issued a concise rebuttal. "There may have been an agreement entered into by the defendants to take the money offered them by scheming gamblers," he later elaborated. "But it has not been shown the players had any intention of defrauding the public or of bringing the game into ill repute." It was true, at least in the case of Joe Jackson. When he agreed to accept $20,000 to take part in the Series fix, he had no earthly idea he was entering into a "conspiracy," and likely never consciously thought he was fleecing baseball fans. Even if he wanted some sort of revenge against Charles Comiskey for the latter's behavior against him during the war, it is a stretch to believe he wanted to hurt baseball in its entirety. He might not have even recognized the consequences until after speaking to his wife following the fourth game of the Series. In terms of purposefully diminishing his own talents to help the Sox lose is another impossible question, and since Jackson denied it in his grand jury testimony, how could he be sent to prison?

As it turned out, the jury didn't buy the prosecution's case. They didn't accept Burns's version of the scandal nor the overall conspiracy theory and acquitted each and every man on trial. Afterwards, William Barry, the foreman, told a journalist that the jury had "voted not to tell what happened in the jury room," but since they came to a decision on their first ballot in less than three hours, it was clear they were on the same page pretty much from the start of deliberations.[44]

Once the jury's verdict was given, the courtroom atmosphere morphed into one of joy and contentment. The players and defense attorneys celebrated with handshakes and smiles, and then turned their attention to the jury, where more of the same continued. Even Judge Friend beamed at the decision, while court bailiffs whistled in approval.[45] It was a unique scene indeed, and Jackson was fully enjoying the moment. Ahead of him, it appeared, was an eventual reinstatement to Organized Baseball and a full pardon. Things couldn't have been better.

While the jury had made their decision, Judge Landis followed with a formal ruling the next morning. He declared: "Regardless of the verdict of juries, no player who throws a ball game, no player who undertakes or promises to throw a ball game, no player who sits in a conference with a bunch of crooked players and gamblers, where the ways and means of throwing ball games are planned and discussed, and does not promptly tell his club about it, will ever play professional baseball."[46] His words stung the acquitted "Black Sox" as suddenly and sharply as humanly possible, delivering a death knell to their collective careers in Major League Baseball. Jackson was ousted, his career statistics rendered valueless, and the future acknowledgments he'd certainly be awarded eliminated from the realm of possibility. Unless the decision was overruled in the future, he'd forever be tied to the 1919 World Series scandal and never fully appreciated for the gifts he brought to baseball.

But that was the punishment. Jackson later voiced his opinion that the vicious feud between Charles Comiskey and Ban Johnson had a lot to do with their criminal prosecution, as the latter wanted nothing more than to damage Comiskey's franchise and reputation.[47] Had the two remained friends instead of waging an irrational war, there was a good chance the 1919 Series controversy would've been handled much differently. In fact, there was even a probability that Landis would not have been named commissioner, at least not in 1920. Nevertheless, their hostilities severed years of friendship and none of it made much sense. Nearly a century later, it is difficult to understand the stubbornness displayed by both men at such a stage in their lives. Why they couldn't bury the hatchet for the best interests of baseball will never be known.

Surprisingly, though, Jackson was prepared to walk away from baseball even before Landis issued his decree. At least that's what he told reporters right after the acquittal. "I'm through with Organized Baseball," Jackson said. "I've got a store here in Chicago. This will be my home. I'm going to play ball with Williams in Oklahoma for a while this summer. At present I'm contemplating taking a position as coach for a university team in Japan. I've also had an offer to go before the footlights."[48] Considering the fact that his last stint on stage didn't end well, perhaps that wasn't the best idea. But he was evidently looking at all his options. His former manager, Connie Mack, liked what Jackson had to say. "To me, it looks like Joe Jackson was the only wise one of the bunch. While others were insisting they would return to Organized Baseball, Jackson had the foresight enough to say he was through."[49]

In the months that followed, Joe continued to consider and accept independent barnstorming dates in a range of small, out-of-the-way towns. He sold his interests in a cigar and billiard room he shared with Lefty Williams on East Garfield Boulevard in Chicago and returned to Savannah. In March 1922, a national report claimed he was nearly bankrupt, but he refuted the assertion, telling a journalist: "I am not asking a cent from anyone, and I am a long ways from being broke. I have offers from leading baseball officials seeking to get me back into the baseball game."[50] One of his offers was from a Chicago promoter named William C. Meek, who wanted Jackson to join four of his fellow major-league castoffs for a tour of Minnesota.[51] But by May, a legal opportunity presented itself and Joe was gung ho on trying to extract monies owed him pertaining to the contract he signed with Comiskey in 1920.

On May 13, 1922, in a Milwaukee Circuit Court, lawyer Raymond J. Cannon filed a suit against the Chicago White Sox franchise on Jackson's behalf. The case was predicated on a desire to obtain back pay and bonus money due, plus damages. Cannon also established a similar suit for Swede Risberg and had previously filed one for Happy Felsch.[52] A few weeks later, Joe signed a deal to play ball with the Scranton (PA) Coal Miners organization at Poughkeepsie, New York. Although his team lost, 12–4, he was a big hit with local fans. "He had a crowd around him all the time," a local reporter wrote, "and made a great hit with the kids."[53] Conversely, columnist Otto Floto of the *Denver Post* offered words of criticism. He wrote: "Joe Jackson, who played a star part with the notorious "Black Sox" around Cincinnati, three years ago, is posing as a coal miner belonging to the Scranton team. Too bad Joe is only posing. What a great idea it would be if Joe actually went to work in a coal mine and earned an honest dollar."[54]

Jackson soon inked a deal with Eddie Phelan, an entrepreneur from New York City and also the president of the New York Semi-Professional Baseball Association. Phelan, who partnered with a wealthy financial backer, had great ideas for Jackson, which included a campaign to modify the public's views of the former major leaguer. For his part, Jackson would receive $1,000 a week.[55] The deal consisted of semipro games throughout the New York metropolitan area. At Hackensack, New Jersey, on June 25, a contest Phelan claimed was booked directly by Jackson, Joe (under the name "Josephs") hit a home run, a double, and a single. His efforts helped Westwood beat Hackensack-Bogota, and thousands of dollars in bets reportedly changed hands.[56] It was believed Jackson had been touring New Jersey under an assumed name for over a month, but was going to be using his correct identity from that point forward.

The crusade to mend public opinion about Jackson was officially commenced on July 15, 1922, at the Polo Grounds, as petitions were circulated outside the stadium and within the grandstand during the first game of the Yankees series with the White Sox. Ever optimistic about the movement, Phelan told the *New York Times* that their goal, after sending petitions to every city involved in Organized Baseball, was one million signatures. From there, the documents would be forwarded to Judge Landis. However, the wording of the appeal was worthy of note. According to the document's text printed in the press, their intention was "to clear [his] professional reputation" and "lift all ban" so Jackson could "solicit without stigma and practice in peace, without hindrance, his honorable livelihood." But the petition wasn't specifically asking for restoration into OB, and actually read: "Joe Jackson seeks no reinstatement in Organized Baseball."[57]

Joseph S. Rogers of the *Washington Times* asserted that the initial day of Jackson's rehabilitation campaign was a failure, as "very few" people were contented to sign. "The cool treatment given those who circulated the petition at the Polo Grounds reflect universal opinion that neither fans, players, nor owners would ever take seriously any movement to reinstate the 'Black Sox,'" he wrote.[58] Kid Gleason, still the manager in Chicago, also spoke out when asked whether Jackson would ever return. "He has as much chance of that as I have of scaling the Washington monument. I don't know what some people call innocence. They seem to forget that Joe admitted his part in the 1919 deal long before the trial. If Judge Landis ever received such a petition, it would be torn up. Baseball is through with men of that stripe."[59]

The next phase of Phelan's plan was a public declaration of Joe's innocence. They booked the Manhattan Casino in Harlem for July 21, 1922, and Jackson stepped before the curious onlookers and declared, "I ain't guilty of nothing. I'm standing on my reputation as a clean-cut, honest ball player and asking the jury of fans for a square deal. I ain't wantin' to get back in professional baseball, but I want to play with the semi-pros. If Landis wants me back in the big leagues, I'll be pleased to go back. I played my hardest in the 1919 World's Series. I fielded 1.000 and batted .375 in the series. You can't throw no ball games that way. On my word as an honest gentleman,

I don't know nothin' about no crooked work. I don't care what Landis or any one says, I'm goin' to keep on playin' baseball if I have to play by myself. I ain't never murdered no one and I ain't tried. I ain't guilty of nothing and I think I ought to be let play baseball because I can't do nothin' else."[60]

His words weren't poetic yet served their purpose, and Phelan boasted 150,000 signatures in less than a month. On evenings, after ballgames on the northeastern indie circuit, Jackson was a fixture at a Harlem cabaret, drawing much attention by his presence.[61] He mingled with patrons, told stories, and delighted locals with his distinctive mannerisms and style. Before the end of the summer, Jackson departed New York for the South and turned up to watch his younger brother, Jerry, a skilled pitcher, perform on the mound in minor league contests. But the additional weight and stress had taken its toll, and Joe's health began to deteriorate. In early October 1922, he went in for surgery, the United Press reported, but didn't specify what type of operation he was experiencing.[62] He recovered sufficiently to start seeking out a new barnstorming squad after the first of the year and landed with the Blytheville, Arkansas, club during the spring of 1923.[63]

Controversy erupted after Jackson and Swede Risberg were identified as members of the team, and several games were subsequently cancelled. Joe moved on to Bastrop, Louisiana, shortly thereafter, again under a false name. This time he was "Joe Johnson," and he reportedly played in more than 30 games before being recognized. Playing for a "nominal salary," he was only identified by his heavy hitting, and it was alleged that Eddie Cicotte was also with the club under the name "Moore."[64] While touring this part of the country, Jackson became infatuated with fishing and observed the writings of Izaak Walton. As the team planned a trip to the Gulf Coast, he looked forward to more opportunities to practice his hobby.[65] But rival clubs continued to complain about his appearances, fearing their own reputations would be somehow damaged by being in the same ballpark as him.

Judge Landis perpetuated that sentiment as well. After Jackson settled in Americus, Georgia, to play in the South Georgia League in July 1923, a statement was issued from Landis's office. It read: "We cannot conceive of any club owner employing a game-thrower. The players involved in a game in which Jackson plays certainly will be liable to punishment."[66] Truthfully, the South Georgia League was not governed by Organized Ball and Landis, and teams had the right to feature anyone they wanted. The threat by Landis still concerned many young players who hoped to one day play in the minor or major leagues. Taking everything into consideration, officials of the South Georgia League hashed the subject out and voted in favor of allowing Jackson to play. Over the next two months, he played in 31 games, batting well over .400 and captained the Americus squad en route to a league championship.[67]

Jackson's standing with fans was unquestionably sustained in the years following his ban, especially for those who witnessed him play in person. Joe's natural charisma and powerful swing were magnets for attention, and rarely did he disappoint in the clutch. People loved to root for him and the fans in Georgia, his adopted home-state, were no different. Although the plan by Eddie Phelan to clear his name evaporated into thin air, keeping his baseball prospects narrow, Joe wasn't without moneymaking options. He was tied to a whiskey business and bowling alley in Savannah at different times, and later operated the Savannah Valet Service, a dry-cleaning company with his wife.[68] Additionally, the intensifying court action in Milwaukee against the Chicago White Sox and Charles Comiskey had considerable financial implications.

Ever since attorney Raymond J. Cannon filed suit in May 1922, things had progressed slowly but surely. There were innumerable hearings prior to the depositions of Comiskey and Jackson in March and April 1923. At that point, the specific details of Jackson's argument were divulged, and it became apparent just how compelling his case was. But many aspects of his deposition were highly disputable and clashed with his 1920 grand jury confession, creating a bizarre alternate reality. For instance, Jackson explained in his deposition: "I knew absolutely nothing about the throwing of the 1919 World Series until two or three days after it was over."[69] But in his 1920 confession, he not only elaborated on when and how he was approached by Chick Gandil before the Series, but admitted taking the $5,000 payment from Lefty Williams after Game Four. On top of that, Shano Collins revealed that Kid Gleason openly talked about the rumors of a fix in a clubhouse meeting prior to Game Three.[70]

How Jackson could now say he didn't know anything about it until after the Series was over was mindboggling. But Cannon and Jackson hung their hats on that precise notion and went into Milwaukee court in January 1924, ready to fight for $18,500 of back pay.[71] Judge John G. Gregory watched intently as the fireworks started from the opening statement and continued at a feverous pitch. Jackson took the stand and "made an excellent witness," according to the *Milwaukee Sentinel*. He was well prepared with his answers and explained the progress of his career in professional baseball, from Greenville to Chicago. With regard to the 1919 Series, he reiterated the fact that he hit the only home run of the games and performed flawlessly in the field. Joe said that Lefty Williams delivered him an envelope of money from "eastern gamblers," pertaining to a fix, but claimed he never agreed to be a part of it. He didn't even know about it until that moment. The next day he tried to see Comiskey, but the latter refused to meet with him.[72]

On cross-examination, Jackson denied nearly everything he originally confessed to in 1920, and again the Milwaukee press felt he performed admirably.[73] Jackson "may not be able to read or write much, but he has a full-witted brain, a mind that fenced evenly on Wednesday afternoon with an able lawyer," a reporter for the *Milwaukee Sentinel* declared. But his repeated denunciation of the 1920 testimony was strikingly irregular. He might have looked and sounded confident, but for those familiar with his previous statements, it was an unbelievable turnaround. A major sticking point in Jackson's case was how he was allegedly duped into signing his three-year deal with the Sox by team secretary Harry Grabiner. According to his account, Grabiner told him the 10-day release clause was not in the contract and had Joe sign the document on the steering wheel of an automobile without Katie having a chance to read it. The Sox version claimed that Jackson did sign the contract in the presence of Katie in their Savannah home.[74]

Jackson also explained that the Sox signed him to a three-year deal in spite of knowing about the Series fix and his alleged participation. He said that Katie, who was adamant about him getting $10,000 a year salary, "bawled [him] out" for accepting $8,000. There were countless nuggets of trivia interspersed throughout Joe's testimony, making for an entertaining spectacle. But of everyone paying attention to the proceedings, no one was more aware of Jackson's contradictions than Judge Gregory. The jury, though, like the one in Chicago that acquitted the "Black Sox," were firmly on the side of the ballplayer. On February 15, 1924, the 12-person panel awarded Joe a victory and $16,711.04 in back pay. But this time, Jackson didn't have even an evening to relish his win. Judge Gregory immediately stepped in and set aside the verdict, castigating the jury for being "derelict in its duty," and cited the perjury of Jackson.[75]

In turn, Jackson was arrested, which completely stunned him and all the onlookers. "Whatever the verdict of the jury may be," Judge Gregory explained, "it will not affect my attitude in ordering the arrest of the plaintiff, Jackson. He stands self-accused and self-convicted of perjury. Either his testimony here or his testimony given before the Chicago grand jury was false. I think the false testimony was given here."[76] Francis C. Richter, a correspondent for *The Sporting News*, wrote about Jackson's case, noting: "So far as vindication is concerned, the attempt was a 'complete failure,' as Jackson not only repudiated sworn statements made before the Chicago grand jury . . . but he also admitted receiving and retaining a part of the plunder from a crooked fellow player, thereby making himself an actual party to the criminal conspiracy even if guiltless of physical wrong-doing as he claimed."[77] The disastrous case was dismissed, and later, Joe reportedly settled with Comiskey, but the financial terms are still unknown.

None of the major players involved in the entirety of the "Black Sox" scandal and the resulting court cases walked away from the controversy unscathed. Everyone was scorched by the flying barbs, accusations, and comments of judgmental pundits. Those players directly tied to the fix were punished by Organized Baseball, while the reputations of Comiskey and Ban Johnson were never the same. Over four years had passed since that fateful Series, and with little chance of being absolved and reinstated, Joe Jackson began to focus on the bigger picture of life, away from the arguments relating to his major league career. Spending time with his family while tending to his businesses were the concerns he wanted to structure his life around. And if he could still play ball locally in the region to make a little extra money, he was all for it. After all, he always loved the cheers of the crowd.

15

"THE ANSWER TO A GAMBLER'S PRAYER"

Few people in baseball history have shared the same kind of legacy and legend as "Shoeless Joe" Jackson. The romantic mysticism that has surrounded his story for decades perpetuated a genuine hero of the game, a man who would've played baseball just for the fun of it, and a true American spirit. He was a smiling and good-natured soul, and gave back to the public each and every day he stepped onto the field. Jackson was always cognizant of his role-model status with kids and spent time reciting tales of the diamond to groups of youngsters every chance he got. The damning nature of the "Black Sox" controversy was a complete injustice in this realm, and Joe should never have been banished from the national pastime. He deserved a place next to the other icons of baseball, enshrined at Cooperstown, in the National Baseball Hall of Fame. Looking at Jackson through a prism of idolization, it is easy to prop him up as an unjustly vilified superstar. But in reality, he deserves acceptance for the flawed man he really was.

Throughout the years, sportswriters either loved Jackson or tended to paint him with a less than flattering brush. When discussing his idiosyncrasies, some journalists had a bit of fun with him, and attempted to capture his remarkable Southern drawl in their columns. "I suah knows how it comes that boy [Roy] Wood can hit that pill so hawd," Jackson explained, interpreted by a *Cleveland Plain Dealer* columnist in 1914. "That boy done gone and used my bat. He's got so many hits out of it that there don't seem to be any left foh me."[1] Joe's intellect was always fodder for conversation in the press. Despite his acknowledged lack of education, an established businessman from South Carolina lauded Joe for his "much more than average intelligence."[2] But sportswriters, particularly, hammed him without mercy. In fact, a correspondent for *The Sporting News* wrote in 1915 that "It used to be the fashion to poke fun at Joe Jackson because he lacks an education."[3] Jackson took a lot of abuse. He was called "brainless" by the *Washington Times,* while that same paper claimed that if he left baseball he'd be forced to return to the cotton mill because he was unable to do anything else.[4] The *New York American,* upon citing his lead in the American League batting race, stated: "This is due to the fact that he never has ruined his eyesight reading literature."[5] James W. Egan in the *Tacoma Times,* in response to the possibility of Jackson beating Ty Cobb for the batting title, remarked: "Think of the awful blow it will be to education. Small boys will refuse to hurt their batting eyes by reading and will forsake desks for the sand lots." Upon learning about Joe's vaudevillian endeavors in 1915, Cleveland manager Joe Birmingham said stories about Jackson's stage career were "worth more to the club in keeping the players in good humor than anything that has happened in five years," according to the report in the *New York Evening World.*[6]

A lot of the time, the criticisms of his intelligence were ingrained within a game recap. Writers would comment that Jackson wasn't able to outguess baserunners from the outfield or think ahead far enough to successfully manage his throw. When he was at bat, he was called selfish for swinging away when a bunt would've been a more-suited scientific play. Essentially, he was critically assessed for not being able to think on his feet when he did just that on a day-to-day basis. He knew the game of baseball, but also relied heavily on instructions from his on-field captain, baseline coach, or manager. But when his natural instincts kicked in, he sometimes found it difficult to maintain that discipline. "That is a thing the player must get used to," Jackson explained in 1917. "When I go up to the plate and am told to sacrifice very often a ball comes over the plate that I feel sure I could paste a mile. But that's where team play comes in. You have to follow orders and never mind about the batting average."[7]

In a way, his nickname "Shoeless" was a source of condescension from the press and other players. It was a constant reminder of his backwoods, Southern upbringing and lack of sophistication. And for that reason, the always prideful Jackson hated it. The newspapermen who were sensitive to his perspective and wanted to remain on his good side called him "General Joe" instead. Jackson was usually pacifistic on the field and let a lot of one-liners tossed his way slide by without a rejoinder. Many of the jokes, he probably laughed at himself, not understanding the intent was to get his goat. He was known by a majority of people as a genial fellow, a guy who didn't take himself too seriously. But there were instances in which Joe was pushed to his limits.

One of his most famous moments came in 1912 at Hilltop Park in New York against the Highlanders. A rowdy spectator in the stands began harassing him as he went to the plate with two runners on. The loudmouth was relentless, projecting his voice at the top of his lungs, finally asking Joe to "spell 'cat.'" Jackson was in no laughing mood. He watched the next ball intently and proceeded to slam it to right for a triple. As he landed on third, Joe looked up to the now humbled spectator and shouted, "Spell triple, you bonehead. Spell triple!"[8] This scene was dramatized a little differently in the film version of *Eight Men Out.*

That same year in Detroit, he was hassled by the right-field bleachers because he'd gone hitless in two plate appearances. Next time around, he confidently told them he was going to hit a double to left, and waved his baseball cap to his tormentors prior to settling into the box. Needless to say, he followed through with his promise and the gang of bullies roundly cheered his astounding act.[9]

Joe normally maintained his cool and let his play speak for itself. He was crafty and clever in his own way, and seemed to always be full of surprises. While with Cleveland, he apparently tried to pull the wool over the eyes of Joe Birmingham after the latter fined him for staying out all night, which was against team rules. Birmingham returned to check on Jackson the next evening, but again found the outfielder missing from his bed. Angry, Birmingham began to rant, only to be stunned when Joe slid out from under the bed. "What are you doing under there?" Birmingham asked. "That's where I sleep, on the floor," Joe replied, "and I was under there all the time last night when you thought I was staying out all night." Lee Fohl, who was a witness, later said: "I don't know yet whether he was telling the truth or had figured out we would be up to see if he was in and was rigging up a belated alibi to square himself for being missing the night before."[10]

His first White Sox manager, "Pants" Rowland, figured Jackson's intellect was underrated, and felt he "never was a dumb ball player." He believed it was the opposite, that Joe "had a natural genius for the game."[11] Joe just wasn't book smart. When Cleveland owner Charles Somers offered to send him to college in 1911, allowing him to learn many of the things he should've picked up in his schoolboy years, Jackson wanted no part of it.[12] However, he made small progress in his reading as he aged. George Stovall, who managed him in Cleveland in 1911, said that teammates found Joe reading the newspaper one day. "We had seen him reading the paper before, but thought that he was just stalling the public," Stovall explained. "But one morning we noticed him looking at the paper, and all at once he got gloomy. Somebody asked him what was the trouble, and Joe replied that Ty [Cobb] had got four hits that day. 'How do you know?' asked the player. ''Cause I can read Cobb's name,'" Joe said.[13]

For years his inability to read and write was a major sore spot, and he went to great lengths to obscure his handicap. At restaurants he'd often stare blankly at a menu, giving the impression of an indecisive man. But he was just trying to fool the waiter and often piggybacked off the order of the man before him, asking for the same thing.[14] He'd scribble his signature into hotel registries and occasionally sat in the lobby holding an open periodical, again trying to give the appearance of a cultured man. He clearly cared what people thought of him, but rather than make the effort to learn to read, he just pretended . . . and he was good at it to a certain extent.

The fact that Jackson learned how to read Ty Cobb's name was not surprising. The two men were intrinsically linked from the instant Joe entered the big leagues as a regular in 1910, and each stood among American League batting leaders. They were natural rivals and since both were from the South, it only added to the nature of their competition. Their head-to-head battle for honors was the most heated between 1911 and '13, and fans were sometimes more focused on their individual performances than on the games themselves. It surely was the case on June 25, 1912, the *Cleveland Plain Dealer* reported, as the local crowd feverishly beckoned for Joe to outperform his Detroit adversary. The cheers grew as fans yearned to see Joe reciprocate a double Cobb had made in the first inning. Jackson repeated the feat in the third, but fell behind in their tit-for-tat routine when Cobb hit a home run in the sixth.

The vocal audience didn't want to see Cobb gain on their hero and nearly combusted in the seventh after Joe blasted a deep drive to center and missed a home run by inches. Cobb scrambled for the loose ball, giving Jackson time to race around the basepaths . . . and he would've crossed home had his base coach not stopped him at third. Altogether, Joe batted .667 on the day, beating out Cobb's average of .500, and Cleveland fans were all too pleased.[15] For Jackson, Cobb was someone he looked up to; a mentor of sorts, like when Ty gave him advice and taught him the hook slide. But Jackson was exceedingly determined to beat Cobb for the batting title, an achievement he never reached. His astronomical .408 average in

1911 was 12 points behind the Detroit outfielder. He hit .395 the following year, but that time finished 14 points behind. Cobb always found a way to outdistance Jackson, sometimes kicking it into high gear in the season's final days. He knew if he let up even a little, Joe was going to take it.

Through it all they remained respectful to each other and held no real animosity. Here and there, though, there was a bit of friendly taunting. In 1912, Cobb, after realizing that Cleveland was entering Washington after Detroit had finished a series there, and that the Naps would be using the same hotel, arranged to have Jackson get the exact room he used. The plan worked, and when Joe entered the room, he was flabbergasted to see the famous George "Honey Boy" Evans Trophy, awarded to baseball's top hitter—and won by Cobb—displayed majestically. The *Cleveland Leader* mentioned that it was an "aggravating sight" for Jackson. A little over a month later, Joe pasted a ball at Cobb during a game at Cleveland. It looked to be the average single, but Jackson rounded first and dashed for second, stretching the hit into a double. The move was more typical for Cobb and, after pulling it off, Joe gave Ty a knowing grin.[16]

As might be expected, Ty was all too curious about Jackson's vaudeville show in 1915, and turned out with a front row seat for an Atlanta performance. Joe was unable to avoid talking about Cobb during his finale speech, saying: "You're a bird, Ty, and a hard one to catch, but I've made up my mind to clip your wings this season." According to the report in *The Sporting News*, Joe humbly mentioned that Cobb was indeed one of the best of all-time, "but," he added with a pronounced wink, "maybe he isn't the greatest after all."[17] Cobb, interestingly, was never bashful about complimenting Jackson, even while the two were active. Years later, he named Jackson the "greatest hitter that baseball ever knew" in a nationally syndicated column by Grantland Rice. It wasn't just a stand-alone proclamation, but Cobb backed up his statement, saying: "I'll tell you why Jackson belongs on top. Back in those years we not only had to swing at a dead ball but also a ball that was doctored in every known way.

"We had the spit ball, the emery ball, the fuzzed-up ball—a ball that would do a lot of queer things and come at you with odd dips and breaks. So the good hitters of that period had to choke the bat and go in for punch hitting. All except Jackson. Joe still took his full swing and he was often up there from .380 to .410. I know I could never have hit above .300 with that type of swing. Only Jackson, old Shoeless Joe, had the eye and the smoothness and the timing to do that. I've often wondered what Joe Jackson would have hit against the pitching and the livelier ball that came in around 1920."[18] Cobb, holder of baseball's all-time greatest average (.366) and easily considered one of the best hitters ever, was known to be a thoughtful speaker. He was immensely intelligent and made sound choice of his words when talking to reporters. For him to give the highest possible accolades to Jackson was something that made people sit up and take note. Cobb's words were golden.

Of course, Jackson respected Cobb in a similar way. In 1913, he advised a Cleveland pitcher to put it over the plate and pray when facing Cobb.[19] And the hurler undoubtedly did. One of the overriding elements of Cobb's reputation was the allegation of racism and, in some aspects, Jackson was painted with the same brush as the typical Southerner, harboring many of the same prejudices. However, after an exhaustive search, there is little public evidence of any such tendencies. He wasn't hateful in that regard, or in any regard for that matter. During spring training in 1914, Jackson and teammate Ivy Olson spent over an hour hitting balls to a reported fifty young African American kids in an impromptu batting practice session in Georgia.[20] But oddly, there were reports in 1918 that black trainer "Doc" William Buckner was released from his duties after years of handling White Sox players because of racial issues spawned by certain members of the team.[21] The names of the players were never confirmed.

Based on his track record of physical altercations, loud arguments, and other hostilities, Ty Cobb was known for his temperamental ways. Jackson's on-field moods were also easily influenced at times. He wouldn't go as far as to fight anyone, but he'd lose much of his own momentum if the crowd shifted against him. While playing for Cleveland, just before the trade to Chicago, Indians fans showered him with one of the worst negative reactions a hometown crowd had ever shown him and, understandably, it affected his game play. A *Washington Times* writer noted: "[Joe] is a temperamental player, one who likes to have the fans with him. Adverse criticism hurts him greatly, interfering with his work. If Jackson has support behind him, he is one of the most dangerous hitters in the game, as well as a wonderful fielder and thrower. But if the fans are against him, he slumps dreadfully."[22]

Jackson liked the fans and was the type of approachable ballplayer that gave the sport a good name. He loved to toss balls into the stands—especially after making the third out—and it got to the point in which fans in Chicago anticipated it with loud merriment. Joe did it on the road as well. A *Chicago Eagle* columnist wrote in 1914 that Jackson would certainly be named the "greatest player in the American League" by the right-field crowd at Sportsman's Park in St. Louis, all because of his generosity in throwing balls to the fans.[23] A baseball official in New Orleans during spring training in 1913 actually got angry at Jackson because he gave a ball to a spectator and demanded that Joe pay for it. Jackson, in his own distinctive way, declined the order, telling the man: "It's on you . . . S'long."[24]

The interaction Jackson gave audiences illustrated his uniqueness in a game which was becoming more and more commercialized. As a result, his fame soared. In 1912, just based on the news reports of Joe's baseball conquests, a Kansas City man decided to name his 12-pound boy after the player, christening him, "Joseph Walker Jackson Harding."[25] Hugh Fullerton, in a 1920 syndicated column, elaborated on Jackson's popularity with kids. "In Chicago, they swarmed to him. He walked the streets with flocks of kid admirers at his heels. He bustled along, good-natured, something of a boy himself, smiling when the kids chorused, 'Hello Joe!' Many of them he called by their names, and sometimes, after the heat of a fierce game, he stopped good-naturedly at the vacant lot near the park and tossed a ball around."[26]

Behind the public face of the esteemed ballplayer, it was obvious Jackson carried a number of quirks and idiosyncrasies that weren't generally broadcast. Yet, some of his eccentricities might have been visible to an attentive onlooker, especially in the form of his many superstitions on the field. In 1912, the *Cleveland Leader* remarked that Joe went to the plate with his cap backwards against St. Louis, in search of good fortune, and lifted a humdrum fly to outfielder Burt Shotton. Lady Luck was on his side that afternoon, and Shotton misplayed the ball, dropping to score a couple runs.[27] After scoring versus Boston in May 1913, he hoped to inspire additional runs by scattering the team's bats in front of the bench.[28] He also felt that hairpins were good luck, and he stuffed his pockets with them, relishing the rusty ones the most. If he entered a slump, though, he wouldn't hesitate to toss out the entire lot and start his collection over. Black bats were another unavoidable essential, as were Piedmont cigarettes.[29]

Keeping with the theme of his exceptionality, Joe thought certain animals brought prosperity. For instance, he attributed his 1910 batting title with New Orleans to the presence of a monkey mascot named Jocko, and, in March 1912, bought a similar monkey to help him with the Cleveland Naps.[30] A different time, a group of railroad men gave him a live possum before a game and players rubbed it for luck.[31] Once, in an exhibition at Lexington, Kentucky, he found a snake slithering its way through the outfield. Joe nabbed it and threatened to put it down the front of pitcher Nick Cullop's jersey if he didn't improve his work on the mound. According to the *Cleveland Plain Dealer*, Jackson's comical threat worked and Cullop quickly improved.[32] There was another notable happening in Lexington. In the ninth inning, Joe, a left-handed hitter, switched to bat righty and produced a single. He admitted that he used to do it all the time in the minors, but couldn't "get [his] bat quick enough [around]" against big-league pitching.[33]

But no one questioned his consistency and power from the left side of the plate. He was a proven commodity against all types of pitchers, and was the type of hitter to learn from his past mistakes against specific pitchers. Only sporadically was he bothered by the same pitcher more than a few times. Earlier in his career, Chief Bender and Jack Warhop presented problems, and teammate Fred Blanding told a journalist "[Joe considered] himself a pretty lucky ball player any time he [got] a hit off either of them."[34] Ralph Comstock of Detroit held him hitless in 12 plate appearances in 1913, and used a clever spitball to keep him off balance.[35] Additionally, Joe marveled at Cy Falkenberg's fadeaway, saying: "I hope the pitchers of other teams are not turning the same trick. If they are, I suppose I won't get anything but the old screw ball all year."[36] These four pitchers were each right-handers, and it was no secret that righties irritated him more than lefties. But righties with a freak delivery and talent were even harder to hit.

The famous Walter Johnson was also a right-hander, and Joe admitted that Johnson had come close to having his number on a few different occasions. "I like him, all right," he explained, "but my batting average goes into convulsions every time his name is mentioned."[37] Johnson struggled with Jackson as well, later declaring Joe the one batter he feared the most during his entire career. "He was one of the greatest natural hitters I ever faced," Johnson said. "Joe loved a high, fast ball, and that was about all I could throw. He gave me plenty of trouble all the time."[38] Jackson, in 1917, talked with *Baseball Magazine* about his pitching preferences, and said: "Personally I like a low ball pretty well, but I don't mind them high. And I don't care whether they are over the plate or not so long as they look good. You can hit a ball just as far as a strike, if you meet it right. Batters, you know, can't be choosers. They have to take whatever the pitchers give them. And pitchers are not at all accommodating these days."[39]

Jackson was a renowned slugger and opposing clubs were always fearful that his long drives would beat them. In defense, outfielders played their positions far deeper than normal when he came up to bat. Surprisingly, in spite of his free swinging style, Joe was exceedingly difficult to strike out. In fact, he was only whiffed 234 times in nearly 5,000 big-league at-bats. His at-bat per strikeout ratio was 21.29, which is among the top 100 of all-time. Ty Cobb, in comparison, struck out once every 16.79 at-bats. In 1919, Joe fanned but 10 times in 139 games and was tops in the majors in at-bats per strikeout with 51.6. The following year, he was fourth with 40.7.[40] His pure ability, dramatic baseball feats, and overall personality made him a legend with the public and with up-and-coming ballplayers. Without question, Babe Ruth was the most prominent athlete to be influenced by Joe's style.

Sportswriter Grantland Rice asked Ruth about his batting stance in 1923, and the home run king answered: "Well, I had tried out a few schemes of my own, until one day I began to watch Joe Jackson. He looked to me about the freest, longest hitter I had seen anywhere. He could take a good, natural cut at the ball without losing his balance and when he landed, the ball usually kept going until it disappeared. If you will remember, he was the first to hit one over the right field stands at the Polo Grounds. So I said to myself, 'If that style works so well with Jackson, why not for me?' And I began keeping my right foot well forward and my left foot well back. I tried this idea out; it worked great—and I've stuck to it ever since."[41]

In the years following his banishment from Organized Baseball, Jackson was content in playing ball on ragged diamonds and in rough outfields across the country. He visited small towns, met people far off the beaten path, and in each place was the same old Joe. Although he was much slower than he'd once been, he retained his skill as a power hitter and often put on a memorable show. Rural newspapers in the South—during his run as player-manager for the semipro Waycross (Georgia) Coast Liners—treated him like royalty, and the public embraced him with hardly a concern for what occurred in 1919. Jackson led his squad to a regional championship in 1924 and, in 51 games, hit .475.[42] But past controversies continued to make news. In December of that year, his perjury charges were dismissed in a Milwaukee court after his attorney filed legal documents to squash the case.[43] The district attorney's office refused to relent in the matter and refiled less than two weeks later, issuing a new warrant for Joe's arrest.[44]

Illness was supposedly the reason why Joe didn't turn up in Milwaukee to respond to the warrant and, in May 1925, he forfeited his $1,000 bail.[45]

In the meantime, he rejoined Waycross for another season of semipro ball. His club toured South Carolina in the spring, and an overly generous report out of Laurens stated that Joe "looked about the same as the day when he left the Chicago White Sox." A Greenwood journalist was more frank, observing his 40- to 50-pound weight gain, and affirmed that Joe did not resemble his former self.[46] His increased dimensions didn't bother fans in the slightest, and he delivered remarkably well versus teams from Georgia, Florida, Alabama, and South Carolina, leading Waycross to a 59–19 record.[47] On October 24, 1925, the Wisconsin Supreme Court dismissed Jackson's appeal against the White Sox, finally putting that issue to bed.[48] The perjury charge was also dismissed.

Joe was still a hot commodity in the eyes of some club owners. The El Paso representative of the independent Copper League was eager to bring him to Western Texas and was offering a sizable salary for 1926. The United States Marine Corps were interested as well, and wanted Jackson to manage their baseball team at Parris Island, South Carolina.[49] He ended up staying in Savannah, where his dry-cleaning operation had expanded to three stores, earning him a "healthy yearly profit."[50] In early 1927, when Swede Risberg, Chick Gandil, and Happy Felsch opened up about another scandal involving the White Sox, pertaining to thrown games against Detroit, Joe advised the press that he "could put straight lots of things in the record which [were] not true." But, he added, his busy schedule offered no opportunity to venture to Chicago to do so.[51] The entire matter was broached years earlier during his trial versus the White Sox, but nothing came of it then, and the same result panned out in 1927.

Harboring heavy resentment toward Organized Baseball, Joe was proud to talk up the success of his business. He didn't care, "Not a whoop," if he was considered for reinstatement. "Why go back?" he asked. "You couldn't pay me to do so even were Judge Landis to reinstate me. Do you blame me? I don't like being called an outlawed player because I fail to see where I am one. I was never convicted of any charge in any court. I was promised full reinstatement if the charges of conspiring to ruin the White Sox were not true. But what happened when I was cleared? I'm out and I'm going to stay out."[52]

Though feeling very strongly, Joe's tone toward reinstatement changed over the next two years. In the summer of 1929, he told writer Quin Hall: "If Judge Landis could see his way clear to reinstate me, I'd like to play again. I'd take a job in any league and if I didn't lead that particular league in hitting, I'd play the season for nothing. You see it isn't the money I'm interested in. I have a good paying business here, but I sure would like to play again."[53]

For Jackson, accepting his restoration into the good graces of Organized Baseball was one thing, especially if the high commissioner came to his senses and corrected the alleged injustice on his own accord. But it was an entirely different thing to even contemplate the possibility of groveling his way back into favor. There was no chance he'd ever sink that low. "They gave me a rotten deal, Judge Landis knows they did," Jackson told a reporter in 1932. "If they want me, they can send for me. I'll never humble myself by asking to be reinstated."[54] He wanted to play and accepted the petitions of others to fight for his cause, but his own pride prevented a hat in hand, bended knee–type situation. He'd didn't want to give Landis the satisfaction.

Baseball was always on his mind. In mid-1932, he discussed helping Savannah return to an organized league by paying off old debts with income derived from a team he was involved with.[55] The idea went nowhere, and Joe and Katie began to study their options. They decided to sell their dry-cleaning operation and considered moving back to Greenville. However, personal tragedy followed, as Joe's mother Martha, who had lived with them for years, passed away on August 25 at the age of sixty-eight.[56] Within two months of her death, the grieving couple picked up and relocated to Greenville to be closer to family and friends. Joe was optimistic, not only about a barbecue business he purchased on Augusta Road, but with the potential of belonging to a local franchise. "I intend to be right there in right field for the Greenville baseball club," he said. "Sure, we're going to have baseball. I've been talking with several men here, and we plan to have a baseball club, and a good one, and play night baseball."[57]

But again, his tarnished status hindered the plan. He was able to tour with his own independent squad, but nothing in terms of a structured league was manageable. Toward the end of 1933, the newly inaugurated Greenville Mayor John M. Mauldin made it his point to fight for Jackson's reinstatement, and began corresponding with Judge Landis. The latter recommended a formal application, and the mayor pressed Joe to fill one out. He did, and based on the letters exchanged and the tone of the conversation between Mauldin and Landis, there seemed to be considerable confidence that Joe was going to be reinstated. Jackson was upbeat about the possibility. He wouldn't have gone the route of filling out the application on his own, but since Mauldin appeared to have the inside track to Landis, he went ahead as advised. "About all I want now is a minor league connection," he explained. "That'll make me happy."[58]

As years passed, the generalizations surrounding Jackson's involvement in the 1919 scandal evolved. Sportswriters as a whole were less inclined to blame him for wrongdoing, and many of the "facts" from the 1924 court case against the White Sox were accepted as truth over and above his 1920 grand jury testimony and the known contradictions. Jackson, either by himself or because of the work of his lawyers, had succeeded in attaining sympathy from the press corps. Several years before the application was sent to Landis, famous columnist Damon Runyon wrote: "The opinion that now prevails among old timers in organized baseball that Jackson didn't know anything about the plot in advance but was cut in on the pay-off by the other conspirators, who took advantage of his illiteracy."[59]

It was a rewriting of history, but this version was becoming more and more accepted. *New York Herald-Tribune* sportswriter Joe Williams voiced his opinion in support of Jackson's restoration. He believed Joe's debt to society was satisfied, noting that 1920 to 1933 was "a long stretch." Williams added: "Jackson today is an insignificant figure, but it seems to me the principle involved in his situation is important. It shouldn't be possible for any self-constituted authority to impose a life sentence as one of its subjects. Such tyranny is inconsistent with the theory of common justice. Even a murderer has his chance for parole."[60] Westbrook Pegler, a syndicated columnist, was against the idea of reinstatement, and felt that Joe and his fellow conspirators "should be made horrible examples of."[61] Judge Landis was of the same belief. After reviewing the submitted documentation and looking over Joe's 1920 confession, he concluded, "This application must be denied."[62]

The news was disheartening for Jackson's supporters and elevated his own bitterness toward Landis. He reminded the press that he didn't seek to be reinstated on his own accord, and wouldn't have done so if Landis didn't advocate the application to Mayor Mauldin. Jackson reiterated that his statistics in the World Series were proof that he didn't participate in the fix, and stated that Landis did "not know the facts in the case." The entire situation was a big letdown and sank his plans to manage a minor league club in Greenville. He didn't plan on reapplying for reinstatement ever again.[63]

Six months later, Joe signed on to manage a team based in Eufaula, Alabama, just over the western Georgia border. But, yet again, the powers-that-be rejected his involvement. On July 1, 1934, the leaders of the Dixie Amateur League voted 5 to 2 in opposition of his participation in the organization, and John Lardner, son of the legendary Chicago writer Ring Lardner, wrote: "I think Joe would lead a happier life if the ball clubs of the south stopped making him offers."[64] But Jackson couldn't walk away from the game completely, enjoying work as an umpire in the Cotton Mill League and as manager of the Winnsboro Mills Royal Cords. He reportedly smashed a 570-foot home run while with the latter club, setting a new personal record.[65] In 1935, he began making arrangements to run a liquor business in Greenville, and was initially denied a license because his proposed location outside the city limits lacked regular police coverage.[66] He found a more suitable site at 1262 Pendleton, north of Brandon Mill, and opened up shop.

Business was good, and as he approached fifty years of age in 1937, Jackson's days of active playing crept to a close. In April 1937, he attended a reunion of the old 1908 Victor Mills baseball squad, and Joe was proud to join eleven of his former teammates for a special tribute event at a Greenville-area stadium.[67] Jackson began to contend with a bad heart and his weakened condition kept him from returning to the field for a benefit game for underprivileged children in 1940. He maintained his celebrity presence, talking with reporters, up-and-coming athletes, and gladly dispensed baseball advice to anyone who inquired. He'd purchase ice cream cones for local children and, although the kids never saw him compete in his prime, Joe was revered. His accomplishments and legacy were pure gospel in Greenville, and yet another generation of youngsters were affected by his friendly disposition and kindness.[68]

Jackson was a big supporter of the American cause during World War II, and graciously responded to any soldiers requesting autographs. One such request came from the Percy Jones Hospital in Michigan, and Joe was more than willing to oblige. The friend of the injured soldier later wrote Carter "Scoop" Latimer in the *Greenville News*, saying, "Oh, yes! 'Shoeless' Joe Jackson sent him two grand autographed photos today—and is the guy happy." An area citizen, Elizabeth Kirksey added, "Joe Jackson will be doubly blessed for his kindness. It is so often the little things in life that make happiness, but the big thing Mr. Jackson did for those boys will ever be a blessing for him."[69]

A series of heart attacks slowed Joe down even further and, while bedridden, he lost more than 30 pounds. He was interviewed at length by "Scoop" Latimer in a piece that was featured on the front page of *The Sporting News* on September 24, 1942. The story was exhaustive, relating memories, factoids, and insightful perspectives. "I have no regrets," he told the reporter. "The world couldn't treat me any better. Regardless of what anybody says, I'm innocent of any wrongdoing. I gave baseball all I had. I think my record in the 1919 World's Series will stand up against that of any man in that series or any other World's Series in all history. If I had been guilty of 'laying down' in the series, I wouldn't be so successful today—for I'm a great believer in retribution. I have made a lot more money since being out of baseball than when I was in it. The Supreme Being is the only one to whom I've got to answer."[70]

Joe repeatedly proclaimed his innocence for years, and used the statistics of the 1919 Series as his proof. But had there not been so many inconsistencies and discrepancies in his stories, and versions reciting either his actions or inactions, it would be easier to support his claims. His 1920 confession to the grand jury was the rawest testimony he ever delivered and, fearing criminal prosecution, he let it all out. It wasn't until later that he began adding details and dismissing earlier parts of his confession to better suit the bid to clear his name. One of the most recent additions to his story was the assertion that he wanted to be suspended before the 1919 Series began because he'd heard teammates plotting to throw games and didn't want to be associated with it. He claimed he went to Charles Comiskey's room and the Sox owner denied his request.[71] This depiction would've certainly boosted his moral credibility in 1920, but it was neglected during his testimony. One might ask why?

Another version of the "telling Comiskey" story was recited in other periodicals and books. As the infamous yarn goes, Lefty Williams gave Joe the crooked money once the Series concluded, but Jackson didn't want it. That started an argument between the two friends, and Joe left the hotel in anger. When he returned, he found the cash-filled envelope still in his room, and decided to do the right thing and take it to Comiskey's office. However, Comiskey refused to see him, wherein Jackson then gave the envelope to the team's business manager, Harry Grabiner.[72] And that was the last he saw of any of the tainted gambling money. This tale portrays Jackson to be the conscientious, honest, All-American ballplayer that people always wanted him to be.

Both sanitized versions reject his 1920 testimony, the comments he made to the press, and the confessions by other Sox players. Overall, it is a whitewash of history with the intent of keeping Jackson's legacy unstained by the gambling scandal. But Jackson was indeed stained. Additionally, his confession revealed that he not only accepted the money, but was eagerly awaiting payment after each of the first four games. He was so impatient about receiving what he was promised that he inquired to Chick Gandil a number of times, pressing him for the cash. He also spoke with Bill Burns the day of the first game and later with Cicotte, and each conversation pertained to different aspects of the fix. While it was true that Joe wasn't in the "inner circle" of the plot's organizers and didn't attend any of the initial meetings, Joe did admit attending one conference in Cicotte's hotel room, remembered specifically because Eddie told him he was a "God damn fool for not getting [the money he was owed] in [his] hand like he did."[73]

Jackson going all the way to Comiskey in order to turn the money in and reveal the fix is also a difficult sell. For one, Joe was on the outs with Comiskey because of the latter's unflattering comments about his jump to the shipyards. The Sox owner was partly responsible for the negative backlash against Joe, essentially calling him unpatriotic during a time of world war. Jackson and Comiskey didn't have a personal history of any kind, nor was the latter all that available to any of his players around that time frame. Going to him would've made a lot less sense than visiting manager Kid Gleason, a person Joe did trust and have an amicable relationship with. It would've been a lot easier to reveal the conspiracy to Gleason, or to anyone other than "The Old Roman" for innumerable reasons.

It's not that Jackson was a liar, but the multitude of explanations and the ever-changing stories draw everything into question. His moral credibility was, in fact, bolstered at one point during his grand jury testimony when he revealed trying to back out of the conspiracy. Feeling uneasy about things, he pulled Gandil aside, telling him: "I am not going to be in it. I will just get out of that altogether." Unwilling to let the heavy-hitting outfielder out, Gandil responded threateningly, telling him: "It wouldn't be well for [you] if [you] did that." He added that since Joe was already involved, it might as well stay that way.[74] The intimidation of Gandil and Swede Risberg, plus not wanting to snitch on his teammates, was a powerful combination, leaving

Jackson relatively helpless. He was not a hardened criminal but, giving him the benefit of the doubt, it was clear he had gotten himself in way over his head. There was no way to right the wrongs developing around him—if that is what he truly wanted to do.

No one knows when Jackson talked to Gandil about getting out of the conspiracy. And if he was truly compelled to do the right thing, he would've gone to any number of officials or sportswriters to break the story open. He didn't need Comiskey or Gleason to do it, nor did he need the approval of Gandil or Risberg. Jackson was a mature man with a lifetime of experiences behind him. If his conscience was truly bothered, Joe was solely responsible for his actions. And his silence was deafening. There is no excuse for his nonintervention.

Jackson's innocence—the innocence he believed with conviction throughout his life—may start and stop at the fact that he played to win in the 1919 Series. He believed it wholeheartedly and it may be 100 percent true. Based on that fact, it is understandable that he'd defend himself to the press and insist he gave it all he had. But Jackson was given the lifetime banishment from Organized Baseball not because of what he did on the field, but because he admitted to being a part of the conspiracy. He admitted to wanting $20,000 to join his crooked teammates and confessed to accepting $5,000. Even if he played every second of the Series with unabashed skill and competence, he still agreed to enter Gandil's conspiracy. That made him equally guilty to those who were actively trying to affect the games through misplay. There is no way to cover this up. It is impossible to place the blame solely on Comiskey, the owner's alleged miserliness, or a general cover-up that will erase what Jackson himself admitted.[75]

It is only possible to distract from the truth. The Chicago and Milwaukee court cases succeeded in doing just that. Altogether, the "Black Sox" players were acquitted and the jury in Milwaukee gave Jackson a verdict over Comiskey, only to see it overturned. None of the men went to jail for the 1919 conspiracy, but each had to live under the shame the crooked event caused. "The only one of the crooks that I could make the slightest excuse for is Joe Jackson," teammate Shano Collins said. "His ignorance and illiteracy lets him out to a great extent. I think he is easily influenced. But for the others I have no sympathy."[76] Like Collins, there were sportswriters and fans who were ready to forgive Joe because of his "ignorance and illiteracy," and people who wondered if he knew the difference between right and wrong when he agreed to join Gandil and the others.

Money was at the root of the scandal and, for Jackson, the importance of greenbacks was established early in his life. As a teenager, he was helping support his family. And not before long was he the central breadwinner for his mother and siblings. If he was blinded by the $20,000 offer and unable to differentiate between what was ethical and what was immoral, that is something to take into consideration. His limitations, after all, are of vital importance to the accurate telling of his story. The combination of his infatuation with money, plus his poor intellect was a perfect storm, and, as John Lardner wrote in 1934, "He was the answer to a gambler's prayer."[77]

Looking over his career, the press was quite ironical with Jackson, but didn't exactly know it at the time. In 1915, a columnist for *The Sporting News* wrote: "Joe Jackson tells them how he turned down $60,000 to play with the [Federal League] for three years. It looked like a lot of money, he said, but there are things in this world to be regarded above money—keeping faith with your friends, for instance. All of which goes to show that you don't have to know how to read and write to be a man of principle and conscience."[78] In another report, J. V. Fitzgerald of the *Washington Post* wrote: "Great player that he is, he can never hope again to take his place with the stars of the game. Ordinarily prone to forget, the American public will not do so in the case of the slugging Chicago outfielder. It seems a shame that a player of Jackson's ability has dug his own grave in baseball. He has no one but himself to blame." Fitzgerald's comments were made in 1918 and related to his jump to the shipyards.[79]

In looking at the life of "Shoeless Joe," it is evident that he faced innumerable forks in the road and was called upon to make split second decisions that sincerely affected his path. Other decisions, however, were out of his hands. It is easy to say that if he was educated or even stayed with the Philadelphia Athletics, the banished Jackson that we are confronted with today would likely have never come to fruition at all. Remember how his early baseball coaches tried to change his batting style to fit the customary approach? Imagine if one of them would have succeeded? Joe was considered great because of his instinctual understanding of baseball and, believe it or not, the naiveté of not being educated was a factor in that success.

Imagine if Jackson had gone to the Chicago Cubs or the Brooklyn Superbas, two teams which also wanted him early in his career, or if Charles

Somers hadn't been so financially strapped in 1914–15, Cleveland would never have let him go to Chicago. But, directed by destiny, he ended up with the Chicago White Sox on a combustible franchise, which was also destined for a fate beyond compare.

Following the death of Judge Landis in 1944, Jackson advocates were primed to petition baseball's next commissioner, Happy Chandler, hoping for leniency. Officials were making headway in their grassroots operation, but their efforts didn't land on the commissioner's desk.[80] In fact, Chandler later said: "They never sent it to me. If they had, I'd have looked into it." It was likely Joe would've gotten a fair deal had the petition gone all the way. In 1988, Chandler announced his support of Jackson's reinstatement, and felt he belonged in the National Baseball Hall of Fame.[81] The Hall of Fame, incidentally, was opened in 1939 at Cooperstown, New York. The inaugural class included Joe's peers: Ty Cobb, Walter Johnson, and Babe Ruth—three men who had the utmost respect for Jackson—plus Christy Mathewson and Honus Wagner. One could only imagine what Joe would've looked like next to his contemporaries, and there is little doubt that Cobb, Johnson, and Ruth would have supported his enshrinement.

Bothered by continued heart trouble, Jackson turned sixty years old in 1948 and was thrilled by a special "Joe Jackson Night" gala at Brandon Mills Park on August 2. An estimated 2,500 spectators were on hand to honor Joe, offering a "tremendous ovation" and watched as friends gave him gifts in tribute. Jackson was humbled by the experience, thanking the crowd and those who put the event together.[82] The following year, he was interviewed at length by Furman Bisher for a piece in *Sport* magazine, and it was clear Joe still had strong opinions about the 1919 scandal. However, he stood by the belief that he was never involved in the conspiracy, tried to compel Comiskey to suspend him prior to the first game, and invoked his Series accomplishments. But altogether, he wasn't resentful and declared that his "conscience [was] clear."[83]

In 1951, the Cleveland Indians wanted to honor Jackson in a similar fashion to what took place in Brandon Mills, but, of course, on a much larger scale. A telegram was sent to Joe in August, notifying him of his inclusion on the club's All-Time, All-Star team, which included membership in the franchise's official Hall of Fame. It was a significant acknowledgment of

CLASS OF SERVICE

This is a full-rate Telegram or Cablegram unless its deferred character is indicated by a suitable symbol above or preceding the address.

WESTERN UNION

W. P. MARSHALL, PRESIDENT

SYMBOLS

DL=Day Letter

NL=Night Letter

LT=Int'l Letter Telegram

VLT=Int'l Victory Ltr.

The filing time shown in the date line on telegrams and day letters is STANDARD TIME at point of origin. Time of receipt is STANDARD TIME at point of destination

1951 AUG 26 AM 11 09

AA043 CTA217

ZCT.CLA342 LONG PD=WUX CLEVELAND OHIO 26 1036A=

JOE JACKSON= 1262 Pendleton St

GREENVILLE SOUTH CAROLINA=

YOU HAVE BEEN SELECTED BY FANS OF CLEVELAND TO ALL-TIME ALL-STAR TEAM OF THIS CITY TO BE HONORED AT OUR AMERICAN LEAGUE FIFTIETH ANNIVERSARY CELEBRATION AT CLEVELAND STADIUM NEXT SUNDAY AFTERNOON SEPTEMBER 2. WE WOULD LIKE VERY MUCH FOR YOU TO ATTEND NEXT WEEK-END'S ACTIVITIES WHICH INCLUDE NIGHT GAME SATURDAY, NATURALLY, WE WILL ASSUME ALL OF YOUR EXPENSES FOR FIRST CLASS TRAVEL, HOTEL AND MEALS. PLEASE TELEPHONE ME COLLECT TUESDAY, AUGUST 28, AT TOWER 1-1200 FOR COMPLETE DETAILS. REGARDS=

NATE WALLACK PROMOTIONAL DIRECTOR CLEVELAND INDIANS=

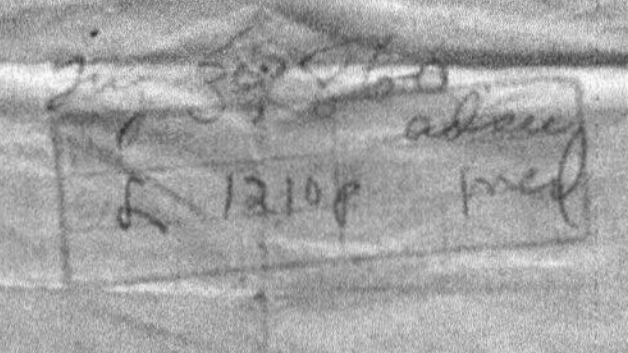

THE COMPANY WILL APPRECIATE SUGGESTIONS FROM ITS PATRONS CONCERNING ITS SERVICE

Notified by telegram that he was named to Cleveland's All-Time, All-Star team in 1951, Jackson was invited to a special ceremony that summer at Cleveland Stadium. Unfortunately, because of health problems, Joe was unable to attend.

his hard work, and Joe wanted nothing more to be in Cleveland to accept the tribute alongside the other honorees. His health was worsening, though, and kept him from making the journey. It was later arranged for Jackson to travel to New York to be awarded a gold clock representative of his honor on Ed Sullivan's *Toast of the Town* television program.[84] Just days before he was supposed to make the trip, Joseph Jackson passed away on December 5, 1951. He was sixty-four years old.[85]

Jackson's death came at 10:15 p.m., and his passing was rapid and unexpected. He actually felt sick days earlier, but went to his store as usual. On December 5, Joe went to bed early, only to be awoken by sharp chest pains, and died before medical assistance could arrive.[86] Katie and the rest of the Jackson Family were showered with an outpouring of affection and sympathy from friends in Greenville and from the larger baseball community.[87] Ty Cobb, who visited Joe briefly at his liquor store five years earlier, sent a message, stating: "Joe is gone. He was a good man and a great man and a great ball player."[88] Telegrams and floral arrangements from all over the country were received, including heartfelt messages from Charles A. Comiskey II and Lefty Williams.[89] Scoop Latimer wrote about his great achievements on the diamond, and added: "Above all, he was a devoted husband and Mrs. Jackson a devoted wife. We will miss him."[90]

Several hundred people braved wintery weather to attend his funeral on December 9, 1951, at Woodlawn Memorial Park in Greenville, among them being Lou Brissie of the Cleveland Indians and former teammates Walter Barbare and Champ Osteen. A preacher declared, "Mr. Jackson had run his race and is now at peace with God."[91] John P. Carmichael of the *Chicago Daily News* memorialized: "Shoeless Joe Jackson has gone upstairs and you ought to hear the old-timers talk about him. Not crying in their beer at his passing, but remembering him with respect and admiration. None of the old-timers—not one—thinks he was guilty in the 1919 series scandal. They exonerate him completely, with the kindly absolution that 'he didn't know what it was all about.'"[92]

Whether he did or didn't will be debated for the rest of time. Columnist Jim Anderson summed it up perfectly. "Joe Jackson was either innocent or guilty," he wrote. "There are those who believe each way. And they will never know for sure."[93] George Landry of the *Columbus Ledger-Inquirer* added: "Chances are people will talk and wonder about 'Shoeless' Joe Jackson as long as kids grow up with a ball and bat in their hands or grown-ups will fill their favorite bleacher seats at baseball games."[94] He couldn't have been more right. Nearly a century after the 1919 World Series, the conspiracy, the players, and specifically "Shoeless Joe" Jackson remain hot button topics with the public. There is an endless stream of fascinating stories relating to these subjects, and fans are always looking for a new perspective on the "Black Sox" and the heroes of the Deadball Era.

Jackson's final active season was in 1920, and at thirty-two years of age batted a remarkable .382 in 146 games, third in the American League behind George Sisler (.407) and Tris Speaker (.388). He achieved 218 hits, 42 doubles, 20 triples, and 12 home runs. These statistics added to his career numbers, which, after 13 seasons, resulted in the following: .356 batting average, 1772 hits, 307 doubles, 168 triples, 54 home runs, 873 runs, 785 RBIs, 202 stolen bases, a .423 on-base-percentage, and a .517 slugging percentage. Most of his numbers were quite pedestrian compared to the sport's leaders, mostly because his career ended after 13 seasons. In comparison, Ty Cobb played twenty-four seasons and doubled many of Joe's stats. But Jackson's .356 lifetime batting average is still third all-time behind Cobb (.366) and Rogers Hornsby (.358), and that figure places him with the most exclusive company in baseball history.

His incredible statistics stand out when compared to those enshrined in Cooperstown, and there is no doubt that he left an indelible mark that cannot be erased from history, even if his numbers have been scrubbed from the official record books. Had he finished his career naturally, there is no telling what kind of stats he would've ultimately put up. In 1912, Tom Terrell of the *Cleveland Leader* predicted that "there [was] a possibility that some day Joe [would] be labeled the 'greatest.'"[95] He was headed in that direction and it is arguable if he would have succeeded, but certainly, at the very least, he would have been just as celebrated as those in the inaugural class of the Hall of Fame. Regardless of what was said and done, Joe did have an innate love for the national pastime, and, as a result of the scandal, Organized Baseball was robbed of the many advantages of having a pure, natural hitter like Jackson around.

The fans were robbed as well. Overall, it is pretty easy to oversimplify the story of Joe Jackson and judge his decision-making by focusing on his lack of education. But in truth, his life was much harder to understand. Sure, he was a fearless hitter, a man who felt every pitcher was the same and swung with a natural ability unrivaled in history, but the complexities of "Shoeless Joe" go well beyond the diamond. The public's fascination with Jackson was immensely strong during his heyday, and continues decades later. There is a certain mystique to his character, there is awe in his achievements, and even his colorful nickname peaks the interest of fans today. His role in the 1919 conspiracy left the leaders of Major League Baseball with no other option but to treat him like the other members of the "Black Sox," as there was no way to distinguish between them. Crooks are crooks on any level.

For the sake of baseball's integrity, they had to be punished. But once you peel back the surface and start examining the specific factors, the statements, and the details of the controversy, there is definitely room to differentiate between the members of the crooked Sox. If anyone, Joe Jackson deserved an impartial review, breaking down his case from his 1920 testimony to the various statements of his teammates. The existing evidence, the statistics, and other mitigating elements might have been enough to alter the public's perception of his role in the conspiracy and perhaps led to his reinstatement. But after all these years, it would take a bold baseball official to take on the challenge. Commissioner Chandler might have been the last man even interested in such a difficult project, and Joe's advocates missed the boat.

The popularity of Jackson didn't waver much as time passed. The 1982 novel *Shoeless Joe* by W. P. Kinsella and later the film *Field of Dreams*, featuring the image of Jackson, are considered classics by the sporting public. Organized movements to clear his name continued, and influential names like Ted Williams and Bob Feller vocally spoke out in favor of Jackson's restoration into the good graces of baseball. The banishment remains in place as of 2016, and the supporters of Joe Jackson hope to one day see him get a fair and thorough reassessment, exploring the depths of his case. For Jackson, over and above any of the other players with lifetime bans, deserves special treatment for the gift he brought to baseball and for the legend he created that remains in place to this day.

STATE OF SOUTH CAROLINA
CERTIFICATION OF VITAL RECORD

Registration Dist. No. 2209-B
Registrar's No. 109
Birth No.

STANDARD CERTIFICATE OF DEATH
Division of Vital Statistics – State Board of Health
State of South Carolina
State File No. 51 016424

1. PLACE OF DEATH: (a) County Greenville
(b) City or town (If outside corporate limits, write RURAL and give township) Rural G'ville
(c) Length of Stay: (in this place)
(d) Full name of hospital or institution: (If not in hospital or institution, give street address or location) 119 E. Wilburn Ave.

2. USUAL RESIDENCE: (Where deceased lived. If institution: residence before admission)
(a) State. S. C. (b) County. G'ville
(c) City or town (If outside corporate limits, write RURAL and give township) Rural G'ville
(d) Street address (If rural, give location) Same

3. NAME OF DECEASED: (Type or Print) a. (First) Joseph b. (Middle) W. c. (Last) Jackson
4. Date of death: (Month) (Day) (Year) Dec. 5, 1951
5. Sex: male
6. Color or race: white
7. Married, never married, widowed, divorced: (Specify) married
8. Date of birth: July 16, 1889
9. Age: (In years last birthday) 62
10a. Usual occupation: (Give kind of work done during most of working life, even if retired) Merchant
10b. Kind of business or industry: Liquor Store
11. Birthplace: (State or foreign country) Greenville Co. S. C.
12. Citizen of what country? USA
13a. Father's name: Elmore Jackson
13b. Mother's maiden name: Martha Ann Jenkinson
14. Husband or wife's name: Katie Wynn
15. Was deceased ever in U. S. armed forces? (Yes, no, or unknown) (If yes, give war or dates of service)
16. Social Security No.
17. Informant: Mrs. Katie W. Jackson

MEDICAL CERTIFICATION

18. Cause of Death: I. Disease or condition directly leading to death (a) Coronary thrombosis
Antecedent causes: Morbid conditions, if any, giving rise to the above cause (a) stating the underlying cause last
Due to (b) Arteriosclerosis
Due to (c) Cirrhosis of liver
II. Other significant conditions: Conditions contributing to the death but not related to the disease or condition causing death
Interval between onset and death: 45 min. / 5 yrs / 2 years

19a. Date of operation: —
19b. Major findings of operation: —
20. Autopsy? YES ☐ NO ☑

21a. Accident Suicide Homicide (Specify) —
21b. Place of injury: (e. g., in or about home, farm, factory, street, office bldg., etc.)
21c. (City, Town, or Township) (County) (State) —
21d. Time of injury: (Month) (Day) (Year) (Hour) m.
21e. Injury occurred: While at work ☐ Not while at work ☐
21f. How did injury occur?

22. I hereby certify that I attended the deceased from Dec 1, 1950 to Dec 5, 1951, that I last saw the deceased alive on Dec 4, 1951, and that death occurred at 10 P m., from the causes and on the date stated above.
23a. Signature: B. M. McLawhon M.D. (Degree or title)
23b. Address: Greenville, S.C.
23c. Date signed:

24a. Burial, cremation, removal: (Specify) burial
24b. Date: 12/9/51
24c. Name of cemetery or crematory: Woodlawn Mem. Park
24d. Location: (City, town, or county) (State) Greenville, S. C.
Date rec'd by local registrar: 1-4-52
Registrar's signature: Thos. V. McAfee, Jr.
25. Funeral director: Thomas McAfee
Address: Greenville, S. C.

FEDERAL SECURITY AGENCY PUBLIC HEALTH SERVICE Form No. VS-5

SC 00588610

ISSUED JUL 23 2009

This is a true certification of the facts on file in the Division of Vital Records, SC Department of Health and Environmental Control.

C. Earl Hunter
Commissioner and State Registrar

Guang Zhao
Assistant State Registrar

This copy is not valid unless prepared on an engraved border displaying the state seal and issuing agency logo.

Revision Date: 05/01/2006

DHEC

ANY ALTERATION OR ERASURE VOIDS THIS CERTIFICATE

South Carolina Certificate of Death for Joe Jackson, who passed away on December 5, 1951, of coronary thrombosis. Jackson was buried at Woodlawn Memorial Park in Greenville.

ENDNOTES

INTRODUCTION

1 *Chicago Daily Tribune,* July 5, 1916, p. 15.
2 *Chicago Examiner,* July 5, 1916, p. 13.
3 *Baseball Magazine,* March 1916, p. 66–67.

CHAPTER ONE: "SHOELESS JOE"

1 James Samuel Jackson's year of birth was either 1805 or 1813, depending on the source. If he was born in 1813, he would've been fifty-one in 1864; the year the Confederate conscription age was raised to fifty, and still would've avoided service. If he was born in 1805, he would've been fifty-six in 1861, at the start of the war. See 1860 and 1870 U.S. Federal Censuses, ancestry.com.
2 Martha was a first generation American-born citizen as well, and her father was also from England.
3 *Durham Sun,* May 3, 1913, p. 3.
4 Jackson's World War I Draft Registration and Certificate of Death are available at ancestry.com. The invaluable resource Baseball-Reference.com cites 1887 as his birth year.
5 *New York Herald,* August 11, 1912, p. 7.
6 *Cleveland Plain Dealer,* April 16, 1912, p. 9.
7 *Growing Up with Shoeless Joe* by Joe Thompson, 1998, The R. L. Bryan Company, p. 6.
8 Jackson's exact quotes were: "There's eleven regular players on our team. Father, mother, six brothers, two sisters, and little 'Joe.'" *New York Herald,* August 11, 1912, p. 7. Joe confirmed having "six other brothers," in another article. *San Francisco Chronicle,* August 25, 1912, p. 7.
9 *Milwaukee Evening Sentinel,* January 29, 1924, p. 1.
10 According to one source, the other brother may have been "Earl Jackson."
11 *Columbia State,* July 8, 1901. The mill was at 25 Draper Street.

12 South Carolina was known for its lax child labor laws.

13 George's illiteracy was confirmed by the 1910 U.S. Federal Census, where it is indicated that he could neither read nor write. Martha and the other children could read, according to the census, but Martha, Lula, and Dave could not write.

14 *Atlanta Constitution*, September 26, 1917, p. 14.

15 *Baseball Magazine*, March 1916, p. 53–67. Also see Greenville City Directories, 1907, 1910.

16 Joe reportedly started playing baseball at nine years of age. *Washington Herald*, March 26, 1917, p. 9.

17 *Baseball Magazine*, March 1916, p. 53–67.

18 *Baseball Magazine*, September 1917, p. 492.

19 *San Francisco Chronicle*, August 25, 1912, p. 7.

20 *Pittsburgh Daily Post*, May 25, 1913, p. 44.

21 Ibid.

22 *Cleveland Plain Dealer*, March 28, 1912, p. 10.

23 *Greenville News*, January 28, 1938, p. 17.

24 U.S. Census records, ancestry.com.

25 *Charleston News and Courier*, February 13, 1913, p. 7.

26 Martin passed away in 1915 and Ferguson in 1916; neither would see Jackson's ultimate fate in MLB.

27 According to one source, W. R. Moseley managed the Victor Mills squad, while others claimed it was Garvin Suttles.

28 *Charlotte Observer*, March 2, 1911, p. 2. Additional Stouch quotes about signing Jackson. *The Sporting News*, April 15, 1909, p. 4. Quotes by Laval about meeting Jackson. *Greenwood Index-Journal*, December 27, 1939, p. 8.

29 *Greenville Daily News*, April 17, 1908, p. 2.

30 *Greenville Daily News*, April 29, 1908, p. 2.

31 *Greenville Daily News*, April 26, 1908, p. 2.

32 *Greenville Daily News*, May 1, 1908, p. 2.

33 *Greenville Daily News*, May 22, 1908, p. 2.

34 *Washington Post*, December 29, 1912, p. 3. Jackson explained it again in 1932, and said he was pitching on this specific occasion. *Franklin News-Herald*, March 10, 1932, p. 8.

35 *Greenville Daily News*, June 5–6, 1908.

36 *Greenville Daily News*, July 10, 1908, p. 2.

37 *Greenville Daily News*, July 21, 1908, p. 2.

38 Memphis wouldn't agree to pay $300 for Jackson. *Delaware County Daily Times*, February 28, 1913, p. 3.

39 *Charlotte Observer*, March 24, 1912, p. 8, *Anaconda Standard*, July 27, 1913, p. 28, *Greenville Daily News*, May 22, 1908, p. 2, *Sporting Life*, July 25 and August 1, 1908.

40 *Greenville Daily News*, August 15, 1908, p. 2.

41 *Greenville Daily News*, August 13, 1908, p. 1. Greenville later dropped its protest and Greensboro was awarded the Carolina Association pennant. *Greenville Daily News*, August 19, 1908, p. 2.

42 *Greenville Daily News,* August 23, 1908, p. 2.
43 *Philadelphia Inquirer,* August 26, 1908, p. 11.
44 *Greenville Daily News,* August 29, 1908, p. 2.
45 One report claimed first baseman Harry Davis went to Greenville to get Jackson back. *Pittsburgh Press,* July 7, 1916, p. 29.
46 *New York Herald,* August 11, 1912, p. 7.
47 *Charlotte News,* June 1, 1912, p. 6.
48 *Greenville Daily News,* September 22, 1908, p. 2.
49 *Greensboro Record,* January 4, 1909, p. 5.
50 *Western Sentinel,* May 11, 1909, p. 2.
51 *Savannah Morning News,* June 11, 1909, p. 8.
52 *Savannah Morning News,* September 2, 1909, p. 8.
53 *Savannah Morning News,* May 13, 1909, p. 8.
54 *Macon Telegraph,* June 11, 1909, p. 6 and *Savannah Morning News,* June 11, 1909, p. 8.
55 Chattanooga won the first half of the 1909 season. *South Atlantic League, 1904–1963: A Year-by-Year Statistical History* by Marshall D. Wright, 2009, McFarland, p. 29–34.
56 *Columbus Daily Enquirer,* July 17, 1909, p. 6.
57 Jackson went 2-for-5 in his last Sally League performance. *Macon Telegraph,* September 1, 1909, p. 6.
58 *Savannah Morning News,* September 2, 1909, p. 8.
59 *Philadelphia Inquirer,* September 8, 1909, p. 10.
60 Jackson went 3-for-17 for Philadelphia in 1909 for a batting average of .176.
61 *Columbia State,* November 23, 1909, p. 12.
62 *Philadelphia Inquirer,* March 1 and March 3, 1910.
63 *Charlotte Observer,* March 7, 1910, p. 2.
64 *Atlanta Georgian and News,* February 2, 1911, p. 10. It was reported that Mack obtained waivers on Jackson. *New Orleans Item,* March 15, 1910, p. 12.
65 *New Orleans Times-Picayune,* March 10, 1910, p. 12.
66 *New Orleans Item,* April 9, 1910, p. 6.
67 *Charleston Evening Post,* June 13, 1910, p. 3.
68 *New Orleans Item,* July 9, 1910, p. 6.

CHAPTER TWO: BOUND FOR THE BIG SHOW

1 *The Sporting News,* June 16, 1910, p. 2.
2 The attendance for the Naps that season was 293,456, which was the sixth lowest (out of eight) in the league, and the team's lowest since 1904 (264,749).
3 *Cleveland Plain Dealer,* April 21, 1910, p. 9. The reconstructed stadium, known as League Park II, opened on April 21, 1910, and the Naps were defeated by Detroit, 5–0.
4 Somers reportedly loaned Charles A. Comiskey money in Chicago, while, at the same time, investing and becoming a stockholder in the Philadelphia Athletics,

Boston Americans, and Cleveland Blues. *The Sporting News*, January 7, 1915, p. 1. The inflation calculator used had a starting year of 1913, and it can be assumed that the real inflation amount for 1900–01 to 2015 is well over $18 million. www.bls.gov/data/inflation_calculator.htm.

5 *Atlanta Georgian and News*, February 2, 1911, p. 10.

6 *Cleveland Plain Dealer*, July 24, 1910, p. 15. Infielder Morrie Rath played six total seasons in the major leagues for Philadelphia, Cleveland, Chicago White Sox, and Cincinnati Reds. He was a member of the Reds 1919 World Series championship club and ended his career with a lifetime .254 batting average.

7 Cleveland Naps Vice President Ernest Barnard went to Philadelphia to negotiate the terms of the deal with Connie Mack shortly before the Lord-Rath deal was announced. *Cleveland Plain Dealer*, July 31, 1910, p. 15. A New Orleans reporter claimed that the purchase price for Jackson was around $5,000 and noted that it was "not an out-and-out cash trade." *New Orleans Item*, August 5, 1910, p. 10.

8 Bris Lord reported to Philadelphia immediately and played in 70 games, batting .280.

9 *New Orleans Times-Picayune*, August 1, 1910, p. 12. Carlton Molesworth, player-manager of the Birmingham Barons, was the only other player in the Southern League with 100 or more hits at the time (108).

10 *New Orleans Item*, August 30, 1910, p. 8.

11 *New Orleans Item*, August 11, 1910, p. 11.

12 *New Orleans Item*, August 16, 1910, p. 8.

13 *New Orleans Times-Picayune*, August 21, 1910, p. 8.

14 *New Orleans Item*, August 28, 1910, p. 17.

15 *New Orleans Item* and *New Orleans Times-Picayune*, August 31, 1910.

16 *New Orleans Item*, September 4, 1910, p. 21.

17 *New Orleans Item*, September 11, 1910, p. 6.

18 The watch fob was awarded to fifteen members of the New Orleans club. It featured a bird-eye diamond and was made of solid gold, hand-crafted by Hausman and Sons. *New Orleans Item*, September 12, 1910, p. 8.

19 Of the eight American League teams, the Cleveland Naps had the second-oldest team with an average age of 28.875. Only the St. Louis Browns were older, with an average age of 29.375.

20 *New Orleans Item*, August 2, 1910, p. 9.

21 *Cleveland Plain Dealer*, July 27, 1910, p. 8.

22 *The Sporting News*, December 21, 1911, p. 2.

23 *New Orleans Item*, September 11, 1910, p. 6.

24 *New Orleans Times-Picayune*, September 5, 1910, p. 10.

25 *New Orleans Item*, August 24, 1910, p. 9.

26 *Cincinnati Post*, October 4, 1910, p. 3.

27 *Cleveland Plain Dealer*, September 13, 1910, p. 10.

28 *Cleveland Plain Dealer*, September 16, 1910, p. 7.

29 *Cleveland Plain Dealer*, September 17, 1910, p. 8.

30 Ibid.

31 *Cleveland Plain Dealer*, September 18, 1910, p. 21.
32 *Cleveland Plain Dealer*, September 20, 1910, p. 8.
33 *Cleveland Plain Dealer*, September 25, 1910, p. 20.
34 *Cleveland Plain Dealer*, October 2, 1910, p. 1C.
35 *Cleveland Plain Dealer*, October 6, 1910, p. 10.
36 Washington sportswriter J. Ed. Grillo commented that Cobb and Lajoie were lucky that Jackson entered the league late in the season because had he been there from the beginning, he most likely would have been in the thick of the fight for league batting honors. *Washington Evening Star*, October 2, 1910.
37 *Cleveland Plain Dealer*, October 9, 1910, p. 18.
38 Henry P. Edwards called the mistakes in the outfield by Jackson and Jack Graney, "awful baseball." *Cleveland Plain Dealer*, October 12, 1910, p. 8.
39 *Cleveland Plain Dealer*, October 19, 1910, p. 11.
40 *Anaconda Standard*, March 28, 1911, p. 2. A report cited that Mack had planned to use Jackson in his outfield in 1911, but sacrificed him for a more experienced player to better his chances for the championship in 1910. *Cleveland Plain Dealer*, November 20, 1910, p. 2C.
41 *Wilkes-Barre Times-Leader*, November 28, 1910, p. 12.
42 *Brooklyn Daily Eagle*, March 31, 1911, p. 25.
43 *Anaconda Standard*, March 28, 1911, p. 2.
44 *Charlotte News*, April 1, 1911, p. 6.
45 *Lincoln Daily News*, January 28, 1911, p. 6.
46 *Washington Herald*, February 15, 1911, p. 10.
47 *Atlanta Constitution*, January 29, 1911, p. 3.
48 *Winnipeg Tribune*, March 24, 1911, p. 6.
49 *The Sporting News*, June 11, 1952, p. 6.
50 *Philadelphia Inquirer*, November 6, 1910, p. 3.
51 *Cleveland Plain Dealer*, November 16, 1910, p. 8.
52 *Philadelphia Inquirer*, April 11, 1911, p. 10.
53 *Cleveland Plain Dealer*, November 20, 1910, p. 2C.
54 Ibid.
55 *Cleveland Plain Dealer*, November 29, 1910, p. 8.
56 *Cleveland Plain Dealer*, February 24, 1911, p. 10.
57 *Winnipeg Tribune*, April 1, 1911, p. 19.
58 *Western Sentinel*, April 18, 1911, p. 8.
59 *New Orleans Item*, March 6, 1911, p. 11.
60 *Cleveland Plain Dealer*, March 7, 1911, p. 8.
61 *Cleveland Plain Dealer*, March 12, 1911, p. 6C.
62 Nap Lajoie's bats were also destroyed in the fire, and he too, had to send a bat to Louisville so that the exact specs could be duplicated. *Cleveland Plain Dealer*, March 24, 1911, p. 10. The J. F. Hillerich & Son fire occurred on December 17, 1910.
63 *Cleveland Plain Dealer*, April 15, 1911, p. 14 and *Cincinnati Post*, April 17, 1911, p. 6.
64 *New York Times*, April 18, 1911, p. 9.

65 *Cleveland Plain Dealer*, April 18, 1911, p. 13.
66 *Cleveland Plain Dealer*, March 25, 1911, p. 8.
67 *The Sporting News*, April 27, 1911, p. 6.
68 *New Orleans Item*, March 26, 1911, p. 18 and *Cleveland Plain Dealer*, March 26, 1911, p. 16.
69 *Cleveland Plain Dealer*, March 7, 1911, p. 8.

CHAPTER THREE: "THAT GUY AIN'T HUMAN"

1 *Colorado Springs Gazette*, April 2, 1911, p. 18.
2 *Cleveland Plain Dealer*, April 13, 1911, p. 13.
3 By May 4, he'd only gone hitless in two games. *Cleveland Plain Dealer*, May 5, 1911, p. 12.
4 *Cleveland Plain Dealer*, April 21, 1911, p. 11.
5 Jackson's blast topped the previous League Park distance mark set by Sam Crawford of the Detroit Tigers. Crawford's hit of July 1, 1910, went a total of 350 feet. *Cleveland Plain Dealer*, April 22, 1911, p. 9–10. Additional details were offered in *Sporting Life*, April 29, 1911, p. 3.
6 *Cleveland Plain Dealer*, May 8, 1911, p. 7.
7 *Boston Herald*, May 11, 1911, p. 4.
8 McGuire's Naps went 6–11 before he resigned. *Cleveland Plain Dealer*, May 4, 1911, p. 9.
9 *Anaconda Standard*, December 17, 1911, p. 23.
10 *Cleveland Plain Dealer*, May 23, 1911, p. 9.
11 *Cleveland Plain Dealer*, June 5, 1911, p. 7.
12 *Washington Times*, June 7, 1911, p. 13.
13 *Sandusky Star-Journal*, July 1, 1911, p. 10.
14 *Cleveland Plain Dealer*, July 5, 1911, p. 7.
15 *Cleveland Plain Dealer*, July 17–18, 1911.
16 *Cleveland Plain Dealer*, July 25, 1911, p. 7.
17 *Twin-City Daily Sentinel*, July 28, 1911, p. 6.
18 *Charlotte Observer*, August 26, 1911, p. 3.
19 Ibid.
20 *Cleveland Plain Dealer*, September 1, 1911, p. 7.
21 *Washington Times*, January 23, 1911, p. 12.
22 *Cleveland Plain Dealer*, June 7, 1911, p. 7.
23 *Charlotte Evening Chronicle*, July 24, 1911, p. 8.
24 *El Paso Herald*, March 11, 1912, p. 5.
25 *Charlotte Observer*, September 23, 1911, p. 3.
26 *The Sporting News*, November 20, 1941, p. 7, September 10, 1936, p. 4.
27 *Ty Cobb: My Life in Baseball* by Ty Cobb with Al Stump, 1993, Bison Book edition, p. 176–177.
28 *Cleveland Plain Dealer*, August 28, 1911, p. 5.
29 The next closest was George Watkins, who hit .373 for the 1930 St. Louis Cardinals.

30 *Cleveland Plain Dealer,* September 10, 1911, p. 17.
31 *The Sporting News,* October 19, 1911, p. 2.
32 *Cleveland Leader,* October 14, 1911, p. 6.
33 *The Sporting News,* October 26, 1911, p. 4.
34 Interestingly, with respect to George Mullin's flawed predictions about Jackson in 1911, a witty journalist asked the pitcher if he had any new prophecies about him headed into 1912. Mullin refused to say a word. *Washington Times,* April 8, 1912, p. 11.
35 *Evening Report,* Lebanon, PA, June 9, 1913, p. 4.
36 *Cleveland Plain Dealer,* January 20, 1912, p. 8.
37 *Cleveland Plain Dealer,* October 4, 1911, p. 7.
38 *Tacoma Times,* September 14, 1911, p. 2 and *Cleveland Leader,* November 15, 1911, p. 7.
39 *Cleveland Plain Dealer,* October 12, 1911, p. 7.
40 *Cleveland Plain Dealer,* September 17, 1911, p. 1C.
41 *Washington Times,* November 7, 1911, p. 14. A report in *Sporting Life* claimed that Jackson backed out of the play because he didn't want to perform in the "role of villain." *Sporting Life,* November 25, 1911, p. 13.
42 *Cleveland Leader,* March 15, 1912, p. 9.
43 *Winnipeg Tribune,* January 23, 1912, p. 7.
44 *Washington Times,* February 10, 1912, p. 10.
45 *New Castle Herald,* March 6, 1912, p. 2.
46 *Cleveland Plain Dealer,* April 14, 1912, p. 1C.
47 Ibid.
48 *Washington Times,* March 12, 1912, p. 13.
49 *Boston Journal,* March 8, 1912, p. 8.
50 *Cleveland Leader,* March 17, 1912, p. 18.
51 *New Orleans Times-Picayune,* February 26, 1912, p. 12.
52 *The Sporting News,* January 18, 1912, p. 2.
53 *Cleveland Plain Dealer,* March 19, 1912, p. 10.
54 *Cleveland Leader,* March 24, 1912, p. 18.
55 *Cleveland Plain Dealer,* April 7, 1912, p. 1C.
56 As stated in the previous chapter, the average age of the starting eight on the 1911 Naps was 28.875. The average age for the 1912 Naps was 26.75, which was over two years younger.
57 *Cleveland Leader,* April 12, 1912, p. 2.
58 *Cleveland Plain Dealer,* April 20, 1912, p. 7.
59 Ibid.
60 *Cleveland Plain Dealer,* April 23, 1912, p. 7.
61 *Cleveland Plain Dealer,* May 9, 1912, p. 9.
62 *Twin City Daily Sentinel,* April 23, 1912, p. 6.
63 *Cleveland Plain Dealer,* May 14, 1912, p. 7.
64 *Cleveland Leader,* May 19, 1912, p. 45.
65 *Cleveland Plain Dealer,* May 23, 1912, p. 9.
66 *Cleveland Plain Dealer,* June 6, 1912, p. 7.

67 *Cleveland Plain Dealer,* June 15, 1912, p. 7.
68 *Cleveland Leader,* June 15, 1912, p. 9.
69 *Cleveland Leader,* June 28, 1912, p. 9.
70 *The Inter Ocean,* July 17, 1912, p. 4.

CHAPTER FOUR: THE PERENNIAL RUNNER-UP

1 *Atlanta Constitution,* February 12, 1911, p. 3.
2 *New York Herald,* August 11, 1912, p. S7.
3 Ibid.
4 *Washington Herald,* August 20, 1912, p. 8 and *Cleveland Leader,* August 28, 1912, p. 7.
5 *Cleveland Plain Dealer,* August 30, 1912, p. 7.
6 *The Sporting News,* October 10, 1912, p. 2.
7 *The Sporting News,* October 17, 1912, p. 4.
8 *Cleveland Plain Dealer,* October 4, 1912, p. 10.
9 *Washington Times,* February 3, 1913, p. 11.
10 *Toledo News-Bee,* September 24,1912, p. 12.
11 *San Francisco Chronicle,* August 25, 1912.
12 *Charlotte Observer,* October 30, 1912, p. 8.
13 *Charlotte Evening Chronicle,* February 11, 1913, p. 6.
14 *The Sporting News,* December 12, 1912, p. 2.
15 *Washington Post,* November 21, 1912, p. 8.
16 *Indianapolis Star,* November 22, 1912, p.10.
17 *Charlotte Daily Observer,* January 4, 1913, p. 8.
18 *Fort Wayne Daily News,* February 17, 1912, p. 9. The family home was at 1752 Burdette Street, which was also spelled "Burdett."
19 *Twin-City Daily Sentinel,* December 7, 1912, p. 9.
20 *Altoona Tribune,* December 10, 1912, p. 10.
21 *Washington Post,* December 29, 1912, p. 3.
22 *The Sporting News,* December 19, 1912, p. 2.
23 *Charlotte Observer,* January 4, 1913, p. 8.
24 Transaction Card Collection, National Baseball Library, Cooperstown, New York. Many newspaper reports incorrectly claimed Jackson earned $4,500 in 1912.
25 *Charlotte Daily Observer,* January 4, 1913, p. 8.
26 Transaction Card Collection, National Baseball Library, Cooperstown, New York. It was speculated that Jackson could receive as much as $7,500 for the 1913 season, but that was far off from the realistic figure.
27 *Cleveland Leader,* February 13, 1913, p. 10.
28 *Cleveland Leader,* March 7, 1913, p. 10 and *Cleveland Plain Dealer,* March 7, 1913, p. 10.
29 *Cleveland Plain Dealer,* March 8, 1913, p. 8.
30 *Cleveland Leader,* April 12, 1913, p. 8.
31 *Cleveland Leader,* May 3, 1913, p. 11.
32 *Cleveland Plain Dealer,* May 4, 1913, p. 2C.
33 Ibid.

34 *Cleveland Plain Dealer,* April 6, 1913, p. 1C.
35 The *Boston Journal* named six of the suspected players involved in the fight, and Jackson wasn't one of them. However, the list was not believed to be complete. *Boston Journal,* May 8, 1913, p. 1.
36 *Cleveland Leader,* May 12, 1913, p. 12.
37 *Washington Times,* May 22, 1913, p. 12.
38 *Arkansas City Daily Traveler,* June 12, 1913, p. 9.
39 *Cleveland Plain Dealer,* May 19, 1913, p. 7.
40 *Brooklyn Daily Eagle,* June 5, 1913, p. 22.
41 *Anaconda Standard,* June 22, 1913, p. 23.
42 *Cleveland Plain Dealer,* July 26, 1911, p. 7.
43 *Cleveland Plain Dealer,* June 21, 1913, p. 10.
44 *Cleveland Leader,* June 25, 1913, p. 11.
45 *Cleveland Plain Dealer,* June 26, 1913, p. 9.
46 *Cleveland Leader,* June 26, 1913, p. 10.
47 *Cleveland Plain Dealer,* June 28, 1913, p. 1.
48 *Fort Wayne Journal-Gazette,* August 10, 1913, p. 19.
49 *Washington Times,* August 18, 1913, p. 10.
50 *Cleveland Leader,* September 11, 1913, p. 12.
51 *Cleveland Leader,* September 13–14, 1913.
52 *Cleveland Leader,* October 5, 1913, p. 20.
53 *The Sporting News,* February 12, 1914, p. 2.
54 *Cleveland Plain Dealer,* October 8, 1913, p. 9.
55 *Bismarck Tribune,* September 25, 1913, p. 3.
56 The team was also acknowledged as "Joe Jackson's Carolina Stars." *Charlotte Observer,* October 19, 1913, p. 10.
57 *Brooklyn Daily Eagle,* October 23, 1913, p. 20.
58 *Indianapolis News,* November 6, 1913, p. 8.
59 *Washington Times,* November 7, 1913, p. 15.
60 *The Sporting News,* October 23, 1913, p. 2.
61 *Athens Daily Herald,* March 10, 1914, p. 5.
62 *New York Evening World,* March 24, 1915, p. 14.
63 *Lewiston Evening Journal,* December 13, 1911, p. 5.
64 *The Sporting News,* March 19, 1914, p. 1.
65 *Cleveland Leader,* March 28, 1913, p. 12.
66 *Athens Daily Herald,* March 10, 1914, p. 5.
67 *The Sporting News,* January 22, 1914, p. 2.

CHAPTER FIVE: BASEBALL'S SCANDALOUS THESPIAN

1 *Baseball Magazine,* June 1912, p. 26–31.
2 *The Sporting News,* January 8, 1914, p. 6.
3 *Charlotte Observer,* January 26, 1914, p. 3.
4 *Charlotte Evening Chronicle,* January 31, 1914, p. 4.

5 *Daily Capital Journal*, February 12, 1914, p. 3. This same story was attributed to Ty Cobb, but it is not known whether he was the original source. *Houston Post*, November 8, 1914, p. 16. Rice's column appeared in the *Washington Times*, February 7, 1914, p. 11.
6 Transaction Card Collection, National Baseball Library, Cooperstown, New York.
7 *Hamilton Journal News*, February 17, 1914, p. 8.
8 *Charlotte Observer*, January 26, 1914, p. 3.
9 The business was at 826 East Main Street. *Richmond Times-Dispatch*, February 11, 1914, p. 8.
10 *Richmond Times-Dispatch*, February 12, 1914, p. 8.
11 *Athens Daily Herald*, March 19, 1914, p. 5.
12 *Pittsburgh Post-Gazette*, April 26, 1914, p. 45.
13 *Cleveland Plain Dealer*, March 4, 1914, p. 9.
14 *Cleveland Plain Dealer*, March 9, 1914, p. 8.
15 *Athens Weekly Banner*, March 13, 1914, p. 1.
16 *Athens Daily Herald*, March 16, 1914, p. 5.
17 *Cleveland Plain Dealer*, March 15, 1914, p. 17.
18 *Athens Daily Herald*, March 20, 1914, p. 5.
19 *Washington Times*, March 24, 1914, p. 10 and *Washington Herald*, March 25, 1914, p. 10.
20 *Cleveland Plain Dealer*, April 8, 1914, p. 10.
21 *New York Evening World*, April 7, 1914, p. 14.
22 Cleveland used 47 players during the 1914 season, eight more than the second highest total in the league.
23 *Cleveland Plain Dealer*, May 10, 1914, p. 20.
24 *Cleveland Plain Dealer*, May 24, 1914, p. 14.
25 *Cleveland Plain Dealer*, June 2, 1914, p. 11.
26 *Chicago Daily Tribune*, June 5, 1914, p. 13.
27 *Cleveland Plain Dealer*, July 13, 1914, p. 9.
28 *Washington Times*, August 31, 1914, p. 9.
29 *Lincoln Daily News*, December 26, 1913, p. 5.
30 *Washington Times*, August 21, 1913, p. 10.
31 *Washington Times*, September 13, 1913, p. 11.
32 *The Sporting News*, November 5, 1914, p. 1.
33 *The Sporting News*, January 7, 1915, p. 1.
34 *The Sporting News*, May 27, 1915, p. 4.
35 *The Sporting News*, January 21, 1915, p. 1.
36 *Asheville Citizen*, February 23, 1915, p. 5.
37 *New York Evening World*, July 31, 1914, p. 8 and *Fort Wayne Daily News*, July 31, 1914, p. 12.
38 *Washington Post*, August 4, 1914, p. 9.
39 *The Sporting News*, November 12, 1914, p. 7.
40 *Fort Wayne Daily News*, February 17, 1912, p. 9.
41 *Twin-City Daily Sentinel*, January 30, 1915, p. 8.
42 *Atlanta Constitution*, February 1, 1915, p. 6 and *Asheville Citizen*, February 17, 1915, p. 7.

43 *Asheville Citizen*, February 21, 1915, p. 8.
44 *Asheville Gazette-News*, February 23, 1915, p. 8.
45 *Winston-Salem Journal*, March 21, 1915, p. 6.
46 *Asheville Citizen*, February 23, 1915, p. 9.
47 *The Sporting News*, April 1, 1915, p. 4.
48 *Chicago Daily Tribune*, August 27, 1914, p. 15.
49 *Washington Times*, December 15, 1914, p. 14.
50 *The Sporting News*, January 28, 1915, p. 1.
51 *The Sporting News*, March 11, 1915, p. 5.
52 *Asheville Gazette-News*, February 25, 1915, p. 2.
53 *Twin-City Daily Sentinel*, March 1, 1915, p. 2.
54 *Greensboro Daily News*, March 8, 1915, p. 6.
55 *New York Evening World*, March 24, 1915, p. 14.
56 *Twin-City Daily Sentinel*, March 8, 1915, p. 5.
57 *Wilmington Morning Star*, July 5, 1914, p. 6.
58 *Cleveland Plain Dealer*, March 15, 1915, p. 9.
59 *Cleveland Plain Dealer*, March 29, 1915, p. 9.
60 *Charlotte Observer*, April 11, 1915, p. 3.
61 *Indianapolis News*, April 6, 1915, p. 11. In one report, Joe said it was his brother-in-law that was sick. *Cleveland Plain Dealer*, April 9, 1915, p. 13.
62 Ibid.
63 *Washington Times*, April 8, 1915, p. 12.
64 *New York Evening World*, April 8, 1915, p. 18. This story originated in the *Atlanta Georgian* newspaper.
65 The response was featured in the *Greenville Piedmont*. Rector's name was not in the original report out of Atlanta, but he assumed the journalist was talking about him because he was the only Greenville County Sheriff. He consulted his lawyer after the piece came out and discussed a civil action against the newspaper for its fabricated content. *Greenwood Daily Journal*, April 9, 1915, p. 2.
66 Katie was going to bring the divorce action in Cuyahoga County (Cleveland), Ohio, because divorces were outlawed in South Carolina. *New Castle News*, April 8, 1915, p. 2. A reporter mentioned that Jackson had an "affair with a chorus girl." *The Sporting News*, August 26, 1915, p. 2.
67 *Twin-City Daily Sentinel*, April 9, 1915, p. 10.
68 *Charlotte Observer*, May 7, 1915, p. 8.
69 *Lima News*, April 10, 1915, p. 5.
70 *Cleveland Plain Dealer*, April 12, 1915, p. 9.
71 *Cleveland Plain Dealer*, April 15, 1915, p. 14.

CHAPTER SIX: THE $65,000 MAN

1 *Cleveland Leader*, March 17, 1912, p. 18.
2 *Cleveland Plain Dealer*, October 16, 1913, p. 9.
3 Ibid.
4 *Cleveland Leader*, August 6, 1912, p. 7 and *Washington Times*, July 3, 1915, p. 14.

5 *Cleveland Plain Dealer,* November 20, 1910, p. 2C.
6 *Lincoln Daily News,* June 19, 1912, p. 3.
7 *Charlotte News,* June 1, 1912, p. 6.
8 *Charlotte News,* June 16, 1911, p. 11.
9 Ibid.
10 *Washington Times,* February 27, 1912, p. 12.
11 *Cleveland Plain Dealer,* April 14, 1912, p. 1C.
12 *Kansas City Star,* August 5, 1911, p. 9.
13 *The Sporting News,* June 3, 1943, p. 10.
14 *Athens Daily Herald,* March 10, 1914, p. 5.
15 *Asheville Citizen,* June 12, 1915, p. 9.
16 *Cleveland Plain Dealer,* May 20, 1915, p. 13.
17 *The Sporting News,* May 27, 1915, p. 1.
18 *Cleveland Plain Dealer,* June 2, 1915, p. 11.
19 *Cleveland Plain Dealer,* June 7, 1915, p. 11. Another report claimed Jackson's injury was caused by "horseplay" in the Cleveland clubhouse when Joe was pushed against a door, causing a serious bruise. This story didn't receive much traction. *Cleveland Plain Dealer,* June 3, 1915, p. 13.
20 *Cleveland Plain Dealer,* June 8, 1915, p. 11.
21 *Washington Times,* May 27, 1915, p. 12. Additional complaints about Jackson's performance at first were reported in *The Sporting News,* June 10, 1915 and June 17, 1915.
22 Baseball-reference.com.
23 *Cleveland Plain Dealer,* July 1, 1915, p. 11.
24 *Atlanta Constitution,* February 3, 1915, p. 10.
25 *Washington Times,* May 22, 1915, p. 13 and *The Sporting News,* June 17, 1915, p. 2.
26 *Cleveland Plain Dealer,* July 8, 1915, p. 11 and *The Sporting News,* July 15, 1915, p. 1.
27 Ibid.
28 Tinker reportedly discussed terms with Jackson and pitchers Bill Mitchell and Roy "Dixie" Walker. *Indianapolis News,* Monday, August 16, 1915, p. 10. It was reported that he also talked with shortstop Ray Chapman. *The Sporting News,* August 26, 1915, p. 4.
29 *The Sporting News,* September 2, 1915, p. 3.
30 Tinker led the Chicago Whales to the 1915 Federal League championship and, in 1946, was inducted into the National Baseball Hall of Fame at Cooperstown, NY.
31 *Cleveland Plain Dealer,* August 22, 1915, p. 17.
32 *The Sporting News,* September 2, 1915, p. 1.
33 *Cleveland Plain Dealer,* August 22, 1915, p. 17.
34 Several different dates, including August 16, August 17, and August 20, 1915, are listed on Jackson's official transaction card with regard to the new contract with Cleveland for 1917 and 1918. Transaction Card Collection, National Baseball Library, Cooperstown, New York. It is important to note that the Cleveland press indicated that the new contract covered the 1917, 1918, and 1919 seasons. However, according to his transaction card, it was only for 1917 and 1918. *Cleveland Plain Dealer,* August 20, 1915, p. 12.

35 *The Sporting News,* August 26, 1915, p. 1.
36 Ibid.
37 *Baseball Magazine,* March 1916, p. 30–32.
38 *Cleveland Plain Dealer,* August 16, 1915, p. 9.
39 *Baseball Magazine,* March 1916, p. 30–32.
40 Ibid.
41 *Cleveland Plain Dealer,* August 21, 1915, p. 10 and *The Sporting News,* September 2, 1915, p. 4.
42 *The Sporting News,* August 26, 1915, p. 2.
43 *Cleveland Plain Dealer,* August 27, 1915, p. 12.
44 *Cleveland Plain Dealer,* August 21, 1915, p. 10.
45 Ibid.
46 *The Sporting News,* August 26, 1915, p. 1.
47 *The Sporting News,* July 22, 1915, p. 4.
48 *Baseball Magazine,* March 1916, p. 30–32.
49 *Chicago Daily Tribune,* August 22, 1915, p. B1.
50 *Chicago Daily Tribune,* August 24, 1915, p. 11.
51 *Chicago Daily Tribune,* August 29, 1915, p. B1.
52 *Chicago Daily Tribune,* September 8, 1915, p. 11.
53 *Chicago Daily Tribune,* September 18, 1915, p. 9.
54 *Chicago Daily Tribune,* September 21, 1915, p. 11.
55 *Philadelphia Inquirer,* September 28, 1915, p. 12.
56 *Chicago Daily Tribune,* September 28, 1915, p. 13.
57 *The Sporting News,* September 9, 1915, p. 1.
58 *The Sporting News,* September 30, 1915, p. 2.
59 *Chicago Daily Tribune,* October 9, 1915, p. 15–16.
60 *Chicago Daily Tribune,* October 11, 1915, p. 14.
61 Ibid.

CHAPTER SEVEN: THE JACKSON OF OLD

1 *Wilkes-Barre Times Leader,* September 27, 1910, p. 13.
2 *Cleveland Leader,* April 12, 1912, p. 2.
3 *Charlotte News,* July 11, 1911, p. 6.
4 *Charlotte Observer,* January 4, 1913, p. 8.
5 A photo of the two in her new car was also featured by the newspaper. *Cleveland Leader,* July 20, 1913, p. 35.
6 *Cleveland Plain Dealer,* June 20, 1911, p. 7.
7 *Pittston Gazette,* June 29, 1911, p. 8.
8 *The Sporting News,* March 21, 1912, p. 7.
9 *Washington Times,* August 31, 1914, p. 9.
10 *Asheville Gazette-News,* February 22, 1915, p. 10.
11 *Chicago Daily Tribune,* January 15, 1916, p. 10 and *The Sporting News,* January 27, 1916, p. 4.

12 *New York Herald,* February 17, 1916, p. 14.
13 *The Sporting News,* October 5, 1916, p. 1.
14 *The Sporting News,* March 8, 1917, p. 1.
15 *The Sporting News,* April 26, 1917, p. 1.
16 *Wichita Beacon,* June 10, 1915, p. 7.
17 *Chicago Inter Ocean,* June 2, 1912, p. 21–22.
18 Ibid.
19 Baseball-reference.com
20 *Chicago Day Book,* January 23, 1917, p. 10.
21 Baseball-reference.com
22 Ibid.
23 *Chicago Daily Tribune,* March 5, 1916, p. B1.
24 *Chicago Daily Tribune,* March 15, 1916, p. 19.
25 *Chicago Daily Tribune,* March 30, 1916, p. 11.
26 *Chicago Daily Tribune,* April 9, 1916, p. B1.
27 *Chicago Daily Tribune,* April 13, 1916, p. 13.
28 *Chicago Daily Tribune,* April 17, 1916, p. 13.
29 *Chicago Daily Tribune,* June 18, 1916, p. B1.
30 *Chicago Daily Tribune,* June 26, 1916, p. 11.
31 *Chicago Examiner,* June 12, 1916, p. 13.
32 *Chicago Examiner,* July 3, 1916, p. 11.
33 *Chicago Daily Tribune,* August 14, 1916, p. 11.
34 Chicago finished the season with an 89–65 record.
35 *Chicago Daily Tribune,* October 8, 1916, p. B1.
36 *Chicago Examiner,* October 10, 1916, p. 12.
37 *Richmond Times-Dispatch,* February 12, 1914, p. 8.
38 *Rockford Daily Register Gazette,* March 10, 1916, p. 12.
39 *Greenwood Daily Journal,* October 11, 1916, p. 5.
40 Ibid.
41 *The Sporting News,* December 7, 1916, p. 4.
42 *The Sporting News,* November 9, 1916, p. 4.
43 *The Sporting News,* December 7, 1916, p. 3.
44 *The Sporting News,* November 23, 1916, p. 7.
45 Ibid.
46 *The Sporting News,* November 9, 1916, p. 4.
47 *The Sporting News,* December 7, 1916, p. 1.
48 *The Sporting News,* December 14, 1916, p. 4.

CHAPTER EIGHT: WORLD SERIES AND WORLD WAR

1 *Washington Post,* March 29, 1914, p. 2 and *The Sporting News,* March 5, 1914, p. 2.
2 For example, Jackson did it in Boston on May 13, 1916. *Chicago Daily Tribune,* May 14, 1916, p. B1.
3 *Brooklyn Daily Eagle,* October 4, 1917, p. 22.

4 *New Orleans Item,* July 29, 1910, p. 10.
5 *Wilkes-Barre Times-Leader,* July 13, 1911, p. 13.
6 *Winston-Salem Journal,* February 25, 1912, p. 14.
7 *Cleveland Plain Dealer,* March 9, 1911, p. 11.
8 *Athens Daily Herald,* March 14, 1914, p. 2.
9 *Cleveland Plain Dealer,* April 5, 1914, p. 39.
10 The Cleveland Indians signed Lou Guisto, a young prospect from Portland. Guisto hit .185 in 1917 and earned a lifetime average of .196 over five major league seasons.
11 *Washington Herald,* September 20, 1910, p. 8.
12 *The Sporting News,* March 8, 1917, p. 1.
13 Ibid.
14 Baseball-reference.com. The purchase was announced on March 1, 1917 and the one reporter claimed the price was in the neighborhood of $5,000. *Chicago Daily Tribune,* March 2, 1917, p. 16.
15 Ibid.
16 *Chicago Day Book,* March 1, 1917, p. 6.
17 *Chicago Daily Tribune,* March 6–7, 1917.
18 *Chicago Daily Tribune,* March 4, 1917, p. A1.
19 *Chicago Daily Tribune,* March 24, 1917, p. 11.
20 A player for the Smithville, Texas, team denied that anyone from their squad had spiked Jackson, stating that Joe "surely spiked himself, as he went to bat only twice in the game." The player added, "[Jackson] hit one so far that our whole club had to go out to relay it back." *Houston Post,* March 28, 1917, p. 5.
21 *Chicago Daily Tribune,* March 27, 1917, p. 14.
22 *New York Tribune,* March 23, 1917, p. 14.
23 *Chicago Daily Tribune,* May 3, 1917, p. 13.
24 *Chicago Daily Tribune,* May 11, 1917, p. 12.
25 *Chicago Daily Tribune,* May 13, 1917, p. 11.
26 *Chicago Daily Tribune,* May 19, 1917, p. 13.
27 *Chicago Daily Tribune,* May 25, 1917, p. 12.
28 *The Sporting News,* June 7, 1917, p. 1.
29 *Wilmington Dispatch,* October 17, 1917, p. 1.
30 sabr.org/bioproj/person/9ea2e3b9
31 *New York Sun,* September 29, 1917, p. 11.
32 *New York Tribune,* October 2, 1917, p. 13.
33 *Chicago Examiner,* October 7, 1917, p. C1.
34 *Chicago Daily Tribune,* August 16, 1917, p. 11.
35 *Chicago Daily Tribune,* August 24, 1917, p. 9.
36 *Chicago Daily Tribune,* August 28, 1917, p. 11.
37 *Chicago Daily Tribune,* June 6, 1917, p. 15.
38 *Chicago Daily Tribune,* July 4, 1917, p. 10.
39 *Chicago Daily Tribune,* July 6, 1917, p. 11 and *The Sporting News,* July 19, 1917, p. 1.
40 According to the *Chicago Examiner,* the White Sox and Red Sox flipped the top position "twelve times" over the course of the 1917 season. *Chicago Examiner,* September 22, 1917, p. 13.

41 Ibid.
42 *New York Sun*, September 28, 1917, p. 11.
43 sabr.org/gamesproj/game/september-27-1917-all-stars-turn-out-tim-murnane-benefit. A photo of Jackson holding the silver trophy he won in the throwing competition was widely featured in newspapers. "In the same picture, he was also holding a second, smaller trophy, which was given to him, reportedly, for outhitting Ty Cobb in a series against Detroit in 1914."
The photo appeared in *The Day*, October 29, 1917, p. 10. "Jackson threw the ball 396 feet, 8½ inches. The smaller trophy was fashioned by Jean Bedini."
44 *Chicago Daily Tribune*, September 30, 1917, p. A1.
45 *Chicago Examiner*, October 3, 1917, p. 11.
46 *Chicago Examiner*, October 1, 1917, p. 11.
47 *Chicago Examiner*, October 6, 1917, p. 10–11.
48 Ibid.
49 *Chicago Examiner*, September 25, 1917, p. 13.
50 *El Paso Herald*, September 29, 1917, p. 14.
51 *Chicago Daily News*, October 4, 1917, p. 2.
52 *Chicago Examiner*, October 3, 1917, p. 11.
53 *Chicago Daily News*, October 4, 1917, p. 2.
54 *Chicago Examiner*, October 6, 1917, p. 11.
55 *Chicago Daily News*, October 6, 1917, p. 1.
56 *Chicago Examiner*, October 7, 1917, p. C2.
57 *Chicago Daily News*, October 8, 1917, p. 2.
58 *Chicago Examiner*, October 12, 1917, p. 7–8.
59 *Chicago Daily News*, October 12, 1917, p. 1.
60 *Chicago Examiner*, October 14, 1917, p. C3.

CHAPTER NINE: FROM BALLYARDS TO SHIPYARDS

1 *Chicago Examiner*, October 12, 1917, p. 9.
2 *The Sporting News*, February 28, 1918, p. 2.
3 *Chicago Daily Tribune*, June 17, 1917, p. A1.
4 *Chicago Examiner*, October 15, 1917, p. 9.
5 *Chicago Examiner*, October 18, 1917, p. 6 and *Chicago Daily News*, October 18, 1917, p. 2.
6 *Chicago Daily Tribune*, October 16, 1917, p. 17.
7 *Chicago Examiner*, October 16, 1917, p. 7.
8 *Chicago Examiner*, October 17, 1917, p. 11.
9 *Chicago Examiner*, October 19, 1917, p. 13.
10 *Chicago Daily News*, October 18, 1917, p. 2.
11 *Cincinnati Enquirer*, October 20, 1917, p. 7.
12 *Lima News*, October 21, 1917, p. 13.
13 It was also reported that Jackson wrote to his mother, telling her that he was given a $1,000 bonus by "Chicago fans" for his sensational Game One catch. *Greenwood Evening Index*, October 23, 1917, p. 7.

14 *Topeka Daily Capital,* January 27, 1918, p. 2.
15 *Mattoon Daily Journal-Gazette,* October 28, 1917, p. 5. Other sources claim Jackson purchased a new Oldsmobile from the Savannah dealership of G. Bingham Bache with a portion of his earnings.
16 Jackson was ordered to appear on August 18 and his draft number was 3778. *Atlanta Constitution* and *Wilmington Morning Star,* August 13, 1917.
17 *Greenwood Evening Index,* August 21, 1917, p. 3.
18 *Sumter Watchman and Southron,* September 29, 1917, p. 3.
19 *Greenwood Evening Index,* October 23, 1917, p. 7 and *Washington Herald,* November 1, 1917, p. 12.
20 *The Sporting News,* January 31, 1918, p. 6 and *The Sporting News,* February 7, 1918, p. 7.
21 *The Sporting News,* February 21, 1918, p. 6.
22 *The Sporting News,* February 28, 1918, p. 1.
23 *Chicago Daily Tribune,* April 14, 1918, p. S1.
24 *The Sporting News,* March 14, 1918, p. 4.
25 *Chicago Daily Tribune,* February 10, 1918, p. S1.
26 *Chicago Daily Tribune,* February 19, 1918, p. 14. A story appeared in the *New York Times* claiming the Sox were willing to trade Jackson or Shano Collins for a "high-class pitcher." *New York Times,* February 18, 1918, p. 8.
27 *The Sporting News,* March 14, 1918 and March 28, 1918.
28 *Washington Times,* February 10, 1918, p. 14.
29 *Chicago Daily Tribune,* March 19, 1918, p. 16.
30 *The Sporting News,* March 28, 1918, p. 1.
31 *Chicago Daily Tribune,* April 3, 1918, p. 13.
32 *Chicago Daily Tribune,* April 8, 1918, p. 13.
33 *Chicago Daily Tribune,* April 16, 1918, p. 11.
34 *Chicago Daily Tribune,* April 14, 1918, p. S1.
35 *Washington Herald,* November 19, 1917, p. 10.
36 *Charlotte News,* April 30, 1918, p. 13.
37 *Greenwood Evening Index,* May 1, 1918, p. 4.
38 *Lincoln Evening Journal,* May 2, 1918, p. 11 and *Greenwood Evening Index,* May 2, 1918, p. 11.
39 Jackson was said to have four dependents at the time. *Washington Herald,* May 31, 1918, p. 8.
40 *San Bernardino County Sun,* May 2, 1918, p. 5.
41 *Washington Times,* May 2, 1918, p. 18.
42 *Cincinnati Enquirer,* May 3, 1918, p. 10.
43 *Washington Post,* May 12, 1918, p. 15.
44 Dozens of newspapers featured this type of headline on May 14, 1918.
45 *Chicago Daily Tribune,* May 20, 1918, p. 10.
46 *The Sporting News,* May 16, 1918, p. 1.
47 *Charlotte Observer,* October 29, 1918, p. 10. Another report claimed Joe had four brothers in the service. *The Sporting News,* May 16, 1918, p. 1.
48 *Washington Times,* May 24, 1918, p. 18.

49 *Ottawa Journal*, May 17, 1918, p. 13.
50 *Warren Times Mirror*, June 1, 1918, p. 7.
51 *The Sporting News*, June 13, 1918, p. 3.
52 *The Sporting News*, May 23, 1918, p. 1 and *Washington Herald*, May 31, 1918, p. 8.
53 *Washington Times*, May 24, 1918, p. 18.
54 *Santa Ana Register*, May 17, 1918, p. 1.
55 *Scranton Republican*, May 17, 1918, p. 16.
56 *The Sporting News*, May 30, 1918, p. 1.
57 *The Sporting News*, July 25, 1918, p. 4.
58 *Delmarvia Star*, October 6, 1918, p. 24.
59 Ibid.
60 *The Sporting News*, July 25, 1918, p. 4.
61 *Harrisburg Telegraph*, May 27, 1918, p. 10.
62 *Delmarvia Star*, June 2, 1918, p. 25.
63 Details of the two teams can be found in this newspaper report. Ibid. The Shipyard League was also known as the Delaware River Shipyard Baseball League.
64 *Delmarvia Star*, June 16, 1918, p. 25.
65 *Delmarvia Star*, June 30, 1918, p. 15. Williams also played for Harlan's Shipbuilding club, as did Byrd Lynn. *Delmarvia Star*, July 28, 1918, p. 25.
66 *Delmarvia Star*, September 15, 1918, p. 23–24.
67 *Delmarvia Star*, September 22, 1918, p. 23.
68 *Delmarvia Star*, September 29, 1918, p. 26.

CHAPTER TEN: CHICAGO'S HOUSE OF CARDS

1 Baseball-reference.com.
2 Initially, it appeared that Comiskey didn't hold Felsch in the same ill-repute that he did the other three men. *New Castle Herald*, July 11, 1918, p. 8. But later, Comiskey expressed his anger toward Felsch just the same. *Washington Times*, January 6, 1919, p. 17.
3 *Chicago Daily Tribune*, June 12, 1918, p. 11.
4 *Louisville Courier-Journal*, July 1, 1918, p. 6.
5 *Chicago Examiner*, September 23, 1917, p. C1.
6 *Chicago Examiner*, October 4, 1917, p. 13.
7 *Chicago Examiner*, October 16, 1917, p. 7.
8 Baseball-reference.com.
9 *New Castle Herald*, July 11, 1918, p. 8.
10 *Chicago Daily Tribune*, January 1, 1919, p. 21.
11 *Reading Times*, November 28, 1918, p. 8.
12 *Reading Times*, December 10, 1918, p. 9.
13 *Washington Times*, December 10, 1918, p. 16.
14 *Indianapolis News*, January 3, 1919, p. 18.
15 *Bridgeport Telegram*, December 21, 1918, p. 4 and *New York Tribune*, December 24, 1918, p. 13.

16 *Washington Herald,* January 14, 1919, p. 4.
17 *New York Tribune,* December 24, 1918, p. 13.
18 *Washington Herald,* January 22, 1919, p. 7.
19 *New Castle News,* January 27, 1919, p. 14.
20 *Chicago Daily Tribune,* January 30, 1919, p. 13.
21 Transaction Card Collection, National Baseball Library, Cooperstown, New York.
22 *Baseball Magazine,* March 1916, p. 30–32.
23 *The Sporting News,* August 26, 1915, p. 1.
24 *The Sporting News,* February 24, 1916, p. 1.
25 *New York Herald,* February 17, 1916, p. 14.
26 *New York Evening Telegram,* February 17, 1916, p. 10.
27 *Chicago Daily Tribune,* October 4, 1915, p. 12.
28 *Chicago Daily Tribune,* October 18, 1916, p. 18.
29 *Washington Times,* August 22, 1917, p. 13.
30 *Chicago Examiner,* April 5, 1916, p. 17.
31 *Chicago Daily Tribune,* March 17, 1916, p. 11.
32 *Chicago Daily Tribune,* July 5, 1917, p. 14.
33 *Chicago Daily Tribune,* March 15, 1917, p. 12.
34 *Chicago Daily Tribune,* October 4, 1916, p. 15.
35 *Chicago Examiner,* September 23, 1917, p. C1.
36 *Fort Wayne Sentinel,* May 28, 1919, p. 9.
37 "Jackson always respected Chicago's captain and referred to him as "Mister Collins."
38 Collins wasn't recognized as the official team captain until April 1916. *Lincoln Daily News,* April 20, 1916, p. 9.
39 *The Sporting News,* May 6, 1915, p. 1.
40 *The Sporting News,* February 13, 1919, p. 1.
41 Ibid.
42 Baseball-reference.com.
43 *Washington Times,* June 21, 1912 and July 9, 1912.
44 *Bisbee Daily Review,* September 18, 1907, p. 8.
45 *Washington Herald,* October 17, 1913, p. 10.
46 *The Sporting News,* March 23, 1916, p. 6.
47 It was claimed in 1916 that manager Clarence Rowland had eliminated the "factional strife" on the Sox. *The Sporting News,* October 5, 1916, p. 1.
48 *Chicago Daily Tribune,* January 1, 1919, p. 21.
49 *New Castle News,* January 27, 1919, p. 14.
50 *Chicago Daily Tribune,* February 11, 1919, p. 18.
51 *Chicago Daily Tribune,* June 17, 1917, p. A1.
52 *Chicago Daily Tribune,* May 23, 1918, p. 11.
53 *The Sporting News,* November 14, 1918, p. 4.
54 *Washington Times,* August 16, 1914, p. 12.
55 *Cleveland Plain Dealer,* June 28, 1913, p. 1.

CHAPTER ELEVEN: THE BIRTH OF THE "BLACK SOX"

1 *Chicago Daily Tribune*, March 18, 1919, p. 13.
2 Ibid, *The Sporting News*, March 13, 1919, p. 1
3 *Chicago Daily Tribune*, February 17, 1919, p. 18.
4 *Reading Times*, February 11, 1919, p. 9.
5 *Chicago Daily Tribune*, February 11, 1919, p. 18.
6 Jackson's contract included traveling expenses for Katie. *The Sporting News*, March 13, 1919, p. 1.
7 *Chicago Daily Tribune*, February 22, 1919, p. 16.
8 *Chicago Daily Tribune*, February 20, 1919, p. 18.
9 *Chicago Daily Tribune*, March 24, 1919, p. 19.
10 *The Sporting News*, April 3, 1919, p. 1.
11 *Chicago Daily Tribune*, April 9, 1919, p. 20.
12 *Chicago Daily Tribune*, April 19, 1919, p. 20.
13 *Chicago Daily Tribune*, April 21, 1919, p. 18.
14 *Chicago Daily Tribune*, April 24, 1919, p. 19.
15 *Chicago Daily Tribune*, April 27 and May 1, 1919.
16 *Chicago Daily Tribune*, May 3, 1919, p. 21.
17 *The Sporting News*, May 8, 1919, p. 1, 4.
18 *Chicago Daily Tribune*, May 16, 1919, p. 13.
19 *Chicago Daily Tribune*, May 18, 1919, p. A1.
20 *Chicago Daily Tribune*, May 19, 1919, p. 19.
21 *Chicago Daily Tribune*, May 31, 1919, p. 19.
22 *Chicago Daily Tribune*, June 24, 1919, p. 18.
23 *The Sporting News*, June 19, 1919, p. 1.
24 *Chicago Daily Tribune*, July 20, 1919, p. A3.
25 *Chicago Daily Tribune*, July 21, 1919, p. 15.
26 *Chicago Daily Tribune*, August 13, 1919, p. 14.
27 *The Sporting News*, August 7, 1919, p. 4.
28 *Chicago Daily News*, September 29, 1919, p. 1.
29 *The Sporting News*, December 14, 1916, p. 4.
30 *Chicago American*, August 30, 1919.
31 *Washington Times*, August 5, 1917, p. 16.
32 *The Sporting News*, March 11, 1920, p. 1.
33 *Salt Lake Telegram*, January 29, 1919, p. 9.
34 *The Sporting News*, February 6, 1919, p. 2.
35 *New York Times*, April 14, 1919, p. 10.
36 *Chicago Daily Tribune*, April 15, 1919, p. 20.
37 Gandil was ready to protest any trade to the White Sox in 1915 because of the "insult" earlier in his career. *The Sporting News*, November 18, 1915, p. 6. Also see *The Sporting News*, December 5, 1912, p. 6.
38 *Chicago American*, August 6, 1919, p. 9.
39 *Chicago Daily Tribune*, June 2, 1919, p. 21.
40 *Chicago American*, September 3, 1919.

41 *Chicago American*, September 9, 1919.
42 Ibid.
43 Joe Jackson Grand Jury Testimony Transcript, Bart Garrison Agricultural Museum of South Carolina, Pendleton, South Carolina.
44 *New York Tribune*, September 30, 1920, p. 2.
45 *Louisville Courier-Journal*, July 22, 1921, p. 6.
46 Cicotte asserted that Gandil was still trying to convince him "for a week before the series started." *New York Tribune*, September 30, 1920, p. 2.
47 *Washington Post*, October 21, 1917, p. 22 and *The Day Book*, March 1, 1917, 6.
48 *The Sporting News*, April 10, 1919, p. 5.
49 *The Sporting News*, March 13, 1919, p. 1.
50 *New York Tribune*, September 30, 1920, p. 2.
51 Joe Jackson Grand Jury Testimony Transcript, Bart Garrison Agricultural Museum of South Carolina, Pendleton, South Carolina.
52 Ibid.
53 *New York Tribune*, September 30, 1920, p. 2.
54 Joe Jackson Grand Jury Testimony Transcript, Bart Garrison Agricultural Museum of South Carolina, Pendleton, South Carolina.
55 *Atlanta Constitution*, September 26, 1917, p. 14.
56 *Winston-Salem Journal*, March 21, 1915, p. 6–7.
57 *The Sporting News*, September 2, 1915, p. 1.
58 *Cleveland Plain Dealer*, August 22, 1915, p. 17.
59 *Lima News*, January 25, 1919, p. 3.
60 *New York Tribune*, September 30, 1920, p. 2.
61 *Boston Post*, November 27, 1920, p. 12.
62 *New York Evening World*, September 30, 1920, p. 2.

CHAPTER TWELVE: THE CONSPIRACY UNFOLDS

1 *New York Times*, August 22, 1887, p. 6.
2 *Chicago Daily Tribune*, October 13, 1917, p. 15, *Chicago Examiner*, October 13, 1917, p. 8.
3 The meeting occurred on September 29, 1919, at the Ansonia Hotel in New York. *Chicago Daily Tribune*, July 22, 1921, p. 1, 8.
4 *Sports Illustrated*, September 17, 1956.
5 *Boston Post*, October 23, 1920, p. 9.
6 *Sports Illustrated*, September 17, 1956.
7 *San Francisco Chronicle*, August 25, 1912.
8 *Washington Times*, May 24, 1918, p. 18.
9 *Chicago American*, September 3, 1919.
10 *The Sporting News*, February 20, 1919, p. 1.
11 *The Sporting News*, January 23, 1919, p. 1.
12 *Chicago Daily News*, September 24, 1919, p. 1.
13 Some fans in Chicago "hissed and booed" the Sox for their performance. *Chicago Daily News*, September 29, 1919, p. 1.

14 *Chicago Daily Tribune*, September 21, 1919, p. A1.
15 *The Sporting News*, August 28, 1919, p. 1.
Robbins also stated, "Probably not in the history of baseball has there been a greater money team than the White Sox."
16 *New York Evening World*, September 29, 1920, p. 7.
17 *New York Tribune*, September 30, 1920, p. 2.
18 *Chicago Daily Tribune*, July 8, 1919, p. 17.
19 *New York Tribune*, September 30, 1920, p. 2.
20 Jackson talked at length about the "promises" made him before the Grand Jury. Joe Jackson Grand Jury Testimony Transcript, Bart Garrison Agricultural Museum of South Carolina, Pendleton, South Carolina.
21 Jesse Barnes of the New York Giants won 25 games in 1919. Cincinnati had the top three pitchers in terms of win-loss percentage in Dutch Ruether (.760), Slim Sallee (.750), and Ray Fisher (.737). Baseball-reference.com.
22 *Chicago Daily News*, September 30, 1919, p. 2.
23 *Chicago American*, August 4, 1919.
24 *Chicago Daily News*, September 11, 1919, p. 1.
25 *Chicago Daily Tribune*, October 2, 1919, p. 22.
26 *Chicago Daily Tribune*, October 2, 1919, p. 22.
27 *Boston Post*, November 27, 1920, p. 12.
28 Joe Jackson Grand Jury Testimony Transcript, Bart Garrison Agricultural Museum of South Carolina, Pendleton, South Carolina.
29 Jackson reportedly told his friend Lefty Williams that it was a "crooked deal" after the first day, and felt Gandil was not being honest with them. Joe Jackson Grand Jury Testimony Transcript, Bart Garrison Agricultural Museum of South Carolina, Pendleton, SC. According to one account, Felsch was, in fact, paid $5,000 after the first game in Cincinnati. *Milwaukee Evening Sentinel*, October 1, 1920, p. 18.
30 *Boston Post*, November 27, 1920, p. 12.
31 *Chicago Daily Tribune*, October 3, 1919, p. 22.
32 *Boston Post*, November 27, 1920, p. 12.
33 Joe Jackson Grand Jury Testimony Transcript, Bart Garrison Agricultural Museum of South Carolina, Pendleton, South Carolina.
34 *Cleveland Leader*, December 21, 1912, p. 7.
35 *Anaconda Standard*, June 22, 1913, p. 23.
36 *New York Times*, July 21, 1921, p. 9.
37 Ibid.
38 *New York Tribune*, September 30, 1920, p. 2.
39 *Chicago Daily Tribune*, October 4, 1919, p. 17–18.
40 Ibid.
41 There were claims that Gandil and his cronies refused to win for "bush leaguer" Dickey Kerr. However, there were allegations that this crew met for a special meeting before the third game, ultimately deciding to win and double-cross the gamblers.
42 Baseball-reference.com.
43 *Chicago Daily Tribune*, October 5, 1919, p. A2.

44 *Boston Post,* November 27, 1920, p. 12.
45 Joe Jackson Grand Jury Testimony Transcript, Bart Garrison Agricultural Museum of South Carolina, Pendleton, South Carolina.
46 *New York Tribune,* September 30, 1920, p. 2.
47 Joe Jackson Grand Jury Testimony Transcript, Bart Garrison Agricultural Museum of South Carolina, Pendleton, South Carolina. Jackson incorrectly told the jury that he was paid the same night they were traveling back to Cincinnati. Games four and five were both in Chicago.
48 *The Sporting News,* October 30, 1919, p. 3.
49 *Indianapolis Star,* October 14, 1919, p. 14.
50 *Chicago Daily Tribune,* October 7, 1919, p. 21–22.
51 *Chicago Daily Tribune,* October 8, 1919, p. 18.
52 *Chicago Daily Tribune,* October 9, 1919, p. 21–22.
53 *Chicago Daily Tribune,* October 10, 1919, p. 19–20.
54 Ibid.
55 Ibid.
56 *Chicago Daily News,* October 10, 1919, p. 2.
57 *Chicago Daily News,* October 11, 1919, p. 2.
58 *Boston Post,* November 27, 1920, p. 12.

CHAPTER THIRTEEN: EXPOSED AND SHAMED

1 *The Sporting News,* October 16, 1919, p. 1.
2 Ibid.
3 *Collyer's Eye,* October 18, 1919, p. 1, 4.
4 *Chicago Daily Tribune,* September 28, 1919, p. A1.
5 *The Sporting News,* April 17, 1919, p. 8. Jackson was considering an investment with Bob Jordan of Mineral Wells, TX. *Chicago American,* September 19, 1919.
6 Jackson was considering an investment with Bob Jordan of Mineral Wells, Texas. *Chicago American,* September 19, 1919.
7 *Boston Post,* November 27, 1920, p. 12.
8 *Collyer's Eye,* December 13, 1919, p. 1.
9 *Collyer's Eye,* November 1, 1919, p. 1, 4.
10 *Collyer's Eye,* October 30, 1920, p. 1, 5. The first batter was actually John "Shano" Collins. *Chicago Daily Tribune,* October 2, 1919, p. 22.
11 *Scranton Republican,* October 13, 1919, p. 14.
12 *The Sporting News,* October 16, 1919, p. 1.
13 *Chicago Daily Tribune,* September 30, 1920, p. 15.
14 Full text of these letters appeared in *Shoeless: The Life and Times of Joe Jackson* by David L. Fleitz, 2001, McFarland & Company, Inc, p. 195–197. It is believed the letters were written by Katie Jackson.
15 *Chicago Daily Tribune,* December 15, 1919, p. 21.
16 *Twin-City Sentinel,* December 17, 1919, p. 12.
17 *Scranton Republican,* November 4, 1919, p. 14.

18 Some researchers have concluded that Comiskey actively conspired to cover up the 1919 fix to protect his own interests. Many of these allegations are examined in Gene Carney's 2007 book, *Burying the Black Sox*.
19 *Collyer's Eye*, February 7, 1920, p. 1, 4.
20 *Collyer's Eye*, March 20, 1920, p. 4, Ibid.
21 Ibid.
22 Full text of these letters appeared in *Shoeless: The Life and Times of Joe Jackson* by David L. Fleitz, 2001, McFarland & Company, Inc, p. 199–204.
23 *Chicago Daily Tribune*, February 17, 1920, p. 13.
24 *Houston Post*, February 27, 1920, p. 11.
25 Transaction Card Collection, National Baseball Library, Cooperstown, New York. *Chicago Daily Tribune*, March 2, 1920, p. 15.
26 *Paris Morning News*, March 17, 1920, p. 1.
27 *New York Evening World*, January 10, 1920, p. 10.
28 *Chicago Daily Tribune*, March 23 and April 11, 1920.
29 *Boston Post*, November 27, 1920, p. 12.
30 *Chicago Daily Tribune*, May 3, 1920, p. 19.
31 *Chicago Daily Tribune*, May 29, 1920, p. 13.
32 *Chicago Daily Tribune*, June 1, 1920, p. 23.
33 *Chicago Daily Tribune*, July 15, 1920, p. 13.
34 *Chicago Daily Tribune*, July 17, 1920, p. 7.
35 *Chicago Daily Tribune*, August 21, 1920, p. 7.
36 *Boston Post*, November 27, 1920, p. 12.
37 *The Sporting News*, August 19, 1920, p. 1.
38 Joe Jackson Grand Jury Testimony Transcript, Bart Garrison Agricultural Museum of South Carolina, Pendleton, SC.
39 *Chicago Daily Tribune*, September 25, 1920, p. 1.
40 *Boston Post*, November 27, 1920, p. 12.
41 *Chicago Daily Tribune*, September 27, 1920, p. 1, 12, 15.
42 Ibid.
43 *Chicago Daily Tribune*, September 28, 1920, p. 17.
44 Ibid.
45 *Chicago Daily Tribune*, September 29, 1920, p. 1.
46 *The Sun and New York Herald*, September 29, 1920, p. 2.
47 Ibid.
48 Joe Jackson Grand Jury Testimony Transcript, Bart Garrison Agricultural Museum of South Carolina, Pendleton, South Carolina.
49 Ibid.
50 *The Sun and New York Herald*, September 29, 1920, p. 2.
51 Ibid.
52 Joe Jackson Grand Jury Testimony Transcript, Bart Garrison Agricultural Museum of South Carolina, Pendleton, South Carolina.
53 Ibid.
54 *New York Tribune*, September 30, 1920, p. 2.
55 Ibid.

56 Ibid. This is one of the most famous quotes in baseball history, and, interestingly, was entirely made up, according to Jackson. He claimed Charley Owens of the *Chicago Daily News* was the creative force behind the legendary statement, which was more famously captioned as, "Say it ain't so, Joe." *Sport*, October 1949.
57 Ibid.

CHAPTER FOURTEEN: BANISHMENT

1 *Chicago Daily Tribune*, September 29, 1920, p. 1.
2 Joe Jackson Grand Jury Testimony Transcript, Bart Garrison Agricultural Museum of South Carolina, Pendleton, SC. According to Cicotte's confession, Williams received $10,000. *Washington Times*, September 29, 1920, p. 14.
3 *Gaffney Ledger*, October 9, 1920, p. 2.
4 *St. Petersburg Daily Times*, September 11, 1920, p. 5.
5 *St. Petersburg Daily Times*, September 23, 1920, p. 4.
6 *Greenwood Index-Journal*, October 12–13, 1920.
7 *Savannah Morning News*, September 29, 1920, p. 12.
8 *Greenwood Index-Journal*, October 19, 1920, p. 6.
9 *New York Evening World*, March 29, 1920, p. 16.
10 *New York Evening World*, September 30, 1920, p. 2.
11 *Logansport Pharos-Tribune*, October 15, 1920, p. 10.
12 *Washington Times*, October 6, 1920, p. 15.
13 *Chicago Daily Tribune*, October 8, 1920, p. 20.
14 *Charlotte News*, November 24, 1920, p. 10.
15 *Collyer's Eye*, December 4, 1920, p. 1.
16 *Atlanta Constitution*, January 31, 1921, p. 6.
17 Jackson was also seemingly in Chicago on December 18, 1920, when he was initially arrested on the charge, "Obtaining Money and Goods by Means of the Confidence Game." He posted a $5,000 bail and was released. *People of the State of Illinois vs. Cicotte, et al.* Case No. 21867, Criminal Court of Cook County, Illinois.
18 *Washington Post*, February 13, 1921, p. 20.
19 *Chicago Daily Tribune*, January 30, 1921, p. S1, S3.
20 *Chicago Daily Tribune*, January 12, 1921, p. 19.
21 Landis was named commissioner on November 12, 1920. *New York Times*, November 13, 1920, p. 1.
22 *Washington Post*, March 13, 1921, p. 20.
23 *Chicago Daily Tribune*, March 17, 1921, p. 14.
24 *Chicago Daily Tribune*, March 18, 1921, p. 20.
25 It was initially realized during the fall of 1920 that the immunity waivers were gone, although it wouldn't be made public until July 1921. However, the prosecution knew about their disappearance when they dismissed the case and decided to reorganize in March 1921. *Chicago Daily Tribune*, July 23, 1921, p. 11 and July 26, 1921, p. 3.
26 Ibid. There have also been claims that Jackson was coerced by Comiskey's lawyer, Alfred Austrian.

27 *Chicago Daily Tribune*, March 27, 1921, p. A1.
28 *Chicago Daily Tribune*, April 5, 1921, p. 23. According to court documents, Jackson was arrested on the new charges on April 9, 1921, and paid a $3,000 bond. *People of the State of Illinois vs. Cicotte, et al.* Case No. 23912, Criminal Court of Cook County, Illinois.
29 *Chicago Daily Tribune*, April 8, 1921, p. 17.
30 *Charlotte News*, April 15, 1921, p. 10 and *Chicago Daily Tribune*, April 17, 1921, p. S1.
31 Ibid.
32 *Oregon Daily Journal*, May 10, 1921, p. 14 and *Boston Post*, May 10, 1921, p. 14.
33 *Washington Post*, May 20, 1921, p. 12.
34 The "Black Sox" played on a field at East 75th Street and South Greenwood Avenue on the South Side. *Washington Herald*, May 17, 1921, p. 9.
35 *New Castle News*, June 14, 1921, p. 12. They also played at the White City baseball field at 65th Street and South Park Avenue.
36 *Chicago Daily Tribune*, July 6, 1921, p. 3. Short was law partners with George Guenther.
37 *Chicago Daily Tribune*, July 7, 1921, p. 7.
38 *Chicago Daily Tribune*, July 20, 1921, p. 1. Burns's cohort Billy Maharg also testified on behalf of the prosecution later in the trial.
39 *Chicago Daily Tribune*, July 26, 1921, p. 3.
40 Ibid.
41 *People of the State of Illinois vs. Cicotte, et al.* Case No. 23912, Criminal Court of Cook County, Illinois.
42 *Chicago Daily Tribune*, July 30, 1921, p. 5.
43 *Chicago Daily Tribune*, July 31, 1921, p. 15.
44 *Chicago Daily Tribune*, August 3, 1921, p. 1.
45 Ibid.
46 *New York Evening World*, August 3, 1921, p. 1.
47 *Sport Magazine*, October 1949.
48 *Chicago Daily Tribune*, August 3, 1921, p. 1.
49 *Washington Times*, August 4, 1921, p. 14.
50 *El Paso Herald*, March 3, 1922, p. 10 and *Washington Post*, March 29, 1922, p. 15.
51 *Twin City Sentinel*, April 22, 1922, p. 7.
52 *Indianapolis News*, May 13, 1922, p. 21.
53 *Poughkeepsie Eagle News*, June 23, 1922, p. 9.
54 *Denver Post*, July 14, 1922, p. 20.
55 *New York Times*, June 30, 1922, p. 12.
56 Buck Weaver and Swede Risberg were also said to be teamed with Jackson on the Westwood club, but manager Eddie Phelan claimed Jackson was the only "Black Sox" player in the east. *Washington Herald*, June 28, 1922, p. 7 and *New York Times*, June 30, 1922, p. 12. The report that thousands of dollars changed hands was later denied by local club officials.
57 *New York Times*, July 16, 1922, p. 23.
58 *Washington Times*, July 17, 1922, p. 16.

59 *Altoona Tribune*, July 28, 1922, p. 10.
60 *Flint Journal*, July 22, 1922, p. 15 and *Fort Wayne News Sentinel*, July 22, 1922, p. 8.
61 The cabaret was at 125th Street and 7th Avenue. *Olean Times Herald*, July 25, 1922, p. 21.
62 *Anniston Star*, October 3, 1922, p. 8.
63 *St. Louis Post-Dispatch*, May 3, 1923, p. 31.
64 *Monroe News-Star*, July 11, 1923, p. 1, 8.
65 Ibid.
66 *Altoona Tribune*, July 20, 1923, p. 9.
67 *Shoeless Summer* by John Bell, 2001, Vabella Publishing.
68 *Decatur Herald*, January 28, 1921, p. 4 and *Lincoln Evening Journal*, March 21, 1923, p. 9. Also see deadballbaseball.com/?cat=328.
69 *Lincoln Star*, April 24, 1923, p. 11.
70 *Boston Post*, November 27, 1920, p. 12.
71 Jackson wanted his $8,000 for 1921 and 1922, $1,500 bonus pay, and $500 due him from the last part of 1920.
72 *Milwaukee Sentinel*, January 30, 1924, p. 1, 9.
73 Jackson's attorney fought to prevent admission of the 1920 grand jury testimony, but lost the argument.
74 Jackson sparred with attorney George B. Hudnall. *Milwaukee Sentinel*, January 31, 1924, p. 1, 6.
75 *Milwaukee Journal*, February 15, 1924, p. 1, 2.
76 Ibid. Happy Felsch, who testified on the plaintiff's behalf, was also arrested on a perjury charge. *Milwaukee Evening Sentinel*, February 13, 1924, p. 1.
77 *The Sporting News*, February 14, 1924, p. 4.

CHAPTER FIFTEEN: "THE ANSWER TO A GAMBLER'S PRAYER"

1 *Cleveland Plain Dealer*, March 15, 1914, p. 19.
2 The businessman was Thomas A. Miller. *Fort Wayne Daily News*, February 17, 1912, p. 9.
3 *The Sporting News*, February 11, 1915, p. 1.
4 *Washington Times*, November 11, 1912, p. 11, December 25, 1912, p. 11.
5 *Cimarron Citizen*, August 21, 1913, p. 3.
6 *New York Evening World*, March 24, 1915, p. 14.
7 *Baseball Magazine*, September 1917, p. 492, 530.
8 *Allentown Democrat*, April 30, 1913, p. 6.
9 *Cleveland Plain Dealer*, June 20, 1912, p. 10.
10 *The Sporting News*, July 4, 1918, p. 4.
11 *Brooklyn Daily Eagle*, October 4, 1917, p. 22.
12 *Elkhart Truth*, June 26, 1911, p. 3.
13 *Oregon Daily Journal*, February 5, 1917, p. 9.
14 *Washington Herald*, July 22, 1914, p. 5 and *The Sporting News*, February 1, 1934, p. 4.
15 *Cleveland Plain Dealer*, June 26, 1912, p. 7.

16 *Cleveland Leader,* May 17, 1912, p. 11, June 27, 1912, p. 9.
17 *The Sporting News,* March 25, 1915, p. 5.
18 *Harrisburg Telegraph,* August 28, 1945, p. 11.
19 *The Sporting News,* March 27, 1913, p. 2.
20 *Cleveland Plain Dealer,* March 5, 1914, p. 7.
21 *The Sporting News,* March 28, 1918, p. 1. Buckner later stated that "Mr. Jackson" was the greatest hitter in baseball, saying, "That's my man. He was the best." *Detroit Free Press,* August 17, 1936, p. 12.
22 *Washington Times,* Wednesday, August 18, 1915, p. 10.
23 *Chicago Eagle,* June 6, 1914, p. 2.
24 *New Orleans Times-Picayune,* March 24, 1913, p. 13.
25 *Cleveland Plain Dealer,* April 16, 1912, p. 9.
26 *New York Evening World,* September 30, 1920, p. 2.
27 *Cleveland Leader,* July 1, 1912, p. 9.
28 *Cleveland Leader,* May 9, 1913, p. 10.
29 Unsourced clipping, Joe Jackson's Personal Scrapbooks, Mike Nola, Shoeless Joe Jackson's Virtual Hall of Fame, www.blackbetsy.com, from Josh Leland of Leland's Auctions. During the 1919 World Series, he carried four new hairpins with him in the fourth game. He got a double and made first on an error, feeding into his belief. *Chicago Daily Tribune,* October 5, 1919, p. A1. Also see *Detroit Free Press,* August 17, 1936, p. 12.
30 *New Orleans Item,* March 3, 1912, p. 25.
31 *Cleveland Plain Dealer,* July 18, 1911, p. 8.
32 *Cleveland Plain Dealer,* April 6, 1914, p. 10.
33 *Cleveland Plain Dealer,* April 8, 1914, p. 10.
34 *Athens Daily Herald,* March 14, 1914, p. 2.
35 *Cleveland Plain Dealer,* November 2, 1913, p. 2C.
36 *Cleveland Plain Dealer,* March 17, 1914, p. 9.
37 *New York Herald,* August 11, 1912, p. 7.
38 *The Sporting News,* September 3, 1942, p. 4.
39 *Baseball Magazine,* September 1917, p. 530.
40 Baseball-reference.com.
41 *Wilkes-Barre Record,* March 15, 1923, p. 21.
42 Research by Mike Nola, Shoeless Joe Jackson's Virtual Hall of Fame, www.blackbetsy.com.
43 *Oshkosh Daily Northwestern,* December 18, 1924, p. 15.
44 *Harrisburg Evening News,* December 29, 1924, p. 1.
45 *Oshkosh Daily Northwestern,* May 20, 1925, p. 9.
46 *Greenwood Index-Journal,* May 9, May 14, 1925.
47 Research by Mike Nola, Shoeless Joe Jackson's Virtual Hall of Fame, www.blackbetsy.com. Another report claimed Jackson's club went 63–21–3 and that Joe had a .556 batting average. *Hamilton Journal News,* November 3, 1925, p. 8.
48 *Zanesville Times-Signal,* October 25, 1925, p. 13.
49 *Greenwood Index-Journal,* March 12, 1926, p. 7.

50 He reportedly was making around $8,500 in 1927. *Franklin News-Herald,* April 2, 1927, p. 8. A 1932 article claimed he had two stores at that time. *Franklin News-Herald,* March 10, 1932, p. 8.
51 *Fitchburg Sentinel,* January 4, 1927, p. 7.
52 *Franklin News-Herald,* April 2, 1927, p. 8.
53 *Greenwood Index-Journal,* June 1, 1929, p. 6.
54 *Statesville Record and Landmark,* August 9, 1932, p. 16.
55 *The Sporting News,* June 30, 1932, p. 5.
56 Georgia Death Index, ancestry.com.
57 *Greenwood Index-Journal,* October 26, 1932, p. 6.
58 *Florence Morning News,* December 19, 1933, p. 6. Mayor Mauldin reportedly obtained the signatures of 5,000 Greenville citizens for his petition to have Jackson reinstated. *The Sporting News,* September 24, 1942, p. 1.
59 *Harrisburg Evening News,* November 5, 1929, p. 19.
60 *Galveston Daily News,* December 24, 1933, p. 17.
61 *Decatur Daily Review,* December 23, 1933, p. 4.
62 *St. Louis Post-Dispatch,* January 19, 1934, p. 22.
63 *Louisville Courier-Journal,* January 21, 1934, p. 30.
64 *Monroe News-Star,* July 2, 1934, p. 7 and *Lincoln Evening Journal,* July 6, 1934, p. 17.
65 *Brooklyn Daily Eagle,* August 19, 1934, p. 11.
66 *Greenwood Index-Journal,* June 18, 1935, p. 3.
67 Unsourced clipping, Joe Jackson's Personal Scrapbooks, Mike Nola, Shoeless Joe Jackson's Virtual Hall of Fame, www.blackbetsy.com, from Josh Leland of Leland's Auctions.
68 Author Thompson wrote at length about Jackson's kindness in his later years. *Growing Up with Shoeless Joe* by Joe Thompson, 1998, The R. L. Bryan Company.
69 Unsourced clipping, Joe Jackson's Personal Scrapbooks, Mike Nola, Shoeless Joe Jackson's Virtual Hall of Fame, www.blackbetsy.com, from Josh Leland of Leland's Auctions.
70 *The Sporting News,* September 24, 1942, p. 1, 8.
71 Specific quotes by Jackson about this topic were found in an unsourced clipping, Joe Jackson's Personal Scrapbooks, Mike Nola, Shoeless Joe Jackson's Virtual Hall of Fame, www.blackbetsy.com, from Josh Leland of Leland's Auctions. Also see *Franklin News-Herald,* March 10, 1932, p. 8.
72 *Growing Up with Shoeless Joe* by Joe Thompson, 1998, The R. L. Bryan Company, p. 2–3.
73 Joe Jackson Grand Jury Testimony Transcript, Bart Garrison Agricultural Museum of South Carolina, Pendleton, South Carolina.
74 Ibid.
75 The White Sox of 1919 had one of the highest salary lists in the majors. Historian Bob Hoie estimated that the Sox payroll might have been around $93,051. "1919 Baseball Salaries and the Mythically Underpaid Chicago White Sox," *Base Ball: A Journal of the Early Game,* Spring 2012.
76 *Boston Post,* November 27, 1920, p. 12.

77 *Lincoln Evening Journal,* July 6, 1934, p. 17.
78 *The Sporting News,* February 11, 1915, p. 1.
79 *Washington Post,* November 29, 1918, p. 9.
80 *Ironwood Daily Globe,* April 25, 1946, p. 11 and *Greenwood Index-Journal,* February 21, 1951, p. 7.
81 *Des Moines Register,* December 3, 1988, p. 12.
82 Unsourced clipping, Joe Jackson's Personal Scrapbooks, Mike Nola, Shoeless Joe Jackson's Virtual Hall of Fame, www.blackbetsy.com, from Josh Leland of Leland's Auctions.
83 *Sport Magazine,* October 1949.
84 Jackson was supposed to be on the program, December 16. Sportswriter Ed Bang and Tris Speaker appeared in his absence and made the presentation of the gold clock to Ed Sullivan, in tribute to Joe. Sullivan, in turn, forwarded the clock to Katie Jackson in Greenville. *Berkshire Eagle,* December 29, 1951, p. 12.
85 Newspapers claimed he was 63, but since a majority of sources claim he was born in 1887, he would've been 64.
86 *Greenville News,* December 6, 1951, p. 1, 22.
87 Katie Jackson died on April 18, 1959, at the age of sixty-six. South Carolina Certificate of Death, ancestry.com.
88 *Greenville News,* December 7, 1951, p. 43–44.
89 *Greenville News,* December 9, 1951, p. S1.
90 *Greenville News,* December 7, 1951, p. 43–44.
91 *Greenville News,* December 10, 1951, p. 9.
92 *Iowa City Press-Citizen,* December 18, 1951, p 20.
93 Unsourced clipping, Joe Jackson's Personal Scrapbooks, Mike Nola, Shoeless Joe Jackson's Virtual Hall of Fame, www.blackbetsy.com, from Josh Leland of Leland's Auctions.
94 *Greenville News,* December 9, 1951, p. S1.
95 *Cleveland Leader,* February 12, 1912, p. 5.

ACKNOWLEDGMENTS

For their eternal support and encouragement, I'd like to thank my family, Jodi Hornbaker, L. W. Hornbaker, Timothy and Barbara Hornbaker, Melissa Hornbaker, Virginia Hall, Sheila Babaganov, Frances Miller, and John and Christine Hopkins.

Additional gratitude goes to my editor Jason Katzman for his patience, sound advice, and tireless efforts. Many thanks goes out to the amazing Interlibrary Loan team at the Broward County Main Library in Fort Lauderdale, Florida, consisting of Amy Miller, Margaret Cruz, Alisa Orange, Deborah Hicks, and Grace Ann Harker. Also, the Main Periodicals Department made up of David Hart, James Onessimo, and William Hubly.

For their assistance in providing material and answering my questions, I'd like to thank: Les McCall of the Bart Garrison Agricultural Museum of South Carolina, Pendleton, South Carolina, the Shoeless Joe Jackson Museum and Baseball Library, Greenville, South Carolina, Wayne Kelley of the Pickens County (SC) Historical Society, Anne Sheriff of the Faith Clayton Room for Family Research at Southern Wesleyan University, Quientell Walker of the Mary Oates Gregorie Historical Room, Pickens County Library System, Rebecca Kilby of the Hughes Main Library, Greenville County Library System, and Mike Nola of the Shoeless Joe Jackson Virtual Hall of Fame.

INDEX

M

N

O

P

T

U

V

W

Y

Z